Framing Literary Humour

Framing Literary Humour

Cells, Masks and Bodies as 20th-Century Sites of Imprisonment

Jeanne Mathieu-Lessard

BLOOMSBURY ACADEMIC
NEW YORK • LONDON • OXFORD • NEW DELHI • SYDNEY

BLOOMSBURY ACADEMIC
Bloomsbury Publishing Inc
1385 Broadway, New York, NY 10018, USA
50 Bedford Square, London, WC1B 3DP, UK
29 Earlsfort Terrace, Dublin 2, Ireland

BLOOMSBURY, BLOOMSBURY ACADEMIC and the Diana logo are
trademarks of Bloomsbury Publishing Plc

First published in the United States of America 2020
This paperback edition published in 2021

Copyright © Jeanne Mathieu-Lessard, 2020

Cover design: Jade Barnett

All rights reserved. No part of this publication may be reproduced or transmitted in any form or by any means, electronic or mechanical, including photocopying, recording, or any information storage or retrieval system, without prior permission in writing from the publishers.

Bloomsbury Publishing Inc does not have any control over, or responsibility for, any third-party websites referred to or in this book. All internet addresses given in this book were correct at the time of going to press. The author and publisher regret any inconvenience caused if addresses have changed or sites have ceased to exist, but can accept no responsibility for any such changes.

Library of Congress Cataloging-in-Publication Data
Names: Mathieu-Lessard, Jeanne, author.
Title: Framing literary humour : cells, masks and bodies as 20th-century sites of imprisonment / Jeanne Mathieu-Lessard.
Description: New York : Bloomsbury Academic, 2020. | Includes bibliographical references and index.
Identifiers: LCCN 2019026043 (print) | LCCN 2019026044 (ebook) | ISBN 9781501356551 (hardback) | ISBN 9781501356568 (epub) | ISBN 9781501356575 (pdf)
Subjects: LCSH: Literature, Modern–20th century–History and criticism. | Wit and humor–History and criticism. | Humor in literature. | Imprisonment in literature.
Classification: LCC PN770.5 .C565 2020 (print) | LCC PN770.5 (ebook) | DDC 809/.7–dc23
LC record available at https://lccn.loc.gov/2019026043
LC ebook record available at https://lccn.loc.gov/2019026044

ISBN:	HB:	978-1-5013-5655-1
	PB:	978-1-5013-7199-8
	ePDF:	978-1-5013-5657-5
	eBook:	978-1-5013-5656-8

Typeset by Integra Software services Pvt. Ltd.

To find out more about our authors and books visit www.bloomsbury.com
and sign up for our newsletters.

*Ce livre est dédié à mes parents
qui ont su créer le cadre essentiel
à la liberté d'esprit*

Contents

Preface and Acknowledgements	viii
Introduction	1
1 Humour and Imprisonment	13
2 Humour in the Cell: Prison Cells and War Camps	43
3 Social Entrapment: Humoristic Characters vs. the World	83
4 Humour in the Cells: Configurations of the Body as Prison	121
Conclusion: A Geometry of Humour	165
Notes	175
References	186
Index	193

Preface and Acknowledgements

The idea behind this book comes from Giovannino Guareschi's imprisonment writings, which I discovered in Italy in 2008 thanks to Simonetta Bartolini. I am very grateful to Guareschi's children, Alberto and the late Carlotta, for their precious help during and after my research trip at the Guareschi Archives in Roncole Verdi in 2014.

I am indebted to Pascal Michelucci, Luca Somigli and Ann Komaromi at the University of Toronto for their intellectual engagement and faith in this project from its inception; to Miranda Hickman for her generous comments at an earlier stage of the project; and to Veronika Ambros, Linda Hutcheon, Lucie Joubert, Jessica Milner Davis and Jill Ross for their invaluable mentorship. This book would not have seen the day without my editor Katherine De Chant's enthusiasm and professionalism and without the two anonymous reviewers' generosity and thoroughness.

Undertaking this research has been greatly facilitated by the support of the Social Sciences and Humanities Research Council of Canada, the Avie Bennett Award, the Jackman Humanities Institute and the Government of Ontario. I am also thankful to the 2014–2015 Jackman Humanities Institute fellows and to the members of the Comparative Literature Students' Tribune/La tribune des étudiant-e-s en littérature comparée and the Canadian Comparative Literature Association/Association Canadienne de Littérature Comparée for their sense of community.

I wholeheartedly thank all my family and friends for their support and encouragement, with special thanks to Élise Couture-Grondin, Katie Fry, Isabella Huberman, Natasha Hay, Nefise Kahraman, Louis-Thomas Leguerrier, Alex Nica, Irina Sadovina, Catherine Schwartz, Terry Skolnik and Julie St-Laurent for their discussions, criticism, revisions and comments at various stages of the research and writing process.

Introduction

In J. K. Rowling's *Harry Potter and the Prisoner of Azkaban*, Harry and his classmates are introduced by Professor Lupin to a shape-shifting entity trapped in a wardrobe: the Boggart. Upon meeting a human being, the Boggart takes the shape of what most frightens that person. To stop the Boggart from impersonating one's fear, one must use the *riddikulus* charm. As Professor Lupin explains: 'The charm that repels a Boggart is simple, yet it requires force of mind. You see, the thing that really finishes a Boggart is *laughter*. What you need to do is force it to assume a shape that you find amusing' (Rowling 1999: 101, original emphasis). For example, Harry's friend Ron, terrified of spiders, ridicules the spider-shaped-Boggart by forcing it into a legless ball that 'roll[s] over and over' (105) and can no longer control its movements.

The Boggart episode brings to mind the Freudian theory of humour, where humour is a means to ridicule fear and to provide a form of relief that is signalled by laughter. In other words, humour strives to dismiss negative affects such as fear through jest (Freud [1927] 1961: 162). Yet Rowling's Boggart also sheds light on a fundamental problem of theories of humour such as Freud's. Fear – or its representation – does not disappear with the wave of a magic wand. The Boggart is a non-being that does not live, and therefore cannot die. It can only be given another shape, and as such, fear is not eliminated, but displaced. Harry and his classmates do not spare themselves negative affects; indeed, the whole novel hinges on Harry's ability not to dismiss his fear but to learn to shape it in order to live with it.

Literary humour is a shape-shifter; it displaces negative feelings by giving them new forms and incorporates the explosion of laughter within the larger frame of the narrative. Our way of conceptualizing literary humour should therefore take into account what happens before and after the moment of relief. This book conceives literary humour as an ongoing process that creates an unstable oscillation in the narrative. Just like the highly unstable Boggart craves 'dark, enclosed spaces' (Rowling 1999: 101), literary humour generates figures of constriction that contain and enable its very existence. The temporality of humour seen as an ongoing process is therefore intimately connected with its spatial setting; humour's oscillation is framed within images of constricted spaces. Studies of literary humour that focus on its potential to liberate rather than its inextricable connection with containment run the risk of forcing humour out of the very conditions that created it.

This book challenges the idea that liberation should be conceived as the endpoint of humour. It reframes the discussion to look at the connection between humour and liberation the other way around: by paying close attention to fictional representations of imprisonment that incite the creation of humour. Twentieth-century literature, born in a context marked by two world wars and the rise of totalitarian political systems, is replete with representations of spaces of imprisonment. Despite the impression that imprisonment might not promote the creation of humour, a careful look at works of twentieth-century literature proves the contrary. This book provides a theoretical framework to grasp the conceptual connection between humour and imprisonment, and detailed literary analyses of selected works of five authors who offer complementary perspectives on this connection: Romain Gary (1914–1980), Giovannino Guareschi (1908–1968), Wyndham Lewis (1882–1957), Vladimir Nabokov (1899–1977) and Luigi Pirandello (1867–1936). Understanding imprisonment as a concrete spatial setting and a metaphorical image, I analyse confinement as an essential structural condition for the emergence of humour. By starting from the most obvious cases of imprisonment (in war camps and prison cells) and moving to the least obvious (in masks and bodies), the analyses demonstrate how 'imprisonment' should be seen on a continuum, and how twentieth-century humour in theory and in fiction cannot be fully understood without a careful look at its connection with the notion of imprisonment.

Conceptualizing humour through imprisonment

My work is grounded in five twentieth-century theories developed concomitantly with the works of fiction analysed. Although they emerge from varied linguistic and cultural contexts, these theories share a common core feature: they frame humour as a phenomenon intrinsically connected with imprisonment. Using the concept of imprisonment as a thread to read the theories of Henri Bergson, Sigmund Freud, Luigi Pirandello, Wyndham Lewis and Mikhail Bakhtin, I develop a comparative framework attentive to historical and terminological distinctions. Chapter 1 presents my theoretical framework in chronological order to give an overview of the period discussed in the book and prepares the ground for the thematical chapters on the prison, the mask and the body.

Studying humour in a comparative context entails a number of conceptual and terminological problems. The most pressing problem was the necessity to settle on a single term to refer to a phenomenon that is far from uniform: humour crosses linguistic, temporal, cultural and stylistic boundaries, and it has been named and understood differently in each context. The theories and works of fiction discussed in this book have been written in five different languages over a period of more than half a century. From Henri Bergson's landmark *Le rire* (*Laughter*) in 1900 to Mikhail Bakhtin's *Tvorchestvo Fransua Rable* (*Rabelais and His World*) in 1965 – roughly the two temporal poles of this book – the word has been used to designate at times very different phenomena. When Bergson writes on the comic at the very end of the nineteenth century, for example, the term 'humour' is not yet widespread in France,[1] and he uses it in a sense that is very different from our contemporary understanding of the term and from what I study here. This is further complicated by the theorists' personal preferences and their idiosyncratic use of key terms. Lewis's 'satire', for example, is almost synonymous to art and does not have the relationship with morality satire generally has.

This book discusses humour not in the common sense of what is funny, but in a restrictive sense, as a specific literary form. My understanding of the phenomenon derives from the Italian *umorismo* as it is defined by Luigi Pirandello, and from the German *Humor* as understood by Freud. Literary humour can be conceived as an endless movement of oscillation between contradictory states. It is more likely to raise a smile than to provoke laughter (Freud [1927] 1961: 166), or it will give rise to a 'troubled' form of laughter (Pirandello [1920] 1992: 127). For this reason, I prefer the adjective 'humoristic' over the more common 'humorous', since the latter is related to humour in general, in the sense of 'amusing, comic, funny' ('humorous', *OED Online*). By using 'humoristic', I refer to humour in the restrictive sense only, as a phenomenon distinct from humour understood as a synonym of the comic and the amusing.

Bergson's theory of the comic helps make this distinction clear. I engage with Bergson to show how the comic can also be defined at times in relation to the notion of imprisonment and how comic laughter differs significantly from the 'humoristic' laughter discussed by other theorists. To Bergson, comic laughter is a collective response meant to free the individual from automatism. Yet the liberating intent of the comic collective laughter does not take into account the perspective of the individual who is the source of laughter. Rather than liberating the individual, this comic laughter is more likely to create a new form of oppression which forces the collective perspective onto the individual. Literary works exemplify this type of use of laughter and provide counterexamples of an individualized laughter which can be best characterized as 'humoristic'.

In his two works on jokes, the comic and humour, Freud also distinguishes between collective and individual uses of laughter, between jokes and the comic on one side, and humour on the other. *Jokes and Their Relation to the Unconscious* (1905) is dedicated mostly to the collective phenomena of jokes and the comic, which necessitate the presence of at least three and two participants respectively. In contrast, humour, discussed both in the 1905 book and in the 1927 article 'Der Humor', is an individual phenomenon. Freud explains the specificity of humour by using the example of the joke of a prisoner heading to the gallows on a Monday and exclaiming 'Well, the week's beginning nicely' (Freud [1927] 1961: 161). Freud develops his theory of *Humor*, distinct from jokes and the comic, as a reaction arising in situations similar to the prisoner's. Humour would become a liberating response which enables one to deflate unbearable situations. I argue that it can also become a tool to construct a new space that allows the humorist to negotiate with reality, without leading to any conclusive moment of liberation. The creation of this space is made possible by the interaction between the ego and the super-ego. This interaction is crucial; in the fictional works I analyse, the condition of imprisonment and the isolation of the characters create the ideal setting for the development of humour through an inner dialogue between two parts of the self, in opposition to the open, collective sites of the comic which promote an outer dialogue.

Freud is considered one of the main proponents of the relief theory of humour. Since John Morreall's *Taking Laughter Seriously* (1983), humour theories are often split into three main branches: the superiority theory (Plato, Aristotle's *Poetics* and *Nicomachean Ethics*, Hobbes, Konrad Lorenz), the incongruity theory (Aristotle's *Rhetoric*, Kant, Schopenhauer), and the relief theory (Shaftesbury, Spencer, Freud) (Morreall 1983: 4–37).[2] The relief theory proposes that laughter is 'a venting of nervous energy' (Morreall 1983: 20) which brings liberation. Freud's theory, based on the analysis of short forms such as jokes, poses one main problem for the study of longer narratives: it does not consider the aftermath of the punchline. Studying narratives puts into question the relief theory of humour, asking us to reframe liberation as a moment in the development of humour rather than the conclusion of its trajectory.[3]

Luigi Pirandello's seminal essay *L'umorismo* views humour as such a process. Pirandello defines humour, in a restricted sense (as opposed to what is generally humorous), as a two-step procedure. The first step is the observation, in life or in art, of a discrepancy (the *avvertimento del contrario*). It is followed by a process of active reflection that leads to an emotional comprehension of the discrepancy observed at first (the *sentimento del contrario*). Humour is the trajectory, the interaction between the two steps, as well as the oscillatory state that results from their interaction. Humoristic narratives are based on the tension between the two steps, and humoristic characters are unstable, incoherent figures. To Pirandello, the power of the humoristic narrative is set against the oppressive force of predetermined 'forms', be they social, artistic, stylistic. The characters' humoristic laughter is generally framed as a rebellious reply to the oppression of their milieu. The answer to the prison of forms is thus the refusal to settle in a definite shape, to stop the oscillatory movement of humour. At the same time, the oscillation often calls for a stable form that will contain it, precisely to enable its perpetuation. The close relationship between humour and configurations of imprisonment stems precisely from the necessity for the oscillatory movement to be contained in order for it to be perpetuated.

Wyndham Lewis's theories of laughter, humour and satire are very close to Pirandello's, a parallel that has not been noted previously. His notion of 'metaphysical satire' recalls Pirandello's *umorismo*, in that the metaphysical satirist has the power to reveal, through laughter, one's inherent imprisonment in social and existential forms. Metaphysical satire builds on Lewis's earlier notions of 'blessed' and 'blasted' forms of humour (Lewis [1914] 1981) and of the comic as 'the sensations resulting from the observation of a *thing* behaving like a person' (Lewis 1927: 246; original emphasis). Generalizing this principle, metaphysical satire is defined as a non-moral satire dealing with all mankind: the mere fact of being human (that is a thing behaving like a person) is the source of laughter for the individual who is able to reflect upon it (Lewis [1934] 1964). Metaphysical satire and *umorismo* are thus developed in interaction with imprisonment. For Pirandello, the humoristic narrative can suspend the prison of forms by creating a 'formless' entity, in terms of both structure and character. Lewis's theory is more pessimistic. Laughter sheds light on a constitutive entrapment without proposing any means to suspend it, even less to liberate oneself from it. It is a theory of enlightenment, not of liberation. Both Pirandello and Lewis's theories move away from the notion of liberation and from relief theories of humour. Theirs are based on the contrast between one's immediate perception, and a deeper understanding of a phenomenon through reflection, distance and artistic creation, and can therefore be related to incongruity theories of humour. Lewis's theory can also be connected with superiority theories, since the person who is able to perceive the incongruous is deemed superior to those who cannot do so.

The fifth theory in my framework belongs to Mikhail Bakhtin. Up to the 1980s, Bakhtin was not included in surveys of humour theories in English, such as Morreall's or Holland's, although he was already discussed in Italy by Giulio Ferroni (1974). Since 'the *bakhtinskii boom* of the 1980s and 1990s' (Emerson 1997: 4), Bakhtin's writings on laughter have been included in discussions of humour in contexts of oppression. His best-known claims on the liberating powers of laughter come from *Rabelais and His World*, yet his reflection on laughter's role in narratives is present in many other works that offer a more comprehensive and nuanced discussion of laughter and humour. From the writings collected in *The Dialogic Imagination* (1930s) to the fragmented 'From Notes Made in 1970–71', Bakhtin developed his observations on the liberating power of laughter and humour with regard to social hierarchies, fear and individual bodily limits, while relating laughter to the development of the genre of the novel. The 1970s 'Notes' also shift the discussion from a collective framework to the intimate one which is most prevalent in the works I analyse. Bakhtin's ideas on laughter and humour can be related to the relief theory, since laughter is pictured either as providing individual relief (mainly in the 'Notes') or, on a larger scale, as a moment of collective relief from socially imposed structures. However, we must not lose sight of the idea that relief can only arise in the wider context of the imposition of structures, that it is a moment within a larger dynamic, and that liberation sheds light on the notion of imprisonment that is truly at the core of Bakhtin's discussions.

Using the notion of imprisonment as a thread, I connect the theoretical perspectives of Bergson, Freud, Pirandello, Lewis and Bakhtin, which are not generally united in the same framework. The reception of the theories also greatly varies between critical contexts in English, French and Italian studies. Bergson and Freud are the most prevalent theorists in humour studies in English and are often compared or mentioned together. Bakhtin has now gained popularity and is often included in comprehensive theories of humour, but that is still not the case for Pirandello. While *L'umorismo* is central to any Italian critical work on humour, it is very rarely mentioned in English humour studies.[4] This is unfortunate, especially in the case of the study of literary humour, since Pirandello's theory is dedicated to explaining the particular form of humoristic fiction. Lewis is also rarely discussed in contemporary studies of humour. When it is the case, he is often compared to Bergson, for example by Simon Critchley in *On Humour* (2002). Critchley only looks at *The Wild Body* and does not consider this book's formulation of the comic within a larger Lewisian framework that would include 'blessed' and 'blasted' forms of laughter and metaphysical satire. Pirandello and Lewis are the only two theorists of my framework who are also writers of fiction. Since their theories are informed by their fiction and vice versa, I discuss both parts of their practice as writers (see Chapter 3). Their attention to literary form might actually explain why liberation is reframed as a moment within the process of humour. Including their theoretical input alongside better-known theories allows me both to insist on the specificities of *literary* humour and to reframe the theories of Bergson, Freud and Bakhtin through the concept of constitutive entrapment that is most central in Pirandello and Lewis.

Sites of imprisonment

By studying humoristic representations of imprisonment in twentieth-century literature, I want to show differences between them and the dominant modes of representation of previous eras and to nuance the bleak portrait of imprisonment narratives often drawn in the twentieth century. After the eighteenth-century picaresque conception of the prison as a step in the pícaro's meanderings, and the Romantic dream for the cell as a lyrical space of self-creation, twentieth-century humoristic narratives present an ambivalent attitude towards imprisonment that oscillates between positive and negative portrayals, combining aspects of both previous perspectives.

In *Les prisons du roman (XVIIe–XVIIIe siècle). Lectures plurielles et intertextuelles de* Guzman d'Alfarache *à* Jacques le fataliste (2000), Jacques Berchtold demonstrates how the prison is viewed as a necessary step in the journey of the seventeenth- and eighteenth-century French and Spanish pícaro, the adventurous hero of picaresque novels. He also argues that the novelistic discourse possesses in itself an 'incarcerating' dimension (751–2), explaining the connection between the representation of imprisonment and the rise of novel, a formless genre looking for its own identity (12). Using the metaphor of the Game of the Goose, a board game in which players compete to attain the last space of a path filled with pitfalls, Berchtold pictures the prison as a 'square' that picaresque characters are bound to step on – and be contained in – at some point in their trajectory. The path is not linear, but curls back on itself, and thus the pícaro's passage in prison can be repeated multiple times. Aside from part of Romain Gary's work, where the picaresque plays an important role, the prison is generally not a banal step in a circular narrative in the works of the authors I study. The space of the cell is both not as common anymore (as it used to be in the daily life of the pícaro), and more common under the circumstances of new war regimes and totalitarian regimes. The arbitrariness of the prison in picaresque narratives is present in some works (especially in *Invitation to a Beheading*), but the prison is not depicted as a common square which is quickly entered and exited. Rather, it is often the setting of long stays that frequently lead to epiphanic revelations. In that respect, imprisonment takes on a place that is closer to the nineteenth-century French novel paradigm exposed by Victor Brombert in *La prison romantique. Essai sur l'imaginaire* (1975).[5]

Brombert shows that the imaginary of the prison is never as prominent as it was in the nineteenth century, when the Romantics poeticize the space of the prison and the cell becomes the setting for a dialectics between oppression and the dream of freedom, fatality and will, limits and the desire of infinity (15) – a series of oppositions also present in my corpus. Except for Fabrice del Dongo's epiphanic laughter at the moment when he realizes the extent of his happiness in prison (Brombert 1975: 71; Stendhal 1864: 276), the narratives discussed do not incorporate laughter, comedy or humour. The dominant tone of nineteenth-century representations is an individualistic 'lyrisme cellulaire', a term Brombert borrows from Camus (Brombert 1975: 177). This lyrical mode is contested by the twentieth-century war camps narratives to which Brombert dedicates the third part of his study, be they survivors' narratives or the fictional works of Camus and Sartre. Those narratives refuse the myth of the happy prison (204) and shift the representation from individual to collective imprisonment. Looking at narratives from the same period as that covered by Brombert in his last section, however, I see that the myth of the happy prison is still present in twentieth-century literature. More significantly, by highlighting the connection between imprisonment and humour, I complement the bleak representations of Brombert's corpus.

Berchtold's and Brombert's studies picture the prison cell as both a distinctive setting of epiphanic moments, and a setting that allows for a condensation of time, highlighting the continuity between the time and space of the cell, and the time and space outside it. Narratives of imprisonment often paradoxically insist on the continuity between life in the prison and life outside of it. In Berchtold's words, 'si un *contraste* peut s'affirmer entre l'enfermement et l'état de liberté; on observe ailleurs, à l'inverse, une *absence de rupture* plus surprenante, qui souligne une *homogénéité* entre le monde carcéral et le monde extérieur égalisés dans une relation d'identité spéculaire' (750; original emphasis) ['if a *contrast* may assert itself between imprisonment and the state of freedom, we notice elsewhere, on the contrary, a more surprising *absence of rupture* that underlines an *homogeneity* between the prison world and the outside world, leveled out in a relation of specular identity']. Berchtold's conclusion is crucial for my argument. This very continuity between the space of the prison and life outside of the cell as a form of prison is at the core of the literary developments of humour. The prison should be understood both as a setting and as a metaphor, as the interactions between spatial imprisonment in a cell and other forms of imprisonment demonstrate. I study this continuity between spaces by looking at three types of fictional sites, which will show that imprisonment should be considered along a continuum: the cell, the mask and the body.

Corpus and structure of the book

Humour in imprisonment is not an accidental phenomenon but rather the sign of an essential connection. My choice of works was motivated by historical, methodological and structural considerations to build a coherent corpus that brings to light this relationship. Most works analysed refer directly or indirectly to the historical and political context of the twentieth century in Europe and Russia. Some works fictionalize the historical context of their imprisoned characters (the Shoah and its aftermath in *La danse de Gengis Cohn*; Second World War prisoner-of-war camps in *Diario clandestino* and *Les racines du ciel*). Others create new settings of imprisonment in non-referential ways that can nevertheless be connected to the political context in which they were written (such as Soviet Russia for *Invitation to a Beheading*). In some other cases, political events have left traces in the characters' lives and contribute to their current feeling of entrapment. This is the case with the First World War for the protagonist of *Snooty Baronet* or the Second World War in Guareschi's autobiographical works. Finally, some works reflect on their social context by picturing characters trapped in their most immediate social surroundings (*Uno, nessuno e centomila*; *Les clowns lyriques*; *Laughter in the Dark*).

By adopting a comparative approach based on close readings, I identify core structural features of literary humour, notably its self-reflexivity, its narrative discontinuity, its recourse to split, double or multiple selves and its use of figures of opposition, reversals and paradoxes like the chiasmus and the syllepsis. Humour is located both within the diegesis (where it is then often signalled by the characters' laughter) and at the narrative level (where it can, but does not necessarily has to, be signalled by the reader's laughter). Close reading entails a solid linguistic competence in the language of the work; hence my choice of works written in French, English and Italian.[6] My comparative approach is also informed by a desire to show a conceptual continuity between works that are stylistically varied and whose critical reception has been markedly different. The corpus strikes a balance between the works of authors who are part of the Western literary canon or of their national literary canon (Nabokov, Pirandello and Lewis) and the works of authors who are not. Giovannino Guareschi and Romain Gary have received little critical attention in English, despite the fact that their translated works have been very popular in the Anglosphere – Guareschi is, in fact, the most translated Italian author of the twentieth century (Perry 2007). Guareschi's exclusion from the Italian literary canon has been influenced by the populist and polemic nature of his works and by his right-wing political orientation, while Romain Gary's popularity and Gaullist allegiance have similarly contributed to his exclusion from the French canon. There have been recent revivals of academic interest in the works of both authors in Italian Studies and French Studies, but still little international attention, with the notable exceptions of Alan R. Perry's work on Guareschi, and David Bellos's and Ralph Schoolcraft's on Gary. Gary's and Guareschi's works have proven the most fruitful to highlight the connection between imprisonment and humour. Gary's novels are discussed in all three thematic chapters, while Guareschi's imprisonment writings bookend the analyses.

Finally, the choice of corpus goes hand in hand with the book's structure. The case studies are chosen and organized in a progression that stresses the continuum of imprisonment. I start by presenting obvious cases of imprisonment, narratives where the relationship between humour and imprisonment is the clearest. This allows me to focus on the literary strategies at play in the fiction and to show

how we can define humour in practice. From cases of political imprisonment, I move to cases of social and personal imprisonment. While the narratives frame political imprisonment by using the recurrent image of the prison, social forms of entrapment are framed thanks to the mask, and personal confinement is delineated by the limits of the characters' bodies. Within each of the sites of imprisonment (prison, mask, body), the analyses are also presented from the most concrete to the most metaphorical cases.

Thus, Chapter 2 deals with three narratives picturing prisoners who use humour within their prison cells or war camps, or within their narration about it. The first case is autobiographical; the second one refers to a historical situation of imprisonment; the third is set in an imaginary totalitarian state. Guareschi's *Diario clandestino 1943–1945* fictionalizes the author's real-life experience of internment in Nazi war camps. From this autobiographical narrative, I move to the fictional representation of Second World War prisoners of war in a passage of Gary's *Les racines du ciel*. Finally, I look at the nineteen days in prison of Cincinnatus C., the protagonist of Nabokov's *Invitation to a Beheading*.

From the setting of the cell and war camp, I reframe the concept of imprisonment to look at situations of imprisonment outside walls and within society (Chapter 3). I argue that the use of humour in prison is directly connected with its use in other, less easily circumscribed but very significant, forms of imprisonment. There is a structural relationship between humour, as it is conceptualized and fictionalized in the twentieth century, and the notion of entrapment. To study 'social imprisonment', I use the frame of the mask, which gives defined boundaries to the character living within it. I look at three masks that Bakhtin singles out as being of crucial importance for the development of the modern novel: the fool, the rogue and the clown (Bakhtin 1981). The fool figure is exemplified by Vitangelo Moscarda, the protagonist of Pirandello's *Uno, nessuno e centomila*. Snooty Baronet, narrator of Lewis's eponymous *Snooty Baronet*, exemplifies the figure of the rogue. Finally, La Marne, one of the many characters of Gary's *Les clowns lyriques*, is the emblematic lyrical clown.

Following the cell and the mask, I conclude with the analysis of the body as a site of imprisonment which elicits humour. Chapter 4 offers three configurations of imprisonment within the body: an immaterial character trapped within another character's body, a character increasingly confined within his own body and a character who contains within himself another self from his past, trapped in his bodily shell. Gengis Cohn (Gary, *La danse de Gengis Cohn*) is a Jewish *dybbuk* who is prisoner of the body of former Nazi officer Otto Schatz. Albert

Albinus (Nabokov, *Laughter in the Dark*) is caught in a process of chance and manipulation that leads him to become a prisoner of his own blind body. Finally, I go back to the first character discussed in the book, the fictional 'Guareschi' who was the subject of *Diario clandestino*. Starting from the war camps narratives, I move to narratives written about the author's imprisonment for libel in the 1950s to show how his fictionalization of imprisonment calls into question the temporal and spatial demarcations generally drawn between a time and space of the prison, and an 'after' and 'outside' of the prison.

I conclude by showing how humoristic narratives stress the continuity between different representations of imprisonment such as the cell, the mask and the body by operating displacements between those sites. Humour sets itself against the comic circle; it is a spiral impulse resisting feelings of entrapment. It does not lead to liberation but provokes an oscillatory movement that needs frames that can contain it. Humour's connection to imprisonment is therefore bidirectional: the humoristic oscillation stems from conditions of confinement and creates those conditions anew.

1

Humour and Imprisonment

To set the stage for the analysis of humour in confinement in fiction, this chapter develops a comparative framework out of five theories that connect humour and imprisonment. Since the theorists conceive and name humour differently, I map out the different meanings of the word and the variations within each theorist's work in chronological order: from Bergson's 1900 essay *Le rire*,[1] through Freud's 1905 *Jokes and Their Relation to the Unconscious* and his 1927 article 'Der Humor', Pirandello's 1908 *Umorismo* (revised in 1920), Wyndham Lewis's theories of laughter, humour and satire from the 1910s to the 1930s, up to Bakhtin's theories of laughter, the carnival and dialogism from the 1930s to the 1970s. In bringing together these theories, I am particularly attentive to draw a distinction between the phenomena of the comic and of humour. While I clarify terminological differences, I am most interested in the conceptual application of the theories.

Bergson

Bergson's theory is not one of humour but of the comic. He discusses humour only on two pages, describing it as a type of satire, itself a sub-category of the comic. However, it is essential to use it as a starting point in my discussion of the connection between humour and imprisonment in the twentieth century for several reasons. Firstly, its impact on other modern theories is indisputable. It has been referenced and debated throughout the twentieth century, and it is still quoted and used as a framework in literary analyses today (see Jardon 1988: 20-1). It has also influenced, directly or indirectly, most of the other authors and theorists I discuss, especially Wyndham Lewis. Second, Bergson's theory of *the comic* acts as a foil to better understand *humour*. It highlights the properties of humour that are not present in the comic, an important difference being the presence of self-reflexivity in humour and its absence in the comic. Furthermore, the comic itself is not absent from the works I analyse, but it does not deal with imprisonment the same way humour does. Finally, Bergson's theory is developed around the ideas of mechanicity, automatism, rigidity – that is around notions of individual, social and bodily confinement. For Bergson, comic laughter arises in a social group in direct reaction to the identification of forms of imprisonment, and it is posited as a way to free the imprisoned self from said imprisonment and to reintegrate this individual into the group. However, *Le rire* stages an inner contradiction between liberation and coercion, as laughter becomes both a possible tool for liberation and a coercive device.

The comic, satire, irony, humour

The crux of Bergson's theory is the social role of laughter as a corrective. Having identified three essential characteristics of laughter (pertaining to humans, accompanied by an absence of feeling and necessarily social), the philosopher pictures laughter as a social gesture which corrects individual rigidity. 'Toute *raideur* du caractère, de l'esprit et même du corps' (Bergson [1900] 1975: 15; original emphasis) ['all *inelasticity* of character, of mind and even of body' ([1900] 1911: 19; original emphasis)],[2] interpreted by the social group as a menacing eccentricity, would call for collective repression:

> Par la crainte qu'il inspire, [le rire] réprime les excentricités, tient constamment en éveil et en contact réciproque certaines activités d'ordre accessoire qui risqueraient de s'isoler et de s'endormir, assouplit enfin tout ce qui peut rester de raideur mécanique à la surface du corps social. Le rire ne relève donc pas de l'esthétique pure, puisqu'il poursuit (inconsciemment, et même immoralement dans beaucoup de cas particuliers) un but utile de perfectionnement général. (Bergson [1900] 1975: 15–16)

> [By the fear which it inspires, [laughter] restrains eccentricity, keeps constantly awake and in mutual contact certain activities of a secondary order which might retire into their shell and go to sleep, and, in short, softens down whatever the surface of the social body may retain of mechanical inelasticity. Laughter, then, does not belong to the province of esthetics alone, since unconsciously (and even immorally in many particular instances) it pursues a utilitarian aim of general improvement. ([1900] 1911: 19–20)]

For Bergson, we laugh when we see a person behave as a thing. Someone behaving mechanically, rather than being fully alive, only imitates life: 'Ce n'est plus la vie, c'est de l'automatisme installé dans la vie et imitant la vie. C'est du comique.' (Bergson [1900] 1975: 25) ['This is no longer life, it is automatism established in life and imitating it. It belongs to the comic' ([1900] 1911: 32)]. Automatism being perceived as an imprisonment in a predetermined form, laughter would lead to the individual's liberation from that form and to increased flexibility. Bergson's essay develops this core idea of punitive/liberating laughter for four categories of the comic: the comic in forms and movements, the comic in situations, the comic in words and the comic in character. For each of these categories, he shows the role of three processes: inversion, reciprocal interference and repetition/transposition.[3]

Bergson's essay deals specifically with *comic* laughter. Yet his category of the comic – located at the intersection of life and art (Bergson [1900] 1975: 17, 103, [1900] 1911: 22, 135) – encompasses all sorts of manifestations, from comedies to novels, from caricature to everyday life. Moreover, the comic includes satire, irony and humour, all treated within the category of the comic in words. Bergson saw the artificiality of this category (Bergson [1900] 1975: 78, [1900] 1911: 103), but still distinguished between 'le comique que le langage exprime et celui que le langage crée' (Bergson [1900] 1975: 79) ['the comic *expressed* and the comic *created* by language' ([1900] 1911: 103; original emphasis)]. The comic in words becomes the 'projection' of the comic of actions and situations 'sur le plan des mots' (Bergson [1900] 1975: 85) ['on to the plane of words' ([1900] 1911: 111)].

Within the all-encompassing category of the comic, Bergson identifies subcategories such as satire, which enacts a transposition between the real and the ideal. Humour and irony would be two possible forms of satire, defined in opposition to one another. Irony is defined as stating what should be done and pretending to believe this is what is being done. Humour, on the other hand, is stating minutely what is being done, and pretending to believe this is what should be done: 'Tantôt, au contraire, on décrira minutieusement et méticuleusement ce qui est, en affectant de croire que c'est bien là ce que les choses devraient être: ainsi procède souvent l'*humour*' (Bergson [1900] 1975: 97; original emphasis) ['Sometimes, on the contrary, we describe with scrupulous minuteness what is being done, and pretend to believe that this is just what ought to be done; such is often the method of *humour*' ([1900] 1911: 127; original emphasis)]. Humour is also distinguished by its 'scientific' character. It is an act of transposition from the moral to the scientific, and the humorist is 'un moraliste qui se déguise en savant' (Bergson [1900] 1975: 98) ['a moralist disguised as a scientist' ([1900] 1911: 128)]. This definition of humour, easily applicable to a tradition of humorists or satirists such as Jonathan Swift or Mark Twain, is, however, too specific to explain the structure of humour in the works discussed in this book. Bergson is conscious of the restrictiveness of his use of the term, specifying that he uses the word 'au sens restreint' (Bergson [1900] 1975: 98) ['in the restricted sense' ([1900] 1911: 128)]. This narrow sense is not what I call humour.

Despite the micro-distinctions, Bergson explains all comic word transpositions (irony, humour, parody, exaggeration [Bergson [1900] 1975: 94–5, [1900] 1911: 123–5]) by going back to the notion of the stiffening of something that should be fluid. Laughter arises as a sign that something is mechanical (or appears to be mechanical), where it should be flowing with what will later be called the *élan vital*. In the comic in words, the comic 'souligne les distractions du langage lui-même. C'est le langage lui-même, ici, qui devient comique.' (Bergson [1900] 1975: 79) ['[the comic] lays stress on lapses of attention in language itself. In this case, it is language itself that becomes comic' ([1900] 1911: 104)].

The comic and imprisonment

Therefore, the role of comic laughter is to be a weapon against rigidity, whatever that rigidity is. All types of mechanicity, or lack of elasticity, should be socially signalled by laughter in order to help the individual displaying them to realign with the *élan vital*.[4] Pictured this way, laughter would be a tool to set free the individual trapped by automatism. Yet the relationship between Bergson's laughter and imprisonment is ambivalent, if not paradoxical. While, on the one hand, laughter should set the individual free, on the other hand, this *social* corrective is exercised from outside, without access to the target's interiority. It asserts the primacy of an external, collective perception of what individual flexibility should look like and is therefore, by definition, normative. What Bergson pictures as a way to liberate the individual from imprisonment in habit and mechanicity is also a coercive tool. This is the contradiction at the core of Bergson's theory.

Part of this contradiction can be clarified by understanding the relationship between laughter and Bergson's central notion of *élan vital*. Although Le rire does not use this concept, it is key to understanding laughter's role. Explained as an 'exigence de création' (Bergson 1970: 708) [a 'creative exigency'] that lies at the origin of life, the *élan vital* opposes itself to repetition. In Paul Douglass's overview of Bergson's concept, the necessity of change or creation in the *élan vital* is explained by a crucial line of Le rire:

> If the universe is both creative and destructive, nonetheless its original and fundamental nature is the creative act implied in the phrase *élan vital*. Thus,

Bergson argues that the vital energy of life is perpetually struggling to overcome materiality (or 'matter'). The universe always seeks a return to its origin in pure energy and protean, radical change. 'To cease to change would be to cease to live', Bergson believes, and 'the fundamental law of life ... is the complete negation of repetition'.[5] (Bergson [1900] 1911: 32) (Douglass 2013: 303; original emphasis)

Thus, life is opposed to repetition, and it is not surprising that Bergson sees repetition as one of the main processes of the comic. Social laughter wishes to correct something perceived by Bergson as un-natural and negative for the human being, a lack of fluidity (*'raideur du caractère, de l'esprit et même du corps'*) (Bergson [1900] 1975: 15; original emphasis) ['*inelasticity* of character, of mind and even of body' ([1900] 1911: 19; original emphasis)]. Bergsonian laughter is thus a negative force, but a negative force applied to another negativity, and assumed to bring 'perfectionnement général' (Bergson [1900] 1975: 16) ['general improvement' ([1900] 1911: 20)] to society and to the individual. It is an attempt to remove constraints (of automatism, of habits, of lack of life).

However, the improvement is always imposed on the individual by the group, and the place of the individual response in front of social laughter remains unclear. The question is therefore whether imposed freedom can be perceived as freedom. The role of individual laughter and its impact on the group are also unclear. The disconcerting aspect of Bergson's theory is that the effect of the *élan vital* appears to be both predicted in time and observed from the outside. Indeed, if the social group is able to 'correct' a behaviour that has stepped out of the 'natural' order, it means that the flowing nature of the *élan vital* can be predicted. Moreover, the perception of what automatisms are and what they are not seems to be a matter of consensus among the ideal group depicted by Bergson. What pertains to the *élan vital* and what pertains to '*du mécanique plaqué sur du vivant*' (Bergson [1900] 1975: 29; original emphasis) ['*something mechanical encrusted on the living*' ([1900] 1911: 37; original emphasis)] does not seem to be open to debate. Finally, the idea that 'nous ne commençons donc à devenir imitables que là où nous cessons d'être nous-mêmes' (Bergson [1900] 1975: 25) ['we begin, then, to become imitable only when we cease to be ourselves' ([1900] 1911: 33)] implies that there would be absolutely no automatism inherent in our 'natural' self, and that this 'natural' self is a given and can be clearly identified.

Bergson insists on several occasions on the absence of freedom within comic situations or in comic characters, an absence that laughter should signal. He compares comic characters to puppets controlled by a mechanism or by strings pulled by an entity they cannot see:

Tout le sérieux de la vie lui vient de notre liberté. Les sentiments que nous avons mûris, les passions que nous avons couvées, les actions que nous avons délibérées, arrêtées, exécutées, enfin ce qui vient de nous et ce qui est bien nôtre, voilà ce qui donne à la vie son allure quelquefois dramatique et généralement grave. Que faudrait-il pour transformer tout cela en comédie? Il faudrait se figurer que la liberté apparente recouvre un jeu de ficelles. (Bergson [1900] 1975: 60)

[All that is serious in life comes from our freedom. The feelings we have matured, the passions we have brooded over, the actions we have weighed, decided upon, and carried through, in short, all that comes from us and is our very own, these are the things that give life its ofttimes dramatic and generally grave aspect. What, then, is requisite to transform all this into a comedy? Merely to fancy that our seeming freedom conceals the strings of a dancing-jack. ([1900] 1911: 79)]

The initial opposition between life and automatism reveals a more elaborate set of contrasts between freedom, seriousness and drama on the one hand, and the comic and unfreedom on the other. Most crucially, the puppet's unfreedom is concealed, or rather, the lack of freedom would stem precisely from the puppet's inability to be conscious of its being manipulated. The comic would end as soon as a puppet realizes it is manipulated and modifies its behaviour in order to free itself.

The comic and humour

This points to the most important aspect of Bergson's theory for my discussion: *Bergson's comic cannot be perceived by the comic target*: 'un personnage comique est généralement comique dans l'exacte mesure où il s'ignore lui-même. Le comique est *inconscient*. Comme s'il usait à rebours de l'anneau de Gygès, il se rend invisible à lui-même en devenant visible à tout le monde.' (Bergson [1900] 1975: 13; original emphasis) ['a comic character is generally comic in proportion to his ignorance of himself. The comic person is unconscious. As though wearing the ring of Gyges with reverse effect, he becomes invisible to himself while remaining visible to all the world' ([1900] 1911: 16–17)]. The type of correction provided by laughter is thus intimately related to a lack of self-consciousness. In Bergson's theory, once comic characters are punished by laughter *and understand why*, they are not comic anymore. They are certainly not freed from imprisonment yet – if they can ever be – but, conscious of their own imprisonment, they can start changing their behaviour or at least hiding it from their group. It is in this way that laughter is a social corrective: 'Disons-le dès maintenant, c'est en ce sens surtout que le rire "châtie les mœurs". Il fait que nous tâchons tout de suite de paraître ce que nous devrions être, ce que nous finirons sans doute un jour par être véritablement.' (Bergson [1900] 1975: 13) ['Indeed, it is in this sense only that laughter "corrects men's manners". It makes us at once endeavour to appear what we ought to be, what some day we shall perhaps end in being' ([1900] 1911: 17)].

The humoristic phenomenon in which I am interested, however, implies self-consciousness on the part of the individual. In both cases, the voice of an individual author or an individual character is at the forefront. The most important difference between the comic (as intended by Bergson) and humour (as intended by Freud and Pirandello, among others) is therefore self-consciousness.[6] In other words, both the comic and humour imply imprisonment, but comic characters do not recognize their own imprisonment, whereas humoristic characters do. This does not mean that being conscious of one's imprisonment necessarily leads to the possibility or even the desire of liberation for the literary character.

Freud

Freud's works on jokes, the comic and humour posit a desire for liberation. Out of the three phenomena, humour would be the most liberating. This liberating power, which might be present in literature but nevertheless cannot explain the form of literary humour, is born out of the context of imprisonment that is also at the core of Freud's theory.[7] To explain what he means by 'humour', Freud uses the example of a prisoner walking to the gallows on a Monday and exclaiming: 'Well, the week's beginning nicely' (Freud [1927] 1961: 162). In an unbearable situation such as the prisoner's, a part of one's self would enter in dialogue with another part to soothe it. Humour would be the dialogue between two parts of a split self. Narrative humour shows this dialogue in action, without expecting liberation to come out of it. Freud's theory, despite its insistence on the notions of psychic relief and liberation, is therefore useful to develop my analytical framework.

Laughter, jokes, the comic, humour

Freud's 1905 *Jokes and Their Relation to the Unconscious* (*Der Witz und seine Beziehung zum Unbewußten*) focuses mainly on jokes, but also deals with the comic and with humour in a few pages at the very end of the book (Freud [1905] 1960:

228–35). In 1927, Freud goes back to humour in the short article 'Der Humor', reworking his understanding of the phenomenon according to the separation of the psyche into the id, the ego and the super-ego developed in the meantime (see Shentoub 1989: 13 and Strachey 1960: 6). Freud's approach complements Bergson's by shifting the standpoint from which laughter is observed from the outside to the inside. According to Bergson, laughter would liberate the individual *towards whom* it is directed (and we have seen that this is problematic). Freud, on the other hand, focuses on the impact of laughter *from the point of view of the one who laughs*. Jokes would 'temporarily free one from inhibition' (Parkin 1997: 41) by economizing the psychic energy normally involved in maintaining inhibitions:

> In laughter, therefore, on our hypothesis, the conditions are present under which a sum of psychical energy which has hitherto been used for cathexis is allowed free discharge. And since laughter – not all laughter, it is true, but certainly laughter at a joke – is an indication of pleasure, we shall be inclined to relate this pleasure to the lifting of the cathexis which has previously been present. (Freud [1905] 1960: 148)[8]

The economy principle and the pleasure principle, although not yet formalized as in later theories (see Parkin 1997: 81), are combined to explain the mechanisms of jokes, the comic and humour. In all cases, laughter, associated with pleasure and release, arises from the economy of psychic expenditure, but the nature of the economy differs for the three phenomena. While the pleasure of jokes derives from an economy of expenditure in inhibition, the pleasure of the comic derives from an economy of expenditure in ideation and the pleasure of humour derives from an economy of expenditure in feeling (Freud [1905] 1960: 236).

Laughter elicited by humour is depicted as a primarily individual feature, rather than a collective one. Whereas jokes and the comic necessarily pertain to the social realm, humour is first of all an individual psychic process: 'Humour is the most easily satisfied among the species of the comic. It completes its course within a single person; another person's participation adds nothing new to it' (Freud [1905] 1960: 229). Freud also pictures humour as less likely to produce 'hearty laughter' (Freud [1927] 1961: 166) than jokes and the comic. Humour might be more likely to raise a smile than to provoke laughter. In spite of this, or because of this, humour is to him the most liberating of the three phenomena studied (Freud [1927] 1961: 166). The specific form of economy associated with humour stresses the connection between humour and feeling. Freud perceives negative emotions as impediments to the comic: 'the release of distressing affects is the greatest obstacle to the emergence of the comic' (Freud [1905] 1960: 228). Humour, on the other hand, arises in the presence of (or in confrontation with) those affects. It is 'a means of obtaining pleasure in spite of the distressing affects that interfere with it' (Freud [1905] 1960: 228). We could say that, for Freud, the comic is located outside of painful emotions; it is developed separately from them. In spatial terms, humour would be positioned above emotions, since, as we will see, it is a way of rising above them to attain a form of elevation. Temporally, we can also consider humour to be located after emotions.

The liberating and rebellious power of humour

Indeed, for Freud, humour arises from the recognition of the presence of painful affects but is created by repressing and in the end by overcoming them: 'The conditions for its appearance are given if there is a situation in which, according to our usual habits, we should be tempted to release a distressing affect and if motives then operate upon us which suppress that affect *in statu nascendi*' (Freud [1905] 1960: 228). In his 1927 article, Freud clarifies this idea by explaining that the producer of humour replaces an expected demonstration of affect by jest: 'There is no doubt that the essence of humour is that one spares oneself the affects to which the situation would naturally give rise and dismisses the possibility of such expressions of emotion with a jest' (Freud [1927] 1961: 162).[9]

The economy of emotion is not the only trait differentiating humour from jokes and the comic. Humour, he explains, possesses a form of 'grandeur' (162), of 'elevation' (162), of 'dignity' (163), that the other two phenomena lack. What is important is not the value statement that the notions of grandeur and dignity imply, but the source of humour's dignity:

> The grandeur in it clearly lies in the triumph of narcissism, the victorious assertion of the ego's invulnerability. The ego refuses to be distressed by the provocations of reality, to let itself be compelled to suffer. It insists that it cannot be affected by the traumas of the external world; it shows, in fact, that such traumas are no more than occasions for it to gain pleasure. This last feature is a quite essential element of humour. (162)

The spatial location of humour over painful affects rather than aside from them is denoted in the ideas of grandeur and elevation. By pushing humorists above the conditions they are rejecting, humour becomes more than a mere defence mechanism or a repressive phenomenon (Freud [1905] 1960: 233). Freud stresses the rebellious force of humour: 'Humour is not resigned; it is rebellious. It signifies not only the triumph of the ego but also of the pleasure principle, which is able here to assert itself against the unkindness of the real circumstances' (Freud [1927] 1961: 163). The rebellious aspect of humour is essential to the treatment of imprisonment by humoristic authors. Humour within imprisonment could be read as a rebellion against reality through jest. As Freud makes clear, though, what matters most is not the jest but the intention behind it:

> the jest made by humour is not the essential thing. It has only the value of a preliminary. The main thing is the intention which humour carries out, whether it is acting in relation to the self or other people. It means: 'Look! Here is the world, which seems so dangerous! It is nothing but a game for children – just worth making a jest about!' (Freud [1927] 1961: 166)

The split self as the foundation of humour

The 'assertion of the ego's invulnerability' opens up the discussion to the psychic instances active in humour. The ego's invulnerability is asserted thanks to the participation of the super-ego. To illustrate this idea, Freud uses the image of a father who would smile in front of the triviality of the suffering of his child (Freud [1927] 1961: 163). Humour would be created by the shift of 'psychical accent' from the ego (associated with the child) to the super-ego (associated with the father). As he makes clear, the part of the self that soothes the other part has a position of superiority, that grants it authority and thus the capacity to reinforce the distance between itself and the inferior part. The association between the two instances and the father and son is a development from the 1905 book where Freud had hinted at the relationship between humour and the infantile:

> It is even conceivable that once again it may be a connection with the infantile that puts the means for achieving this [transforming the energy of the possible negative affects into pleasure] at its disposal. Only in childhood have there been distressing affects at which the adult would smile to-day – just as he laughs, as a humorist, at his present distressing affects. The exaltation of his ego, to which the humorous displacement bears witness, and of which the translation would no doubt be 'I am too big (too fine) to be distressed by these things', might well be derived from his comparing his present ego with his childish one. (Freud [1905] 1960: 233–4)

In 1927, the relationship between the two parts of the self is given clear familial correlatives and structured into a hierarchical relationship.

> Genetically the super-ego is the heir to the parental agency. It often keeps the ego in strict dependence and still really treats it as the parents, or the father, once treated the child, in its early years. We obtain a dynamic explanation of the humorous attitude, therefore, if we assume that it consists in the humorist's having withdrawn the psychical accent from his ego and having transposed it on to his super-ego. To the super-ego, thus inflated, the ego can appear tiny and all its interests trivial; and, with this new distribution of energy, it may become an easy matter for the super-ego to suppress the ego's possibilities of reacting. (Freud [1927] 1961: 164)

Freud's insistence on the necessity of the scission of the self in the creation of humour sheds light on the frequent presence of split selves and doubles in humoristic fiction. In the works I analyse, the split self is often embodied, depicted as two separate characters who can dialogue with each other. The multiple occurrences of split selves in these texts cannot however be reduced to the image of father and child so dear to Freud. While the Freudian categories of ego and super-ego reduce all possible forms of the split self to the dynamic of a father figure admonishing a child figure, the interaction between the humoristic doubles in the texts I study takes on multiple shapes and is negotiated in diverse ways by the narratives. More often than not, the two parts are given the shapes of a bodily self and an immaterial self, as in Guareschi's *Diario clandestino* (Chapters 2 and 4), Nabokov's *Invitation to a Beheading* (Chapter 2) or Gary's *La danse de Gengis Cohn* (Chapter 4).

Pirandello

Pirandello's theorization of humour is not as well known as Bergson's and Freud's, especially outside of Italy. It is mentioned or briefly discussed in overviews of theories of humour such as Denise Jardon's *Du comique dans le texte littéraire* (1988) or Norman Holland's *Laughing, a Psychology of Humor* (1982). Written in 1908 in the hope of getting a tenured position, and assembled mostly from already existing material (Marcheschi 1992: viii), *L'umorismo* is split into two uneven parts: a long historical overview and a shorter exposition of his theorization of humour, entitled 'Essenza, caratteri e materia dell'umorismo' ['The Essence, Characteristics, and Substance of Humor'].[10] In 1920, Pirandello revised the book. One short passage added to this version is of particular significance to understand his vision of humour as a two-step process, involving first an observation of a discrepancy, and then a feeling of that discrepancy. This process makes it possible to consider humour (especially Pirandello's *umorismo*) and the comic (especially Bergson's) as two phenomena sharing the same temporal spectrum. The comic could appear as a step within the overarching process of humour.

Another significant aspect of *L'umorismo* is Pirandello's attention to literary form, and his attempt to distinguish a form proper to humour and to humoristic characters. Pirandello sets humoristic prose in opposition to other literary traditions that would limit stylistic freedom and trap literary characters in non-fluid structures. The point of departure of his protagonists is their own feeling of entrapment in the prison of their roles, their names and their bodies, and their trajectory is framed as a rebellion against them, helped by humour's fluidity. The protagonist of his last novel, which will be discussed in Chapter 3, best exemplifies this need to break free. He is 'compreso dall'orrore di chiuder[s]i nella prigione d'una forma qualunque' (Pirandello [1926] 1973: 868) ['filled already with horror at shutting [himself] up in the prison of any one form' (Pirandello 1992: 127)]. Formally, humour creates the possibility to avoid congealing a character, a story or a figure in a polished and closed form precisely by the creation of a dialogue with the entrapment that humour contests.

Umorismo: a two-step process

In the first part of his essay, Pirandello distinguishes between humour in a large (and 'erroneous') sense and humour in a narrow sense (27). The latter is the centre of Pirandello's interest, and it involves two stages. The first is a perception of the opposite, of a discrepancy in life or art: it is the '*avvertimento del contrario*'. What leads to the second stage is the key concept of the essay: reflection. Pirandello explains that by reflecting on the observed contradiction one should develop a *feeling* of the opposite ('*sentimento del contrario*'), understood as a conscious feeling. The state that arises from this movement is what Pirandello names humour. The two stages do not always have to be perceived as taking place in succession – sometimes the result of the two stages is directly presented in art.

The 1920 passage I alluded to is the best-known and the best-explained example of the process. It presents an old lady wearing abundant make-up.

The grotesque aspect of the lady would lead to spontaneous laughter on the part of the spectator. In this case, the *avvertimento del contrario* leads to the comic. However, once reflection has played its role, this laughter would stop (or be mixed with a feeling of uneasiness), and a humoristic understanding of the event could arise. Indeed, reflection about the reasons why the old lady might be wearing such a ridiculous mask could reveal her suffering, caused for example by an attempt at keeping the favours of a younger husband:

> Ma ora se interviene in me la riflessione, e mi suggerisce che quella vecchia signora non prova forse nessun piacere a pararsi così come un pappagallo, ma che forse ne soffre e lo fa soltanto perché pietosamente s'inganna che parata così, nascondendo così le rughe e le canizie, riesca a trattenere a sé l'amore del marito molto più giovane di lei, ecco che io non posso più riderne come prima, perché appunto la riflessione, lavorando in me, mi ha fatto andar oltre a quel primo avvertimento, o piuttosto, più addentro: da quel primo *avvertimento del contrario* mi ha fatto passare a questo *sentimento del contrario*. Ed è tutta qui la differenza tra il comico e l'umoristico. (Pirandello [1920] 1992: 161–2; original emphasis)
>
> [But if, at this point, reflection interferes in me to suggest that perhaps this old lady finds no pleasure in dressing up like an exotic parrot, and that perhaps she is distressed by it and does it only because she pitifully deceives herself into believing that, by making herself up like that and by concealing her wrinkles and gray hair, she may be able to hold the love of her much younger husband – if reflection comes to suggest all this, then I can no longer laugh at her as I did at first, exactly because the inner working of reflection has made me go beyond, or rather enter deeper into, the initial stage of awareness: from the beginning *perception of the opposite*, reflection has made me shift to a *feeling of the opposite*. And herein lies the precise difference between comic and humor. ([1920] 1974: 113; original emphasis)]

In Pirandello's explanation, the movement is thus one from the outside to the inside ('più addentro'), with active reflection enabling the transition.

Pirandello's theory corroborates Bergson's idea that the comic arises only in the context of 'une anesthésie momentanée du cœur' (Bergson [1900] 1975: 4) ['momentary anesthesia of the heart' ([1900] 1911: 5)]. Pirandellian humour, distinguished from the comic, would de-anaesthetize the heart to reach the 'feeling of the opposite'. Paradoxically, the means to attain humoristic feeling is an unsentimental reflection. In 'On Pirandello's Humorism',[11] Dante della Terza specifies that the *sentimento del contrario* 'is not a sentiment at all, since its activity is overwhelmingly critical, analytical, and rational' (della Terza

1972: 20). Della Terza seems to conflate reflection, as a step in the process of humour, and the *sentimento del contrario* itself. Feeling, and especially the capacity to feel pain for oneself or for someone else, is certainly present in *umorismo* – the case of the old lady demonstrates it. Nevertheless, della Terza correctly reads reflection as the movement of return towards the self that recalls the reflexive capacities of surfaces like mirrors. This movement is key to enabling the oscillation of humour. In the lives of Pirandellian protagonists, reflection is to be intended as that capacity to self-criticize that can transform them from comic to humoristic beings. Pirandello's own literary creation indeed provides many examples of movements from a comic, external recognition of contrast to a humoristic feeling of contrast. In the first pages of *Uno, nessuno e centomila*, the external stimulus is a remark by the protagonist's wife about his nose being askew. Quite importantly, the scene takes place in front of a mirror, and it is literally the protagonist's *reflection* that becomes the starting point of his humoristic transformation (see Chapter 3).

The process of humour is also a shift from stability to instability: Pirandello makes it clear that the outcome of the movement from the observation to the feeling of the contrary is not a stable state. Precisely because of the transformation that has occurred between the two different states, the resulting feeling is one of perplexity, caused by an oscillation: 'Questo stato d'animo, ogni qual volta mi trovo innanzi a una rappresentazione veramente umoristica, è di perplessità: io mi sento come tenuto tra due: vorrei ridere, rido, ma il riso mi è turbato e ostacolato da qualcosa che spira dalla rappresentazione stessa' (Pirandello [1920] 1992: 127) ['This state of mind, in each case that I deal with a genuine work of humor, is one of perplexity: I feel as if I were suspended between two forces: I feel like laughing, and I do laugh, but my laughter is troubled and obstructed by something that stems from the representation itself' ([1920] 1974: 117–18)]. The association of the desire to laugh and the impossibility of laughing is only one of the many juxtapositions of antithetical states present in humour.

Indeed, the initial moment of recognition of a contrast, the *avvertimento del contrario*, does not necessarily hinge on the perception of the comic. Another example discussed by Pirandello is Giuseppe Giusti's poem 'Sant'Ambroglio', in which the poet first experiences hatred towards German soldiers he meets in a church (Pirandello [1920] 1992: 122–3). The hatred is however transformed while the poet listens to a German canticle and reflects on the soldiers' personal hardships, until he leaves the church, greatly moved by his experience, which led to the development of a specifically 'humoristic' disposition. Although

Pirandello's examples are mainly dedicated to explaining the passage from the comic to humour, the process of humour can thus deal with the transformation of any sentiments into their opposite. Following his discussion of the process itself, Pirandello insists on humour's capacity to split in two (128) and to associate contrasts (129). This opens up to the main formal characteristic of humoristic works according to Pirandello: their constant association of contraries.

The 'form' of humour; the 'form' of the humoristic character

We can hardly use the term 'form' when dealing with Pirandello's attempt to reject the prison of forms. However, formal analysis is a significant aspect of *L'umorismo*. The two-step formation of humour leaves traces – or rather is embodied – in the formal aspect of humoristic works:

> È stato tante volte notato che le opere umoristiche sono scomposte, interrotte, intramezzate di continue digressioni. [...] Ma se questa caratteristica è stata notata, non se ne son vedute chiaramente le ragioni. Questa scompostezza, queste digressioni, queste variazioni non derivano già dal bizzarro arbitrio o dal capriccio degli scrittori, ma sono appunto necessaria e inovviabile conseguenza del turbamento e delle interruzioni del movimento organatore delle immagini per opera della riflessione attiva, la quale suscita un'associazione per contrari [...]. (Pirandello [1920] 1992: 128-9)

> [It has often been observed that humoristic works are disorganized, disconnected, interrupted by constant digressions. [...] But if this characteristic has received attention, its underlying causes have yet to be clearly seen. The disorganisation, the digressions and divergencies do not derive from the writer's eccentricities or personal whim, but are precisely the necessary and inevitable consequence of the disturbance and disruption which are produced in the organizing movement of the images through the work of the active reflection, which evokes an association through contraries [...]. ([1920] 1974: 119)]

The humoristic character, for its part, is described as a character who cannot be 'composed', in whom the elements cannot form a logical whole. Indeed, in one of the strongest statements of the essay, Pirandello asserts that 'l'umorista non riconosce eroi' (152) ['the humorist does not recognize heroes' (143)], since heroes would be seen to have a predictable and unified personality. By playing its role in the creation of the humoristic character (or of the humorist *tout court*), reflection ensures that the character will be decomposed rather than composed, deconstructed rather than constructed:

> Sì, un poeta può rappresentare un suo eroe, in cui si mostrino in lotta elementi opposti e repugnanti; ma egli di questi elementi *comporrà* un carattere, e vorrà coglierlo coerente in ogni suo atto. Ebbene, l'umorista fa proprio l'inverso: egli non *compone* di quegli elementi un carattere; ma *scompone* il carattere nei suoi elementi; e mentre quegli cura di coglierlo coerente in ogni atto, questi si diverte a rappresentarlo nelle sue incongruenze. (Pirandello [1920] 1992: 152; original emphasis)
>
> [Yes, an epic or dramatic poet may represent a hero of his in whom opposite and contrasting elements are shown in conflict, but he will *compose* a character from these elements and will want to represent him as consistent in every action. Well, the humorist does just the opposite: he will *decompose* the character into his elements and while the epic or dramatic poet takes pains to picture him as coherent in every action, the humorist enjoys representing him in his incongruities. ([1920] 1974: 143; original emphasis)]

In Pirandello, humoristic deconstruction takes either the form of a scission of the self in multiple parts, or a multiplication of the self (Pirandello [1920] 1992: 142) – ideas that recall Freud's definition of humour.

The structure of the movement between contraries or parts of the character is not dialectical, but oscillatory: the observation of the contrary and the feeling of the contrary do not move towards a synthesis, but create an endless flow of reflection, 'un oscillare fra poli opposti' (144) ['an oscillating between [...] extremes' (136)].[12] And this is where Pirandello's conception of imprisonment steps in; the creation of a synthesis (or the 'composition' of a character) is a type of imprisonment to which the humoristic creator refuses to subject the character. The same goes for the very form of humoristic writing, which enables the author to be freed from (certain) constraints of literary forms. The oscillating movement of humour becomes the only way to suspend the imprisonment of literary structures.

Pirandello's preference for humour in its narrow sense, in opposition to a wider 'comic-humoristic' tradition, relies precisely on humour's higher capacity to open up literary forms (see Marcheschi 1992: xvi). The relatively shapeless form of the humoristic narrative is intimately connected with the humorist's use of language: 'L'umorismo ha bisogno del più vivace, libero, spontaneo e immediato movimento della lingua, movimento che si può avere sol quando la forma a volta a volta si crea' (Pirandello [1920] 1992: 43) ['Humor needs a highly spirited, free, spontaneous, and direct movement of language – a movement that can be achieved only when form creates itself anew each time' ([1920] 1974: 35)].

Forms are deconstructed by the humorist to unveil their inadequacy to inner life. Humour becomes – in a way that anticipates Bakhtin's dialogism – a rejection of linguistic and literary finalization. The subtitle of the last section of Pirandello's last novel asserts it quite bluntly: 'Non conclude' (Pirandello [1926] 1973: 310) ['No conclusion' (Pirandello 1992: 159)]. Yet the formlessness of humour and its refusal to settle are paradoxically enabled by the recourse to figures that displace the imprisonment in forms to another realm. The fight against forms that stop the flux of life, such as social roles, names, bodies (Pirandello [1920] 1992: 145, [1920] 1974: 137), is framed in the narratives by those spatial figures we find time and again in humoristic prose: the rooms, shelters, cells, barracks and other prisons.

Lewis

The possibility of humour thus rests on the ability to recognize the presence of varied types of imprisonment. For Wyndham Lewis, humour is a process of self-consciousness that cannot free individuals from what they perceive as entrapment but that stresses the role of bodily, social and individual confinement in life and art. His reflection on laughter, humour and satire, developed in multiple works of theory and fiction, casts them in multiple forms and attributes them different possible roles. The development of his thought on the subject is marked by three key moments. As part of the avant-garde group of the Vorticists, Lewis co-signed[13] the group's manifesto published in the first issue of the journal *Blast* (1914). Humour and laughter already occupy a prominent place in the manifesto. The Vorticists present two types of humour: a social, gregarious humour, and an opposed form of humour that is a marker of the exceptional, brilliant mind. In the 1920s, Lewis further developed his vision of humour and laughter in the short story and essay collection *The Wild Body* (1927). The concept of tragic laughter, already present in the manifesto, comes back both in the essays and the fiction. The relationship between body and mind that is instrumental in Lewis's understanding of humour is also elaborated and instantiated in the types of 'laughing observers' and 'Wild Bodies'. Lewis's theory of satire proper is coherently formulated in *Men Without Art*, published in 1934. Lewis presents the concept of a metaphysical satire, clearly distinct from a more traditional 'moral satire' and marked by the tragic laughter of self-consciousness. Metaphysical satire can recall some aspects of Freud's *Humor* and Pirandello's *umorismo* while distinguishing itself from them.

Blast humour, bless humour (Vorticist manifesto)

The first work of importance for the development of Lewis's thought on humour is the 1914 Vorticist manifesto. The manifesto proper is preceded by a longer section of 'blasts' and 'blesses' following the model of Apollinaire's manifesto 'L'antitradition futuriste' in which he awarded 'merde' to people, places or concepts of which he disapproved and 'rose' to those he approved (Somigli 1995: 21). One section in each category pertains to humour. 'Blast' number 5 depicts humour as a

> Quack ENGLISH drug for stupidity and sleepiness.
> Arch enemy of REAL, conventionalizing like
> > gunshot, freezing supple
> > REAL in ferocious chemistry
> > of laughter. (17)[14]

The manifesto directly addresses the readers, cursing those who will react to it by this particular form of laughter: 'CURSE those who will hang over this/ Manifesto with SILLY CANINES exposed' (17). A tool of the crowd, it recalls Bergson's comic laughter of conformism, although its anaesthetic effect is opposed to Bergson's idea about the role social laughter *should* have.

'Bless' number 3, on the contrary, shows humour – again more particularly English humour – as 'the great barbarous weapon of/the genius among races' (26). It is associated with wisdom and unconventionality, with Swift and Shakespeare as two of its exponents. This humour of the enlightened, opposed to gregarious 'blasted' humour, is more reminiscent of Freud's humour or Pirandello's *umorismo*, and isolates the exceptional within society. The solitude inherent to 'blessed humour' is spatially portrayed as a wall enclosing the individual:

> BLESS this hysterical WALL built round
> > the EGO.
> BLESS the solitude of LAUGHTER.
> BLESS the separating, ungregarious
> > BRITISH GRIN. (26)

Humour as a 'wall built round the ego' is one of election, of a desired and provoked segregation. Here, the manifesto addresses indirectly the potential readers, somehow contradictorily encouraging the diffusion of this humour of the happy few:

BLESS ALL ENGLISH EYES
>   that grow crows-feet with their
>   FANCY and ENERGY. (26)

Several sections of the Manifesto (the fourteen pages following the Blasts and Blesses) expand on the Vorticists' conception of humour and connect humour with tragedy. The martial tone of the section depicts humour as a weapon, a fighter, an explosion, a violent phenomenon resulting from the confrontation of the comic and the tragic (37), but with a particular insistence on the latter: 'We only want Humour if it has fought like Tragedy' (31).

Wild Bodies and laughing observers

In *The Wild Body* (1927), laughter and its relation to tragedy take the foreground, although the words humour, comic and satire are also used, at times in an unclear way.[15] The fiction and essays of the collection extrapolate on the physicality of laughter, already present in the exposed canines and the crows-feet eyes of the Manifesto. In his Afterword to *The Complete Wild Body*, Bernard Lafourcade observes that Lewis, 'quite naturally, opted for forms of comedy closely associated with the body – farce, horseplay, practical jokes and the burlesque – wrongly considered as "low" forms, whereas they are in fact more profound than intellectual wit through being – as with Jonson or Swift – near to sheer physical reality, or the unconscious' (410). Lafourcade's statement highlights the importance of a profound or primitive impulse in Lewis's theory and fiction, incarnated here in 'that small, primitive, literally antediluvian vessel' (Lewis 1927: 237) that is the Wild Body, described by Lewis as 'the generic puppet of all' (232). The Wild Body's laughter is both his 'song of triumph' (236) and the most profound 'spasm' (238) of this creature that is characterized by its body's manifestations. It is fundamental, primitive and as such is also associated with the tragic and the martial – as was the case in the Manifesto – but also with a form of primitive religiosity. The Wild Body's role, fictionalized throughout the collection, is indeed explained in 'Inferior Religions', in which the 'puppets' of the fiction are described as 'carefully selected specimens of religious fanaticism' (234).

In order to fully understand the role of the Wild Body, we need to position it in a dynamic relationship with another of Lewis's puppets (that is types of characters), the 'laughing observer', described in the following essay, 'The

Meaning of the Wild Body'. The first lines of the essay clarify the role of the mind/body duality and its relationship with the two entities:

> First, to assume the dichotomy of mind and body is necessary here, without arguing it; for it is upon that essential separation that the theory of laughter here proposed is based. The essential us, that is the laughter, is as distinct from the Wild Body as in the Upanisadic account of the souls returned from the paradise of the Moon, which, entering into plants, are yet distinct from them. Or to take the symbolic vedic figure of the two birds, the one watching and passive, the other enjoying its activity, we similarly have to postulate *two* creatures, one that never enters into life, but that travels about in a vessel to whose destiny it is momentarily attached. That is, of course, the laughing observer,[16] and the other is the Wild Body. (243–4; original emphasis)

A few pages later, building on the capacity of a 'laughing observer' to perceive what is comic in the 'Wild Bodies', Lewis states what he now calls the 'root of the Comic': 'The root of the Comic is to be sought in the sensations resulting from the observation of a thing behaving like a person. But from that point of view all men are necessarily comic: for they are all *things*, or physical bodies, behaving as *persons*' (247; original emphasis). This definition clearly brings to mind Bergson's theory, and appears as a simple inversion of his statement: '*Nous rions toutes les fois qu'une personne nous donne l'impression d'une chose.*' (Bergson [1900] 1975: 44, original emphasis) ['*We laugh every time a person gives us the impression of being a thing*' ([1900] 1911: 58; original emphasis)]. More than an inversion, however, Lewis's explanation is an extension of the comic principle to human existence itself.

Indeed, laughter signals the acknowledgement of life's inherent absurdity. Whereas Bergsonian laughter is corrective, Lewisian laughter does not correct anything, but is a 'risposta necessaria' ['necessary response'] in the face of the fact that all humans are things (Somigli 1995: 31). As the enumeration of the attributes of laughter makes clear in 'Inferior Religions', laughter becomes a signal of the consciousness of the laugher: 'Laughter is the climax in the tragedy of seeing, hearing and smelling self-consciously' (236). As Luca Somigli explains: 'La risata si profila come strumento di autocoscienza che non porta liberazione ma solamente conoscenza; l'artista si distingue quindi dalla "massa" proprio per il suo maggiore grado di autocoscienza: gli altri appaiono tanto più ridicoli quanto più dimostrano di non rendersi conto della propria materialità.' (32) ['Laughter is described as a tool of self-consciousness that does not bring liberation but only knowledge; the artist distinguishes himself from the "mass" precisely by his greater degree of self-consciousness: the others appear all the more ridiculous as they demonstrate that they are not conscious of their own materiality.'] The laughter of the laughing observer, in opposition to the Wild Body's laughter, is not unconscious, subconscious or primitive, but a developed signal of self-consciousness.

From the laughing observer to the metaphysical satirist

The collection of essays *Men Without Art* (1934) presents Lewis's new theory of satire, a term almost absent from the Manifesto and *The Wild Body*. The new theory builds on some of the attributes of laughter that were introduced earlier, but includes new facets. The theory of satire itself is defended in the second part of the book, in a section that reuses part of the material from an earlier text, *Satire and Fiction*, published in 1930. The most important feature is the capaciousness of Lewis's notion of satire. As he makes clear in the introduction, satire is to be understood in a very broad sense: 'This book has, in fact, been written, to put it shortly, to defend Satire. But to "Satire" I have given a meaning so wide as to confound it with "Art". So this book may be said to be nothing short of a defence of art – as art is understood in the most "highbrow" quarters today' (10). The new vision of satire which Lewis is introducing has almost nothing to do with the traditional 'moral' satire, although in preceding works Lewis had asserted that satire was essentially ethical (Somigli 1995: 63). The first chapter of Part II, 'The Greatest Satire Is Non-Moral', explains Lewis's rejection of the primacy of morality in the creation of satire. The true artist cannot remain caught within a 'purely moral code': 'It could perhaps be asserted, even, that the greatest satire cannot be moralistic at all: if for no other reason, because no mind of the first order, expressing itself in art, has ever itself been taken in, nor consented to take in others, by the crude injunctions of any purely moral code' (108; original emphasis). First named 'non-ethical satire' (107), this type of satire is framed in the conclusion of the book as a 'metaphysical satire occupied with mankind' (289).

The rejection of the moral prerequisite of satire goes hand in hand with the place that Lewis gives to what I would call the 'metaphysical satirist' (i.e. 'artist'): outside of society, outside of the natural flow of life. From this position, similar to the laughing observer's, the metaphysical satirist can make use of tragic laughter, 'a healthy clatter' (114), as a sign of the recognition of the tragic quality of life. As in the Manifesto, tragic laughter is therefore opposed to another form of banal laughter: 'there is laughter and laughter. That of true satire is as it were *tragic* laughter. It is not a genial guffaw nor the tittilations [sic] provoked by a harmless entertainer. It is tragic, if a thing can be "tragic" without pity and terror, and it seems to me it can' (113; original emphasis). Crucially, though, this laughter is not only directed to what is observed but is always put in relation with one's own humanness: 'We should after all only be laughing *at ourselves!*' (113; original emphasis).

The different points of view of Wild Bodies, laughing observers and metaphysical satirists give rise to diverse uses of laughter. The Wild Bodies' laughter, a physical, unconscious manifestation, is entirely confined in the laughable event. On the opposite side, the laughing observers' standpoint is withdrawn and external. This distancing can be likened to the reflection that steps in between the observation of the contrary and the feeling of the contrary in Pirandello's *umorismo*, or to the process at play between the ego and the super-ego in Freud's humour. However, the metaphysical satirist is truly the one who adopts a position comparable to a Pirandellian humorist, in that the reflection always backfires and enables the self-consciousness of humour. Thus, contrary to Bergson's comic, and in the same way as Freud's humour and Pirandello's *umorismo*, Lewis's metaphysical satire involves the capacity of the humoristic subject to perceive humour within their own situation. The self-consciousness that highlights without liberating, the notion of metaphysical satire as the satire of all mankind, as well as the distinction between a 'blasted' and a 'blessed humour' give us tools for the analysis of literary humour.

Bakhtin

Mikhail Bakhtin's work is generally brought up in discussions connecting humour and liberation. In *Rabelais and His World*, Bakhtin stresses carnivalesque laughter's 'indissoluble and essential relation to freedom' (89). His vision of a collective, cosmic laughter and his insistence on its liberating power might seem at odds with the theories discussed so far. Yet they need to be read in the context of his whole production. As Gary Saul Morson and Caryl Emerson note in *Mikhail Bakhtin: Creation of a Prosaics* (433–70), Bakhtin's discourse on laughter predates and postdates *Rabelais and His World* (written in the 1940s but first published in Russian in 1965). The essays 'From the Prehistory of Novelistic Discourse' (from the late 1930s) and 'Forms of Time and of the Chronotope in the Novel' (1937–1938, with 'Concluding Remarks' from 1973) are already concerned with the possible roles of laughter, while writings subsequent to the *Rabelais*, such as 'From Notes Made in 1970–71', also deal with the concept. 'Epic and Novel. Toward a Methodology for the Study of the Novel' (1941), written in the same period as *Rabelais and His World*, also discusses the role of laughter in connection to the development of the novel. Morson and Emerson remark on an important shift from a more individual and more historical vision of the carnival (in 'From the Prehistory' and 'Chronotope', in the 1930s), to the more utopian, collective and generally ahistorical carnival of the *Rabelais* (1940s). In a subsequent shift (1950s to 1975), Bakhtin goes back to his former vision, dealing with the possible impact of the carnival not only on the collectivity but also on the individual. For the purpose of my analyses, both *Rabelais and His World* and Bakhtin's other works are useful. Even more importantly, Bakhtin's claims on the potential liberatory powers of laughter stem from his attention to the conditions of constraint that make the emergence of laughter possible at all. Bakhtin's work should be read not only for the connection it draws between laughter and liberation, but precisely for its attention to what laughter might liberate from: laughter would free one from social hierarchies, the imposition of a norm and a false unity of perception; it would free one from fear; and it would free one from the limits of the individual body. These three sets of constraints – society, fear and the body – are at the core of the humoristic narratives this book studies.

Freedom from hierarchies

The most prominent and best-known aspect of Bakhtin's theory of the carnival is probably the contestation and reversal of social hierarchies. The liberating force of the carnival and its laughter is set in opposition to the regulating force of oppressive social structures, as well as to conceptions of human beings that limit both social roles and bodies to a circumscribed space. For the time of the carnival, the usual rigidity of the normative society is destroyed – this destruction being somehow sanctioned by the official society that has allowed the carnival to materialize. Two types of social structures, two temporalities, are thus opposed. To Bakhtin, the carnival (and by extension the grotesque) always 'discloses the potentiality of an entirely different world, of another order, another way of life. It leads men out of the confines of the apparent (false) unity, of the indisputable and stable' (Bakhtin 1984b: 48).

Masked figures play a key role in the universe of the carnival. Their ambivalence enables them to unveil the truth behind the imposed social rigidity. Discussing the masks of the rogue, the clown and the fool in 'Chronotope', Bakhtin demonstrates their potential to enact liberation from conventions, from logic, from literalism of the word, from measure and from masks themselves:

> In the struggle against conventions, and against the inadequacy of all available life-slots to fit an authentic human being, these masks take on an extraordinary significance. They grant the right *not* to understand, the right to confuse, to tease, to hyperbolize life; the right to parody others while talking, the right to not be taken literally, not 'to be oneself'; the right to live a life in the chronotope of the entr'acte, the chronotope of theatrical space, the right to act life as a comedy and to treat others as actors, the right to rip off masks, the right to rage at others with a primeval (almost cultic) rage – and finally, the right to betray to the public a personal life, down to its most private and prurient little secrets. (163; original emphasis)

With such figures as the clown, the rogue and the fool, and with practices such as abuse-praise or the inside-out and upside-down logics, the carnival opens up a breach – but only for a given time. Carnivalesque social freedom is not absolute; it cannot exist outside of the norm that enables it. Bakhtin mentions two important limitations of the freedom gained through laughter: it is relative and it is ephemeral (Bakhtin 1984b: 89). Nevertheless, he perceives in these limitations (relativity and ephemerality) the source of an even stronger power: 'For a short time life came out of its usual, legalized and consecrated furrows and entered the sphere of utopian freedom. The very brevity of this freedom increased its fantastic nature and utopian radicalism, born in the festive atmosphere of images' (89). Laughter gains a constructive and regenerating aspect thanks to this utopian impulse, even if only during the social time of popular feasts. Indeed, in 'Chronotope', Bakhtin integrates the regenerative movement within the twofold aspect of folkloric laughter and of the carnival. Laughter both destroys and constructs; it destroys the old matrices in order to rebuild new ones.

Freedom from fear

The subversive capacity of carnivalesque laughter is connected to its relationship with fearlessness. The official culture is by its very nature related to authority and the power to intimidate and frighten: it 'always contain[s] an element of fear'

(Bakhtin 1984b: 90). Bakhtin sets laughter in direct opposition to this officially imposed fear, in the tone characteristic of the 'greatly increased binariness of thought' of *Rabelais and His World* (Morson and Emerson 1990: 445): 'Laughter, on the contrary, overcomes fear, for it knows no inhibitions, no limitations. Its idiom is never used by violence and authority' (Bakhtin 1984b: 90). Bakhtin scholars have highlighted this claim's lack of nuance (see Emerson 1997: 164–5; Averintsev 2001: 85–6), since laughter and violence can be and are indeed often connected. In other works such as 'Epic and Novel', Bakhtin analyses specific ways in which laughter and fear's relationship has been articulated in literature. Laughter would defeat fear by rendering familiar that which looked alien. It would destroy narrative distance – this is what happens in the transition from the epic to the serio-comical genres – just as it destroys the hierarchical distance between social positions. Proximity is thus a key for understanding the carnivalesque: 'As a distanced image a subject cannot be comical; to be made comical, it must be brought close. Everything that makes us laugh is close at hand, all comical creativity works in a zone of maximal proximity' (1981: 23). This might appear counter to the theories of laughter and humour that see humour as possible only at a distance, be it from the one who is laughed at (Bergson), from the painful affects (Freud) or from the world observed (Lewis's laughing observer). Yet the contradiction is only apparent. In the carnivalesque, the proximity is perceptual; it is related to the senses, and the capacity to connect with the physical reality of the world. Through this form of proximity, however, *a conceptual distance* with the 'serious', 'official' culture is made possible. Thus, reconnecting with what is close to the human makes possible a distanciation from pain or from fear. In that regard, the frequent use of the first-person narrator in twentieth-century humoristic fiction might contribute to the reduction of narrative distance and produce another form of distanciation that is necessary for the creation of humour.

By recalling that medieval fear did impress people and led to a constant struggle between fear and laughter, Bakhtin also nuances laughter's capacity of defeating fear. Therefore, 'victory over fear is not its abstract elimination' (Bakhtin 1984b: 90); in the world of the carnival (and of humour), fear does exist, but it is countered by a new understanding of life enabled by the carnivalesque (and the humoristic) vision. The partial victory of laughter over fear is similar to Freud's theory of humour, in which humour enables the individual to cope with fear or pain, not to eliminate the possibility of fear or pain. By freeing a person from fear, carnivalesque laughter, in a way similar to Freud's humour, helps overcome individual pain. However, whereas the individual in Freud's theory is generally alone in the process, Bakhtin's individual rejects fear because it isolates, and opts for laughter in its capacity to unite: 'laughter only unites; it cannot divide' (1986: 135). Still, the uniting power of laughter has to be filtered through the individual consciousness in order to combat fear:

> Laughter liberates not only from external censorship but first of all from the great interior censor; it liberates from the fear that developed in man during thousands of years: fear of the sacred, of prohibitions, of the past, of power. It unveils the material bodily principle in its true meaning. Laughter opened men's eyes on that which is new, on the future. (Bakhtin 1984b: 94)

The physical emanation of laughter becomes a starting point that allows the individual to re-centre around the 'material bodily principle'. While Bakhtin insists on the collective aspect of this focus, it is important to note that the connection with one's body is a significant feature of 'individualist' humour too. Moscarda's focus on the appearance of his nose (Chapter 3) and Guareschi's use of his 'mal di stomaco' and his moustache as bodily symbols of his past imprisonment (Chapter 4) show how bodily conscience is instrumental in the individual humoristic process.

Freedom from individual bodily limits; freedom and the individual

The perceptual connection with 'the material bodily principle' does not mean that the body becomes the sole focus of carnivalesque crowds. On the contrary, Bakhtin is insistent on clarifying the link between the bodily and material, and a conceptual world of possibilities where the individual body could dissolve: 'This bodily participation in the potentiality of another world, the bodily awareness of another world, has an immense importance for the grotesque' (Bakhtin 1984b: 48). The comprehension of the grotesque body leads to this potential other world that we find time and again in humoristic prose. Cincinnatus C.'s 'other world' (Chapter 2), Vitangelo Moscarda's final connection with nature (Chapter 3), or the realm of Guareschi's other self (Chapters 2 and 4) presents us with other worlds the characters have been able to create through their new negotiation with bodily limits. Thus, for these characters, the freedom from bodily limits passes through a laughter that recalls carnivalesque laughter, but that is not built solely (or, in some cases, at all) around a collective endeavour.[17]

In an elliptical statement in 'From Notes Made in 1970–71', Bakhtin asserts the possibility of the co-presence of intimacy and laughter: 'laughter can be combined with profoundly intimate emotionality (Sterne, Jean Paul, and others)' (135), an idea that he, unfortunately, did not fully develop. However, another central idea of the 'Notes' is the necessity of the 'other' in the constitution of one's consciousness and one's own freedom. Contrarily to the carnivalesque texts, the 'Notes' explore the liberation of the self not in a grand collectivity, but in the dialogic collectivity of an 'I' and a 'thou'.

> Something absolutely new appears here: the supraperson, the *supra-I*, that is, the witness and the judge *of the whole* human being, of the whole *I*, and consequently someone who is no longer the person, no longer the *I*, but the *other*. The reflection of the self in the empirical other through whom one must pass in order to reach *I-for-myself* (can this *I-for-myself* be solitary?). The absolute freedom of this *I*. But this freedom cannot change existence, so to speak, materially (nor can it want to) – it can change only the *sense* of existence (to recognize it, to justify it, and so forth); this is the freedom of the witness and the judge. It is expressed in the *word*. Authenticity and truth inhere not in existence itself, but only in an existence that is acknowledged and uttered. (137–8; original emphasis)

The constitution of one's freedom in the dialogue with the other has implications for the self in situations of imprisonment. Deprived of the other, the imprisoned self can use fiction to create a double and establish an otherwise impossible dialogue. Bakhtin has been attentive to the presence of doubles and the possibility of dialogue with oneself in modern fiction, that he traces back to the Menippean satire (1984a: 117). Dialogism in fiction and the preservation of the I's positionality in 'benevolent demarcation' (1986: 136) with the other's make possible the 'absolute freedom' to change not existence but its meaning.

Oscillatory humour: Humour as an unstable mode

The position of the self is a key element for the understanding of theories of humour. The five theories presented in this chapter differ in the position they attribute to the individual. Both Bergson and Bakhtin start with an emphasis on the collective, but in a radically different way. For Bergson, laughter is a social corrective aimed at an individual who has gone astray. In this case, the individual's exclusion from the group is highlighted by laughter, with the goal of transforming the exclusion into an inclusion, if and only if the individual corrects the improper behaviour. In Bakhtin's carnival of *Rabelais and His World*, on the contrary, social laughter is inclusive from the start, so much so that individual positions do not matter within the world of the carnival. Laughter remains a unifier throughout Bakhtin's theories: 'laughter only unites; it cannot divide' (1986: 135). Yet in his earlier and later writings, Bakhtin also stresses the possibility and importance of laughter for the individual. This laughter, which has the potential to free from hierarchies, fear and bodily limits, also makes the individual enter into a dialogue with the other's consciousness, in a process that I term humour. The clear identification of the position of the self is indeed essential for dialogism to happen. Freud's humour and Pirandello's *umorismo*, on the other hand, are dedicated to explaining the phenomenon from the position of a self-reflexive and somewhat isolated individual. Their theories focus on an intimate form of humour that might deal with collective situations, but always observed from the standpoint of the individual. Of the five theorists, Lewis is the most comprehensive in his treatment of individual and collective forms of humour. The Vorticist manifesto presents both a more collective, gregarious form of humour and a more individual, elitist form. Even if this second form (the 'blessed' humour) is the most developed afterwards, it does not stay in the realm of the individual. Its scope is widened in *Men Without Art* to encompass all humankind as the object of humour, or rather of 'metaphysical satire'. Although practised individually, metaphysical satire is given a potentially universal significance.

The shift from an individual, elitist standpoint to a universal characteristic comes from the central role Lewis gives to physicality. Since every human has a body, everyone can be a humoristic object and, potentially, a humoristic observer or creator: 'The root of the Comic is to be sought in the sensations resulting from the observation of a *thing* behaving like a person. But from that point of view all men are necessarily comic: for they are all *things*, or physical bodies, behaving as *persons*' (1927: 246; original emphasis). Lewis is not the only one to identify the body either as the cause of humour or as the location where humour can be developed. His awareness of a person as body and of a body as thing highlights the role of the body in theories of humour. Bergson certainly makes of the mechanization of the body one of the most important causes of the comic. For Pirandello, bodily awareness often becomes the epiphanic first step in the two-step process of *umorismo*, as in the example of the old woman. The body is also at the core of Bakhtin's theorization. The 'material bodily principle' is instrumental in the development of a collective participation in laughter *and* in the connection between an individual body and the potentiality of another world (Bakhtin 1984b: 48). Freud is probably (and strangely, if we think about the place the sexualized body has in Freud's thought in general) the theorist for whom the body is least significant in the development of humour.

For Simon Critchley (2002), it is precisely the clash between the physical and the metaphysical that would be the source of humour and laughter: 'What makes us laugh, I would wager, is the return of the physical into the metaphysical, where the pretended tragical sublimity of the human collapses into a comic ridiculousness which is perhaps even more tragic' (43). Alenka Zupančič (2008) complicates this reading by showing that the movement can also go the other way around, and that both directions cohabit in comedy (Zupančič's concept of comedy being at times close to what I define as humour): 'comedy always moves in both directions: not only from pure discarnate spirit to its material, physical conditions, but also from the material to forms of pure discarnate intellect, wandering around quite independently' (46). The movement in both directions is yet another opposition that creates the oscillation of humour. In the theories discussed, the oppositions are at time blended into single concepts, such as Lewis's tragic laughter, and at times split, as in Pirandello's two-step *umorismo*, which separates them temporally in a process that however results in their co-presence. The oscillation of humour cannot be solved by the creation of a third term and humour is not a dialectics that could create a synthesis putting the oscillating tension to an end. The unfinalizability and instability of humour, often set in opposition to fixed political, social or literary structures, highlight precisely the indissociable relationship between humour's oscillatory movement and figures of imprisonment that can contain it. Humour in the 'narrow' sense I have defined so far emerges as both a formal method for literary creation, and a mode of understanding and living individual, social and bodily confinement.

2

Humour in the Cell: Prison Cells and War Camps

Humorists in their prisons

This chapter explores some ways in which life in political imprisonment can be depicted through the eyes of a humorist. The three works discussed represent the literal imprisonment of an individual, but they differ in terms of the context of imprisonment and the mode of depiction. Giovannino Guareschi's 1949 *Diario clandestino* provides an example of an autobiographical depiction of imprisonment, constituted of pieces written from 1943 to 1945 while the Italian journalist was in Nazi war camps in Poland and Germany. Romain Gary's *Les racines du ciel* (1956; revised in 1980), and more precisely a particular episode of this long, Goncourt-winning novel, gives a fictional account of the imprisonment of French men in Second World War camps. Finally, Vladimir Nabokov's *Invitation to a Beheading* (1935–1936 in Russian, 1959 in English), although reminiscent of contemporary political endeavours, presents the entirely fictional imprisonment of Cincinnatus C.

The discussion of these works does not follow a chronological order, neither in terms of the time of writing nor in terms of the events represented. Rather, their succession presents three humoristic stances that are located at different positions of the same spectrum. This spectrum starts with Guareschi's stance of self-declared humorist. Indeed, *Diario clandestino* is introduced as 'la prigionia vista da un umorista' (Guareschi [1949] 2009: xv) ['a humorist's account of his prison' ([1949] 1958: 15)] and humour plays a role both in the diegesis of the work and in its narration. Guareschi's stance is found in Robert Duparc, a secondary character in *Les racines du ciel* and the leader of the episode of imprisonment discussed in this chapter. Robert's posture in the novel's diegesis shares many features with that of Guareschi's *persona*. Humour at the narrative level is however scarce both in this novel and in this episode. Nabokov's *Invitation to a Beheading* presents a humoristic stance very similar to Guareschi's and Robert's, but in a veiled form: it is almost entirely dissociated from the comic, which is not the case in Guareschi's and Gary's works.

Notwithstanding these contextual and textual differences, the three works have crucial features in common. This chapter's goal is to highlight them and explain their role in the relationship between humour and imprisonment. More precisely, this chapter deals with key processes leading to the construction of a humoristic discourse within imprisonment, such as falsely logical deductions, abundant repetitions, doublings, euphemisms and figures of opposition. It also explores the relation between myth creation and humour, as well as the presence of temporal and spatial distanciations in the development of humour. Most crucially, this chapter draws a connection between the separation of selves and the creation of two contrasted spaces: the space of imprisonment and a space of negotiation of that confinement. The representation of the literal space of imprisonment is filtered through literary humour, which creates another space designed to dialogue with it, setting in motion an oscillation between the two.

Giovannino Guareschi: The choral diary

Guareschi's involvement in the social and political life of twentieth-century Italy was marked by two imprisonments: in Nazi camps (September 1943 to April 1945) and in Parma's San Francesco prison (June 1954 to July 1955) following a condemnation for libel against former Prime Minister Alcide De Gasperi (see Chapter 4). The first was a collective imprisonment, and Guareschi's main publication about it insists on that aspect. *Diario clandestino 1943–1945*, written during his incarceration in Nazi war camps in Poland and Germany following the capitulation of Italy in the Second World War, was published in 1949. According to Guareschi's children, Alberto and Carlotta, this 'diario corale' ['choral diary'] is perhaps the author's most important work, although unfortunately the least well known (A. and C. Guareschi 2009: 207). It is generally overshadowed by the popular *Mondo piccolo* (Little World) stories that tell the adventures of the Catholic priest Don Camillo and the communist mayor Peppone. And yet the space of the war camp and the textual space of the *Diario* are necessary starting points for understanding Guareschi's humour, which became so popular with the Don Camillo series. Not only does *Diario clandestino 1943–1945* feature the textual techniques essential to the development of Guareschi's humour, but it also sets into motion a new understanding of humour influenced by the author's experience of war imprisonment as an Italian Military Internee.

The Italian Military Internees and the birth of *Diario clandestino 1943–1945*

The fall of 1943 constitutes a major turning point in Italy's involvement in the Second World War. In July 1943, the Italian state, then part of the Axis, saw the invasion of Sicily by the Allied troops. On 24 July, 'the Fascist Grand Council, in a gesture of defiance against Mussolini, asked King Victor Emmanuel [III] to assume "effective command" of Italy's armed forces, and called for the responsibilities of Crown and Parliament to be "immediately restored"' (Gilbert 1989: 446). Mussolini was transported outside of Rome to the island of Ponza and Marshal Pietro Badoglio was named as the head of the Government of Italy. Continental Italy was invaded at the beginning of September and the country surrendered on 8 September 1943, officially remaining in the war on the side of the Allies. While the Allied forces continued to advance from the south to the north, Germany seized control of the northern and central parts, and liberated Mussolini. On 23 September 1943, Mussolini became head of a newly formed state, the Italian Social Republic (RSI, Repubblica Sociale Italiana, a name adopted in November of the same year), commonly known as the Salò Republic, so called for the name of the location of its unofficial capital. The RSI remained in power until 25 April 1945.

The military members serving northern Italy in September 1943 were given a choice: they would either remain in Italy to serve under Mussolini's Salò Republic, and thus fall under the German rule, or be sent away to detention camps in Germany and Poland. The men who refused to swear an oath to Mussolini and were sent to the camps were at first considered Prisoners of War (POW). In September 1944, however, Mussolini abandoned the prisoners to the German state, thus leading to the loss of their POW designation and of the rights associated with it (Cotta 1977: 87). Their new status of 'internees' would impede the International Red Cross's ability to offer them the same help it afforded to those labelled POW according to the 1929 Geneva Convention (Perry 2009: 624). These men, an estimated six hundred thousand (Cotta 1977: 86), are nowadays recognized as Italian Military Internees (Internati Militari Italiani).

More than thirty thousand of them died in the camps (Cotta 1977: 88). The peculiar status of the Italian Military Internees impacted them both during and after the war, when their role as 'resistenti' failed to be acknowledged. The IMI's resistance was distinct from the official Italian Resistance. It took mainly two forms: their refusal to serve the Nazi power in Italy, and their subsequent refusal to accept any offer of work from the Nazis (in order either to improve their conditions or to go back to Italy) (Perry 2009: 632). They formed a 'resistenza bianca' (white resistance) (Lugaresi 2011: 6) paradoxically apart from and a part of Italian history, imperceptible but necessary.

In September 1943, Guareschi was an artillery lieutenant in Alessandria, Piedmont. Captured by the Germans, he refused to swear allegiance to Hitler or Mussolini, and was sent to an internment camp in Poland (Perry 2009: 624). From September 1943 to April 1945, he was imprisoned in four different camps: Czestokowa and Beniaminowo in Poland, and Bremerwörde-Sandbostel and Wietzendorf-Bergen in Germany (Gnocchi and Palmaro 2008: 49–50). In the camps, Guareschi reasserted his choice of imprisonment on several occasions: 'Guareschi himself refused the Nazis twice, once with the offer to become a journalist in Berlin and again with the chance to return to Milan and resume his editorial duties with Bertoldo, the humorous newspaper he directed before the war' (Perry 2009: 632). He remained in the camps until the end of the RSI, and after, during the uncertain times that followed. In fact, it was not until 28 August 1945 that he finally left Germany (Gnocchi and Palmaro 2008: 53). In all writings related to his experience in the camps, whether they were written during or after the war, Guareschi keeps insisting on the importance of his choice – a choice, he explains, guided by his conscience. This idea is central in the 'Istruzioni per l'uso' ['Instructions for Use'] of *Diario clandestino*, where Guareschi designates his imprisonment as a 'volontaria prigionia' (xiii) ['voluntary prison'].

During those two years spent away from Italy, Guareschi never stopped writing; upon his return, his diary could have constituted a book of around two thousand pages (Guareschi [1949] 2009: vii). But this hypothetical book was never published. In the 'Istruzioni per l'uso' ['Instructions for Use'], Guareschi explains his decision not to publish the document after having typed it, instead choosing to throw the original and the copies into the fire (Guareschi [1949] 2009: viii). We learn from Guareschi's children that this is not true. Most of the typed diary was actually used as rough paper. Parts of it were rediscovered by Alberto and Carlotta Guareschi and published with some of the original notebooks in the *Grande diario* (the big diary), not translated into English (A. and C. Guareschi 2011: 4).

Yet the diary is not the only thing Guareschi produced as a prisoner in the camps. Many short stories, reflections and comments were written with the intention of being read aloud to his comrades from barrack to barrack. These, he explains, constitute the only 'approved material', and thus the only material worth publishing:

> Il quale diario, come dicevamo, è tanto clandestino che non è neppure un diario, ma secondo me potrà servire, sotto certi aspetti, più di un diario vero e proprio a dare un'idea di quei giorni, di quei pensieri e di quelle sofferenze.
>
> Perché è l'unica roba valida, sicuramente valida che possa oggi essere pubblicata.
>
> È l'unico materiale autorizzato, in quanto io non solo l'ho pensato e l'ho scritto dentro il Lager: ma l'ho pure letto dentro il Lager. L'ho letto pubblicamente una, due, venti volte, e tutti lo hanno approvato. (Guareschi [1949] 2009: x–xi)[1]

> [As I have said before, it is a diary so secret as not to be a diary at all. Yet, in many ways, it seems to me to give a better picture of those days, and their thoughts and sorrows than my huge original compendium. Nothing else, I repeat, is valid or deserving publication. This material is what you might call 'authorised'. I thought it out and wrote it in the Lager; most of it[2] I read aloud a dozen or more times, and it won general approval. ([1949] 1958: 11)]

In fact, *Diario clandestino 1943–1945*, published in 1949, alternates between short stories and diary entries. These entries are not to be conflated with the original journal entries. They are the ones Guareschi shared with others around the barracks, accompanied by the musician Arturo Coppola and the actor Gianrico Tedeschi (Lugaresi 2011: 7). Guareschi's humoristic techniques should be read in the context of this 'choral' diary written in and about imprisonment. Falsely logical deductions, repetitions, multiplications (doublings or 'triplings') and euphemisms become tools to hint at other layers of representation and meaning that open his discourse unto new planes.

'Istruzioni per l'uso' ['Instructions for Use']

Guareschi's introduction to the *Diario* features most of these techniques. The very first sentence sets the tone: 'Questo "Diario clandestino" è talmente clandestino che non è neppure un diario' (vii) ['This *Secret Diary* is so secret that it isn't a diary at all' ([1949] 1958: 9)]. The structure of the assertion recalls that of the 'Jonathanisms' described by Nash in *The Language of Humor* (1985).[3] Jonathanisms are structured in three clauses: 'a declarative clause of the type Subject-BE-Complement'; a result-clause; and 'an explanation-clause of infinitive or adverbial pattern' (47). Nash's first example, 'My uncle Sam is so tall that he has to climb a ladder to shave himself'; follows the same structure as Guareschi's sentence, with a small difference. Guareschi's sentence is composed of a clearly identifiable declarative clause ('This *Secret Diary* is so secret') and result-clause ('that it isn't a diary at all'). However, the explanation-clause ('to shave himself' in Nash's example) is not as local, but rather diffused in the following paragraphs. This modification of a typical comic structure constitutes a perfect example of a device Guareschi is fond of: suspending the meaning by presenting an incomplete or incomprehensible statement. Both the meaning and the importance of the first sentence are only revealed later. In fact, Guareschi repeats the statement in a slightly different form a few pages later, after having described how *Diario clandestino* came into being. In the second instance, he adds that not only is the diary not a real diary, but that it is more than a real diary: 'Il quale diario, come dicevamo, è tanto clandestino che non è neppure un diario, ma secondo me potrà servire, sotto certi aspetti, più di un diario vero e proprio a dare un'idea di quei giorni, di quei pensieri e di quelle sofferenze' (xi) ['As I have said before, it is a diary so secret as not to be a diary at all. Yet, in many ways, it seems to me to give a better picture of those days, and their thoughts and sorrows than my huge original compendium' ([1949] 1958: 11)]. The repetition serves to introduce, in a condensed and striking form, this plus, this more, that has been explained in the gap between the first element and its repetition, namely that it originated as a collectively shared chronicle of war imprisonment.

Repetitions are central to Guareschi's style. Their function goes beyond the need to insist; they are essential to the formation of humour. In the following excerpt, an apparently non-logical statement, 'Non muoio neanche se mi ammazzano!' ('I won't die, even if they kill me!'), is explained and repeated, imperceptibly taking on new meanings:

> L'unica cosa interessante, ai fini della nostra storia, è che io, anche in prigionia conservai la mia testardaggine di emiliano della Bassa: e così strinsi i denti e dissi: 'Non muoio neanche se mi ammazzano!'.
> E non morii.
> Probabilmente non morii perché non mi ammazzarono: il fatto è che non morii.

> Rimasi vivo anche nella parte interna e continuai a lavorare. (Guareschi [1949] 2009: x)

> [For the present purposes, the only thing of interest is that, even in prison, I remained a stubborn native of the province of Emilia, of the lower reaches of the Po valley; I gritted my teeth and said to myself: 'I won't die, even if they kill me!' And I didn't die, either, probably only because they didn't kill me, but at any rate I didn't die. I stayed alive in spirit as well as in body, and kept on working. ([1949] 1958: 11)]

The repetitive structure is built by short sentences separated by line breaks giving a poetic quality to the passage. Here as on many other occasions, repetition is used to establish a contrast between the reality of imprisonment and its poetic treatment, a gap through which the humoristic surplus can be introduced.

Guareschi also repetitively uses the word 'volontari' ['volunteers' or 'voluntary', depending on the context] in describing himself, his companions and their state of affairs. 'Voluntary imprisonment', which would in other contexts be a paradox, becomes in this case a powerful oxymoron. This example must be linked with a more widespread use of contrasting pairs, and in general of elements grouped in twos. Guareschi contrasts life in the camps and life after the camps in a striking way; to him, the men in the camps gave birth to the only real Democracy (generally written with a capital letter), only to find a false version of democracy once back in Italy.

> Non abbiamo vissuto come bruti: costruimmo noi, con niente, la Città Democratica. E se, ancor oggi, molti dei ritornati guardano ancora sgomenti la vita di tutti i giorni tenendosene al margine, è perché l'immagine che essi si erano fatti, nel Lager, della Democrazia, risulta spaventosamente diversa da questa finta democrazia che ha per centro sempre la stessa capitale degli intrighi e che ha filibustieri vecchi e nuovi al timone delle varie navi corsare.
>
> Sono i delusi: forse i più onesti di tutti noi volontari del Lager. (Guareschi [1949] 2009: xiv)

> [We did not live like brutes; out of nothing we built our own Democratic City. If now, many ex-internees are shocked by the spectacle of everyday life and hold themselves aloof, it is because the image of Democracy which they came to cherish in imprisonment was so different from the false version they see around them, the usual sea of intrigue, with pirates, old and new, at the helm of the pirate crafts of yore. These disappointed men are doubtless the most honest among us.[4] ([1949] 1958: 14)]

In this introduction, Guareschi assumes two identities: Giovannino Guareschi, and the number 6865. When addressing himself to his former companions, Guareschi adopts his former 'numerical' identity, which acquires a positive connotation and authenticates his testimony: 'È la voce del numero 6865 che parla. È la stessa voce di allora. Sono gli stessi baffi di allora' (Guareschi [1949] 2009: xiv) ['The voice of No.6865 is speaking, the same voice, coming out from under the same handle-bar moustache' ([1949] 1958: 14)]. This first dissociation is later complicated by the intervention of many other selves, as *Diario clandestino* alternates between the perspective of Guareschi as IMI, as father, as husband, as man, as humorist, as journalist and as others. The multiplication of the selves, some of which tend to be depicted as masks (like the Italian bourgeois), some of which are shown as 'real', is a central Guareschian theme. It is also present in *Ritorno alla base*, a posthumous collection of pieces written in the camps or about the camp experience. When presenting Bertoldo, his 'Giornale umoristico chiacchierato e sonorizzato' (Guareschi [1989] 2011: 25) ['chattered and sonorized humoristic journal'] from barrack to barrack, Guareschi introduces the team as 'composta da me, da Giovannino Guareschi e dal corrispondente numero 6865' (Guareschi [1989] 2011: 29–30) ['composed of me, of Giovannino Guareschi and of the correspondent number 6865']. Each part of the trinity highlights a specific aspect of himself, while also resonating with his deep and explicit Catholic faith.

The division of the self allows at least one of the selves to escape the concreteness of the situation of imprisonment, in a way that recalls the dynamic of humour according to Freud. If we position the voice of the prisoner as the primary instance representing the author's *persona* or ego, we can see how the division into a multiplicity of voices (the prisoner, the narrator, the father etc.) enables the 'victorious assertion of the ego's invulnerability' (Freud [1927] 1961: 162). The ego-prisoner 'refuses to be distressed by the provocations of reality, to let itself be compelled to suffer' (Freud [1927] 1961: 162). Separating himself into characters who pertain to different spaces both inside and outside of the boundaries of the prison, Guareschi creates spaces of freedom outside of the camps, while remaining fully anchored in the camps' reality and in the communicative act with his fellow prisoners.

Repetitions and oppositions thus act on a structural level to hint at something intangible that can be found within the concrete situation of imprisonment. A similar process takes place at the linguistic level, in the choice of vocabulary.

Guareschi's style is famous for its apparent simplicity. The author tends to prefer generic terms to precise ones, in that they can often convey a more comprehensive meaning. These words will on many occasions acquire the quality of euphemisms. The Second World War, for example, is at first introduced as the 'ultimo grosso pasticcio che ha rattristato il nostro disgraziatissimo mondo' (Guareschi [1949] 2009: viii) ['the most recent of the messes into which our unfortunate world has got itself' ([1949] 1958: 9)], 'pasticcio' being one of Guareschi's favourite euphemisms, used to designate a wide variety of situations. Similarly, 'Istruzioni per l'uso' ends with the laconic depiction of two years of war imprisonment as an 'umile avventura' ['humble adventure']. This euphemism reproduces at the linguistic level the division of the selves that enables the creation of a freer space for one of the selves, outside of the main setting of imprisonment described by the text. Indeed, euphemisms and repetitions with additions embed hidden, elusive surpluses in the sentence. Therefore, all Guareschian techniques presented so far introduce a surcode that lies outside of the boundaries of the word, of the sentence or of Guareschi's *persona*. To Denise Jardon, literary humour is defined precisely by its use of a surcoded language: humour says A in order to imply A^{+x}, that is A with an addition (1988: 145). Humour therefore distinguishes itself from lies or irony: 'Le menteur dit A, pense non-A et veut faire entendre A./L'ironiste dit A, pense non-A et veut faire entendre non-A./[...] L'humoriste dit A, pense A^{+x} et veut faire entendre A^{+x}' (145). ['The liar says A, thinks non-A and wants us to hear A./The ironist says A, thinks non-A and wants us to hear non-A./[...] The humorist says A, thinks A^{+x} and wants us to think A^{+x}'].

The hidden surplus contained in humoristic statements distinguishes them from comic ones, since the surplus is generally connoted negatively and reveals the subject's dysphoric state (Morin 2006: 9). In the case of Guareschi's Jonathanism quoted above, for example, the 'explanation-clause' is hidden, and then revealed to be collective imprisonment. Humoristic statements thus unveil an important underlying movement in the narratives: the movement from dysphoria to euphoria. As Morin explains, 'L'humour implique donc un sujet passionné dysphoriquement, par son rapport avec ce qui l'entoure, d'où la présence d'une certaine tristesse dans ce type de discours' (Morin 2006: 9). ['Humour implies a dysphorically passionate subject, in their relationship with what surrounds them, hence the presence of a certain sadness in this type of discourse.'] Guareschi's humour becomes 'a means of obtaining pleasure in spite of the distressing affects that interfere with it' (Freud [1905] 1960: 228), to move from a dysphoric to a euphoric (or less dysphoric) state. This movement is more clearly perceptible in the short stories of *Diario clandestino*. Addressed to Guareschi's companions, they combine an inward, introspective outlook and the desire to raise morale by transforming the perception of present conditions. One of the 'Lettere al postero' ['Letters to my Descendant'] also has an additional fictional addressee: Guareschi's son Alberto. The presence of this child intermediary strongly underlines the transformation of dysphoric events into their euphoric narration.

'Lettere al postero' ['Letters to my Descendant']

The movement constitutive of humour is most felt in the stories involving communication between Guareschi and his family, be they short stories in the form of letters, stories about the writing of letters, or about packages to be sent, or stories about packages just received. Some of the fictive letters are part of a series entitled 'Lettere al postero' ['Letters to my Descendant']. Although only two have been selected to appear in *Diario clandestino*, the author wrote other ones, with at least a seventy-page one published in *Il grande diario*. In the first of these letters, which is also the very first short story of the book, Guareschi intends to explain to his descendant (conflated with his three-year-old son, especially at the close of the letter), how exactly he came to be in the camps. The characteristic tone of the story, the use of repetitions and of a powerful punch line are some features that contribute to make 'Lettere al postero' one of the best examples of Guareschi's humour, in that they all displace the focus of the story from the dysphoria of the situation to the euphoria of its narration.

The stories revolving around communication with the outside world take into account the gap separating the two realities. Guareschi's position often creates a distancing effect. The fact that the 'Lettere al postero' ('Letters to my descendant') are addressed to a child increases that effect, favourable to the development of humour. Guareschi opts from the start for a falsely naïve tone, which he immediately abandons in the second paragraph:

Postero mio diletto,
    dopo una tremenda esperienza come l'attuale, l'umanità è ben decisa a non lasciarsi trascinare in avventure belliche, e questa – come tutti sanno benissimo – sarà l'ultimissima guerra che affliggerà l'orbe terracqueo.
    Per la qual cosa anche tu, postero mio diletto, un bel giorno troverai nella casella della posta una cartolina che t'inviterà a presentarti immediatamente a una determinata caserma, dove ti forniranno di utensili atti a danneggiare il

prossimo tuo come te stesso. E, in seguito, per un determinato susseguirsi di vicende, forse ti troverai – come ora si trova il tuo sciagurato padre – in un campo di concentramento.

[...] E per questo io ritengo utile cosa spiegarti, sulla base delle mie esperienze, come si possa andare a finire in un campo circondato da un filo spinato. (Guareschi [1949] 2009: 3)

[Dearly beloved Descendant:

After an experience as harrowing as the one it has just lived through, the human race is hell-bent on keeping out of all future war. The present scourge, then, is definitely the last of its kind to afflict us.

Thus you too, beloved descendant, may some day find in your letter-box a summons to appear at such-and-such army barracks, where you will be equipped with tools enabling you to do unto your neighbour just as much harm as you can do unto yourself. And eventually, after a long train of vicissitudes, you may wind up, like your unfortunate forefather, in an internment camp.

[...] And that is why there is some point to my explaining, on the basis of my own experience, how and why you may land behind a barbed-wire fence. ([1949] 1958: 17)]

The irony of this passage is clearly not meant for a child, but for the adult public, and primarily for the men listening to the verbal rendition of the story. After this preamble, Guareschi goes back in time, as he says, to explain his presence in the camps. What he has in mind by 'explanation' is however not necessarily what one might expect.

The main story is developed on two additional temporal levels. The narrator first declares that an extraordinary event happened to him one morning, when, in soldier's gear, on a parade ground, his heels 'cozzarono l'un contro l'altro e diedero uno schiocco formidabile' (Guareschi [1949] 2009: 4) ['snapped together with a resounding click' ([1949] 1958: 17)]. He then goes further back in time to explain why this fact is significant. The following account will be the one of his 'scarsa attitudine militare' (Guareschi [1949] 2009: 4) ['unsoldierly attitude' ([1949] 1958: 17)]. Set in an unnamed Italian town, the story depicts the narrator as he goes through a series of military vicissitudes. Left to fend for himself as a newcomer on a military base, the narrator seems never to find the solution that is appropriate for a military man. Episodes like the 'fattaccio del cappuccino' (Guareschi [1949] 2009: 7) ['the coffee crime' ([1949] 1958: 19)] (in which, in order to remedy the fact that the sixty men under his supervision have not been given coffee that morning, he brings them all out to the nearest cafés) all end up discredited as being 'unsoldierly'. Yet the biggest problem arises when he finds himself unable to make the typical heel-clicking sound a soldier should produce when saluting his superior. Heel clicking becomes his obsession. As he explains, 'ben sapevo che, solamente con una adeguata serie di buoni schiocchi, avrei potuto sfatare la leggenda della mia "scarsa attitudine militare"' (Guareschi [1949] 2009: 8) ['I knew that only a succession of successful clicks could destroy the myth of my "unsoldierly attitude"' ([1949] 1958: 21). But even a deal with an army lieutenant who would 'dub' in the heel clicking does not turn out to be successful. The narrator even reports seeing over every soldier's head 'una di quelle nuvolette famose dei giornali per bambini e, dentro ogni nuvoletta, era scritto a caratteri fiammeggianti:/"Scarsa attitudine militare"' (Guareschi [1949] 2009: 9) ['a sort of comic-book legend, in letters of fire, reading: "Unsoldierly!"' ([1949] 1958: 21)].

In repeating the same formulas over and over again, 'Lettere al postero' expands the stylistic device already at play in 'Istruzioni per l'uso' to build the story around it. The use of repetition culminates with the resolution of the story within the story, that is with the explanation of the reason why making a clicking sound is extraordinary. The following conclusion repeats almost exactly the first paragraph of the embedded story, except for the addition of a punch line:

> Ma una mattina d'autunno, mentre io ero 'nei ranghi' in mezzo al cortile d'una caserma, squillò l'attenti e – come dicevo al principio della mia storia – accade qualcosa di meraviglioso.
> I miei tacchi cozzarono e si udì uno schiocco formidabile:
> Takk!
> 'Finalmente!', esclamai trionfante.
> Poi guardai i miei piedi e tutto fu chiaro, e io mi sentii meno trionfante: non calzano più i soliti stivali, ma due zoccoli con suole di legno alte sei centimetri.
> Ero prigioniero. (Guareschi [1949] 2009: 11)

> [One autumn morning, when I was standing in line in the barracks courtyard, and the bugle called me to attention, something miraculous happened. My heels came together with a resounding click. Tac!
> 'At last!' I exclaimed triumphantly.
> Then I looked down at my feet and saw the reason why. All my cockiness faded away. I was wearing not my regulation boots, but a pair of wooden shoes whose soles where three inches above the ground. I was a prisoner of war.[5]
> ([1949] 1958: 22)]

With this punch line, Guareschi reveals the added values of his opening statement, which he had strategically suspended. While the suspension had first created a distancing effect, the final revelation forces the reader to go beyond this effect, and to reread the entire passage from a totally different perspective. In a way that recalls Pirandello's two-step analysis of his reaction in front of the old lady, our reading of the story can first remain at the level of the narrative's comic effect. Rereading, however, brings in a second level of understanding that goes beyond the comic, while retaining it at the same time. The outcome is an incessant passage between the euphoric retelling of the narrator's military vicissitudes and their underlying painfulness.

The story within the first of the 'Lettere al postero' does not provide a clear explanation, a response to the 'how' or 'why' the narrator was sent to war camps. This will only be explained in the second letter. In the first one, the story seems to elude both questions, to bypass the painfulness of the event and to transmute it into a comic tale that has only a slight relation to the aforementioned event. However, Guareschi's peculiar way of answering the two questions cannot be seen as an omission. The legend of the narrator's 'scarsa attitudine militare' ['unsoldierly attitude'] should first be connected to Guareschi's own relation to the military: the author was in fact forced to join the army when, having learned that his brother had 'disappeared' in Russia (which was in fact not true), he publicly insulted Mussolini and got caught by the police (A. and C. Guareschi 2009: 201). This 'legend' must also be read as a general critique of the absurdity of the demands brought about by an illogical system. In the story, the narrator always finds a solution that enables him to solve a problem, but the representatives of the system – of the army in this case – never find it suitable.

The fact that this narrative is inscribed within the frame of a letter addressed to a child must also be taken into account. Using the child as an intermediary between himself and his fellow prisoners helps Guareschi to transmute the dysphoria of war into a game-like universe. The perceivable intention behind this humoristic gesture aligns with the Freudian explanation of humour: 'the jest made by humour is not the essential thing. It has only the value of a preliminary. The main thing is the intention which humour carries out, whether it is acting in relation to the self or other people. It means: "Look! Here is the world, which seems so dangerous! It is nothing but a game for children – just worth making a jest about!"' (Freud [1927] 1961: 166) The 'Letter' also underlines the importance for Guareschi to transmit his experience, and the impossibility or the choice not to transmit it by means of a matter-of-fact, explanatory narrative. The importance of transmission is manifest at the close of the letter, where the narrator gives advice to the 'postero' ['descendant'] who assumes the particular traits of his son:

> Fu così, postero mio, proprio così. E la prossima volta ti racconterò come ci arrivai, nel cortile di quella grande caserma polacca.
>
> Nel frattempo saluta la mamma, la nonna e la Carlottina, e fa il bravo a scuola, e impara a contare fino al numero 6865. Che poi sono io, tuo padre. (Guareschi [1949] 2009: 10)

> [That, dear descendant, is the whole story. Next time I'll tell you how I came to be in the great central yard of a *Polish* barracks. Meanwhile, give your mother, grand-mother and sister my love; be a good boy at school and learn to count up to 6865. Which is the number of your devoted
> Father. ([1949] 1958: 22; original emphasis)]

The word for word translation equates Guareschi with his number: 'learn to count up to 6865. Which, besides, *is* me, your father'. By amalgamating his identity as a father with his identity as a political prisoner, Guareschi condenses the different spatialities (of the home and the camps) and temporalities (of the past and present) that coexist within the letter to the descendant. Transmission is thus made possible by the incorporation of distinct realms within key images containing more than first appears, such as the prisoner's number.

This transmission is accompanied by another theme that acts as a connecting thread throughout the book and that works in a similar fashion: that of the dream. Here, the narrator uses the dream to reinforce the opposition between his lack of military propriety and his superior's request for military rectitude, extending this desire for rectitude to the free space of dreaming: 'Non esiste nel regolamento restrizione alcuna al riguardo dei sogni, e non è raro perciò il caso di colonnelli in Servizio Permanente Effettivo i quali sognano addirittura angeli. [...] Angeli [...] che, atterrando davanti ai colonnelli, si mettono sull'attenti con uno schiocco di tacchi secco e preciso' (Guareschi [1949] 2009: 7–8) ['Army regulations are not concerned with dreams, and many an old-time colonel dreams about angels. [...] [W]hen such angels land at a colonel's feet, they draw themselves to attention with a sharp click of their heels' ([1949] 1958: 20)]. Yet this extension of the power to control the space of the dream uses the initial opposition to create a new movement between two realms essential to the creation of humour. In the short story 'Il sogno' ['The Dream'], Guareschi brings this idea to another level by using the dream at both the thematic basis and the structure of the narrative.

'Il sogno' ['The Dream']

The short story 'Il sogno' ['The Dream'] is not dissimilar from the series of stories about letters and packages, in that it constitutes another type of imagined contact with the writer's loved ones. Once again, the contact is double: the narration of the imaginary contact, performed in front of the group of internees, helps create a bond between people sharing the same situation, the same longing for home and for their families. This second type of contact is also implicitly inscribed in the story, and especially in its preamble, where the whole group is included in the 'we' employed by the narrator:

> A noi è concesso soltanto sognare. Sognare è la necessità più urgente perché la nostra vita è al di là del reticolato, e oltre il reticolato ci può portare solamente il sogno.
>
> Bisogna sognare: aggrapparsi alla realtà coi nostri sogni, per non dimenticarci d'esser vivi.
>
> Di queste inutili giornate fatte di grammi, di cicche o di miseria, la sola parte attiva, la sola parte vitale saranno i nostri sogni.
>
> Bisogna sognare: e, nel sogno, ritroveremo valori che avevamo dimenticato, scopriremo valori ignorati, ravviseremo gli errori del nostro passato e la fisionomia del nostro avvenire. (Guareschi [1949] 2009: 58)

[Our only privilege is to dream. Dreaming is necessary to us, because our life is outside the barbed-wire enclosure, and we have no way of getting there except in our dreams. Only through them can we maintain a hold on reality and remember that we are still alive. After futile days, measured by ounces of food and numbers of cigarette butts, dreams offer us the only real activity we know. Dream we must, for in our dreams we recover forgotten values and find new ones we had never known before; we detect the errors of our past and catch a glimpse of the future. ([1949] 1958: 55)]

A number of contrasts are introduced here, which force the auditor and the reader to go beyond the conventional way of thinking about dreaming. Here, dreaming is given concreteness: it is 'la sola parte vitale' ['the only real activity'] for the internees. Instead of being seen as a way to escape reality, it is perceived as the only way to retain it. Finally, it is presented as the necessary intersection between past and future. This insistence on the importance of always keeping in mind one's past and one's future is at the core of Guareschi's narrative of the camps. (It is also closely related to his conception of humour, as I will explain in the next section.) Although it deals with the situation of the men in the camps, the imprecise way in which this preamble is written also makes it possible to read it as a general statement about humanity.

The preamble is distinct from the actual story in many ways. The point of view moves from the plural to the singular, with the narrator enacting just what has been suggested in the preceding part: 'costruendo noi stessi la trama della vicenda immaginaria, soggettisti, registi, attori, operatori e spettatori del nostro sogno' (58) ['let us write our own plot and scenario and be directors, actors, camera-men and spectators of our own imaginary story' (55)]. This story is introduced to the reader/spectator by degrees, in a slow unfolding that possesses a dream-like quality. The narrator first describes the setting, an unnamed Italian city. Then, the main character of the dream, Giovannino, moves in the city, in military gear, and starts conversations with places and objects and people (Verdi's monument, a sign posted on the street, his old café, the echo of his footsteps, his late grandmother). Some of these offer striking comments on the shock between the two realities depicted in Guareschi's book: the reality of the camp and the one of the 'ordinary citizen' in Italy. The sign 'Pedoni sul marciapiede!' (Guareschi [1949] 2009: 60) ['Pedestrians should keep to the pavement' ([1949] 1958: 56)] acts, precisely, as a sign, a symbol of the shock inherent in the meeting of the two spaces. When the narrator explains 'È tanto tempo che sogno di camminare libero in mezzo a una strada assolata! Torno adesso dai campi di concentramento ...' ['For a very long time I have dreamed of walking down the middle of a sunlit street. After all, I'm just back from an internment camp'], the sign only replies 'Sì, ma torni a piedi, e quindi, per me, sei un pedone e i pedoni debbono camminare sul marciapiede!' (Guareschi [1949] 2009: 60) ['Yes, but you've come back on foot and so, as far as I'm concerned, you're a pedestrian and have to obey the regulations!' ([1949] 1958: 56)] The sign operates as evidence of a clash between two frameworks, as a means to normalize the former situation of the main character, and as a reminder that the world outside the camps also has its rules.

When, after many pages of events of this type, Giovannino finally arrives in front of his house, the narration suddenly shifts. The point of view adopted up to this point, the 'I' of the protagonist, is replaced by an external voice – the voice of the director of the dream/story.

> Giovannino – dunque – è giunto finalmente davanti a casa sua. Ma proprio qui il nostro eccellente personaggio è colto da viva perplessità.
>
> Il finale ha un'importanza straordinaria, e non varrebbe certamente la pena d'aver sofferto lunghi mesi per costruire una delicata vicenda sentimentale, per poi rovinare tutto con un finale sciatto.
>
> Bisogna pensarci.

La prima idea, quella di emettere urla scomposte, è da scartare senza discussione. Così facendo si sveglierebbe di soprassalto questa povera gente che ha invece tanto bisogno d'essere dolcemente distolta dal sogno cupo che dura da mesi e mesi. (Guareschi [1949] 2009: 63-4)

[And so Giovannino has finally come home. But at this very moment he finds himself in a dilemma. The last scene is of capital importance. It would be a complete waste of time to have suffered for months and months, with only sentimental illusions to sustain him, and then to ring down the curtain on a fiasco. The matter requires thought.

His first idea of making a loud noise[6] is quickly discarded. By so doing he would inflict a rude shock upon good people who need to be quietly awakened from the bad dream which has for so long held them in thrall. ([1949] 1958: 59)]

This passage shows how the dream acts in this story both as structure and as theme. In a way that is typical of Guareschi, what was first presented as a dream undergoes a complete reversal. In the protagonist's dream, the family members are waiting for the prisoner's return but they are the ones imprisoned in a dream. With this idea in mind, the hero decides to gently call his wife with a 'voce pacata e lontana come le voci dei sogni' (Guareschi [1949] 2009: 64) ['a far-away, positively dream-like voice' ([1949] 1958: 59)]. His precaution does not have the anticipated effect, and the 'finale sciatto' ['fiasco'] that he tried to avoid finally happens.

For the denouement, a truly comic part of the story, the tone of the story changes completely. The ethereal quality of the stroll in town gives way to a more pragmatic (although not fully realistic) tone, and the speed of the narration increases extremely quickly in only a few paragraphs. The character's wife, surprised by his arrival, shrieks loudly and provokes a chain reaction of shrieks, jumps and falls that involves the whole household, from the baby girl to the cat and fish. This finale, compared to the 'Rivoluzione Francese' and the 'Terrore' (Guareschi [1949] 2009: 64) ['the French Revolution' and 'the Reign of Terror' ([1949] 1958: 60)], culminates with the desperation of the hero: '"No! No!", singhiozza Giovannino davanti alle rovine fumanti della famiglia. "Così non può andare!"' (Guareschi [1949] 2009: 65) ['"No, no", sobs Giovannino, before the smoking ruins of his family. "This will never do!"' ([1949] 1958: 60)]. The only way to remedy the situation is for the director of the dream to rewind the events before the eyes of the protagonist. The story ends when Giovannino concludes 'Mio Dio, com'è difficile ritornare!' (Guareschi [1949] 2009: 65) ['Lord help us! How hard it is to come home!' ([1949] 1958: 61)].

The punch line of 'Il sogno' is even more powerful than the one in 'Lettere al postero'. While the Russian doll structure of the 'Letter' (with its story within a story, enclosed in the frame of a letter) circumscribes the punch line within another framework, 'Il sogno' foregoes such mirroring. The ending returns to the power of direction of one's dream, but the opening reflection on the general power of dreams is not paralleled by closing remarks, and the inclusive 'we' disappears. Greater emphasis is therefore placed on the catastrophic ending. By choosing not to insist on the positive characteristics of the home his interlocutors long for, but rather on the importance of preparing one's return in imagination, the humorist turns an otherwise intolerable wait into a euphoric moment of storytelling, setting up an oscillation between the narrative euphoria and the dysphoria of the conditions depicted.

Guareschi's humorist: One who can backdate one's actions

The movement at play in 'The Dream' actualizes humour's rebellious potential, leading to 'the triumph of the ego but also of the pleasure principle, which is able here to assert itself against the unkindness of the real circumstances' (Freud [1927] 1961: 163). The dream blurs the boundaries between the reality of the camp and the reality of the Italian town, enabling the creation of humour to lighten the situation of the men in the camp. Yet from the point of view of the reader/auditor, the whole story rather insists on the distinctions between the two realities, even increasing the gap between them. The euphoric effect nevertheless remains present, and the gap need not provoke desperation, but rather lucidity. In using the dream both as theme and as structure, Guareschi creates an oscillatory movement between two orders of reality, and between opposite attitudes, such as desperation and hope, resulting in the co-presence of euphoria and dysphoria.

This oscillatory movement is central to the development of the author's new definition of humour. As Perry explains, 'before the war, [Guareschi] had seen his craft on a strictly literary plane; now, imprisonment brought him to see humor as a way of life. [...] He realized that as a humorist, he must use humor to assign positive meaning to events in the present. He should not wait for a future time to reconsider the significance of past events' (2001: 69). Guareschi's new conception of humour is grounded in a particular understanding of time. Indeed, in 'Umorismo razionato' ['Rationed humour'], another public talk given in the camps, published posthumously in *Ritorno alla Base* (1989) and in *L'umorismo* (2015), Guareschi explains how crucial it is to be able to make one's future present. It is, to him, the key feature of the humorist and of humour seen not as a literary genre but as a way of life. To him, 'umorista è chi sa retrodatare le sue azioni e le sue sensazioni' (Guareschi [1989] 2011: 64) ['the humorist is one who can backdate their actions and their sensations']. By adopting the point of view of the future, as is the case for example in the short story 'The Dream', Guareschi succeeds in uncovering unsuspected positive aspects. The focus on temporality is interwoven with Guareschi's particular conception of the space of imprisonment, which assumes porous boundaries. The multiple dissociations within the space of the war camp (dissociation of the self, of the storytelling, of the word) are rendered possible by the new understanding of humour's role.

The role of humour in Guareschi's world is multiple; a means of coping with pain and of helping others to cope with theirs, it is also an act of resistance, and a way to fathom the situation. It must not be conflated with the comic, as is clearly stated in this passage of 'Umorismo razionato': 'Non fissiamoci che umorismo e comicità siano due termini equivalenti. Comicità è una faccenda puramente accessoria. Escludo che l'umorismo *debba* far ridere, come escludo che un uomo, per essere tale, debba – ad esempio – avere il capelli biondi e gli occhi azzurri. Come un uomo *può* essere biondo o con gli occhi azzurri, così l'umorismo *può* essere comico' (Guareschi [1989] 2011: 66; original emphasis). ['Let us not think that humour and the comic are two equivalent terms. The comic is a purely secondary matter. I refuse to admit that humour *must* make one laugh, just like I refuse to admit that a man, to be a man, must – for example – have blond hair and blue eyes. Just like a man *could* be blond or have blue eyes, humour *could* be comic']. By drawing a parallel with the Nazis' ideal of Aryan uniformity and supremacy, Guareschi criticizes both political and textual rigidity and totalitarianism, that would not leave space for a human genre or a literary genre with porous and changing boundaries. Guareschi's comment also recalls both Pirandello's and Freud's distinctions between humour and the comic. Guareschi's pre-war humour can best be described as generally 'comic', whereas the postwar production is closer to a Freudian understanding of humour and does not necessarily always strike the reader as 'comic'. Guareschian humour becomes above all a new way of life that will continue to be reflected in his subsequent works. Remembering life in the Lagers, and the insight it has rendered possible for him, will be a chief concern in the rest of his production.

Romain Gary: The roots of humour

Criticism regarding Romain Gary's works always highlights the impact of the Second World War on the author's life and work. Most straightforwardly, Guy Amsellem declares: 'C'est peu dire que la guerre eut, pour Gary, une importance décisive. Elle transforma sa vie d'homme, détermina sa création romanesque, décida de son avenir' (Amsellem 2008: 39) ['It is an understatement to say that the war had, for Gary, a decisive impact. It transformed his life as a man, it determined his novelistic creation, it decided his future']. In his first Goncourt-winning novel[7] *Les racines du ciel*, the impact of war is perceptible implicitly throughout the work. Set in Africa in the 1950s, the novel deals with the aftermath of the Second World War on human consciousness. According to David Bellos (2010), while it may seem like the core of the novel is African (Gary's working title for the novel was *Éducation africaine*), in truth 'the heart of Gary's African novel is in Europe and in the healing of its wounds' (245). A short section of the novel, which might seem very circumscribed and almost anecdotal at first glance, is central in light of Bellos's comment. Set in a Nazi camp, it is reported as an analepsis within an analepsis (a flashback within a flashback). The episode is a striking example of the power of humour in surviving war imprisonment, with the stance of the main character of the episode calling to mind the one of Guareschi's *persona*. Moreover, the episode informs the protagonist's choices and attitude and makes possible the creation of the myth that surrounds him, and ultimately of the novel itself. Understanding the workings of Gary's humour therefore means grasping the relationship between humour and myth-making, and the role of the communal sharing of humour in camps, a feature that was present in Guareschi's war diary.

The episode (alluded to on page 55 and fully developed on pages 205 to 215) relates the story of Robert, a companion of the protagonist Morel in Second World War camps, later known as Duparc, owner of a cotton plantation. The reader learns the whole story in the second part of the novel, when Duparc is asked to appear at the trial where Morel's acolytes are being prosecuted for their actions against plantation owners and elephant hunters. The narration shifts to the memory of Minna, a German waitress in Africa and follower of Morel. Minna recalls the moment she learned about Duparc. After having heard about him on several occasions, Minna asks Morel to explain the story. The reader discovers the story in an analepsis from Morel's point of view, itself inserted in another analepsis from Minna's point of view (205–13). The final meeting between

Duparc and Morel is also told from a point of view external to the protagonists, as the bar owner Habib comments on it in front of the trial's audience (213). A last shift in point of view closes the episode with Morel's voice, still in Minna's narration (215). As I will show, the multiplication of voices in the episode and in the novel has a significant impact on the relationship between humour and myth-creation.

Robert's story can be summarized as follows: a prisoner in a Nazi camp, Robert reacts to his fellow prisoners' discouragement by creating an imaginary woman whom all must respect and in front of whom all should behave. First perceived as absurd, the idea is quickly accepted by his comrades, who understand that 's'il n'y avait pas une convention de dignité quelconque pour nous soutenir, si on ne s'accrochait pas à une fiction, à un mythe, il ne restait plus qu'à se laisser aller, à se soumettre à n'importe quoi et même à collaborer' (Gary [1980] 2010: 207) ['if there wasn't some convention of dignity left to sustain us, if we didn't cling to some fiction, to some myth, there would be nothing left but to let ourselves go, submit to anything, including the Nazis, to give in and to betray' ([1958] 1964: 163–4)].[8] The Germans also strongly react to Robert's creation by trying to have him hand over the imaginary woman. Having refused to do so, he is imprisoned in an individual cell, where he comes up with the image of free elephants as a source of strength to fight claustrophobia, another idea that will be adopted by his companions, and especially by Morel. Years after the war, Robert's idea has led to Morel's attempt to raise awareness about the unregulated hunt for elephants in Africa. Morel's collaborators set Duparc's house on fire, as the latter is a rich plantation owner known for unjustly killing elephants. Morel comes face to face with Duparc and recognizes him as Robert. Habib witnesses Morel's astonishment.

Humour's role in the camps

Humour and laughter are present at different levels of the story: the reaction of Robert's companions, Robert's own attitude and Habib's response at the end of the episode. Robert's fellow inmates' first reaction is one of incomprehension and is expressed by 'quelques rires glauques' (Gary [1980] 2010: 207) ['a few hoarse laughs' ([1958] 1964: 163)]. Robert's invention can first be read as a typical case of incongruity humour, highlighting the discrepancy between the repulsion of the situation and the beauty and dignity evoked by the imaginary woman. Not all prisoners in Robert's 'Block K' will come to understand the revolutionary power underlying this attitude, but most of them will. When they do, a shift occurs between their incredulity and an attitude I identify as humoristic, in the Guareschian sense of the term.

Indeed, Robert's stance recalls Guareschi's definition of humour and Gary's own comments on humour dispersed throughout the novel. Briefly summarized, we can say that Gary distinguishes two forms of humour: humour as a weapon or a tool helping to survive, and humour as deception. The first type, often used by the British Colonel Babcock, is described as 'une dynamite silencieuse et polie qui vous permet de faire sauter votre condition présente chaque fois que vous en avez assez, mais avec le maximum de discrétion et sans éclaboussures' (Gary [1980] 2010: 242) ['a silent and polite dynamite which enables you to blow your own way of life sky-high every time you have had enough of it, yet with the maximum discretion and without making a mess' ([1958] 1964: 191)]. Yet, Babcock's humour is criticized by the American Forsythe for its deceptive power: 'Votre maudit sens de l'humour est une façon de tricher, d'apprivoiser cette vérité au lieu de vous mesurer avec elle' (Gary [1980] 2010: 64) ['Your damned sense of humour is a way to cheat, to tame this truth instead of confronting it' (my translation; this passage is missing from the 1958 English edition)].

This distinction recalls Lewis's two types of humour exposed in *Blast*: 'blasted' humour, and 'blessed' humour. On the one hand, the imposture, deception and anaesthesia that Forsythe criticizes in Babcock's humour are key elements of the style of humour that Lewis 'blasts' for its conventionalism and stupidity. On the other hand, Lewis 'blesses' the wise and unconventional type of humour that can act as 'the great barbarous weapon of the genius among races' (26) and that is compared in the manifesto to a bomb (31), or to nitrogen (38). The explosiveness and strength of this type of humour break down the common understanding of everyday life and recall many of Gary's affirmations on humour, such as the comparison with dynamite quoted above. However, whereas for Lewis there are two distinct types of humour, for Gary, the same type of humour is perceived differently by two characters. Babcock's use of humour is presented by the narrator as 'silent dynamite', but this very same use of humour is criticized by Forsythe for being deceptive.

Robert's use of humour can be best described as silent dynamite and as a means of survival, and it clearly assumes a positive value. The first encounter with Robert, still unnamed, depicts him laughing through his imprisonment: ' – et, chaque matin, les Allemands le trouvaient en pleine forme, en train de rigoler: il était devenu increvable' (55) [' – and, every morning, the Germans would find him in top shape, laughing: he had become indestructible' (my translation; this passage is missing from the 1958 English edition]. Just like Ostrach, another character of *Les racines*, Robert possesses 'cette antique et impérissable gaieté qui est une garantie de survie' (203) ['that ancient, imperishable human gaiety, like a guarantee of survival' ([1958] 1964: 160)]. In Morel's words, it is 'de la gaieté de qui est allé au fond des choses et en est revenu rassuré' (206) ['the cheerfulness of a man who has gone deep down into things and come back reassured' ([1958] 1964: 162)]. Robert's gaiety becomes the strength that makes him the leader of Block K. When the Nazi commander asks Robert to hand over the imaginary woman, the Block enters into a debate around the belief in this common myth. Morel, narrating the story, explains that no matter what the arguments are, the final decision will be solely Robert's, and there is no doubt what it will be.

> Il n'y avait qu'à le voir: il jubilait. [...] [I]l refusait, lui, de renoncer et il nous observait de ses petits yeux moqueurs, *prisonnier d'une puissance autrement formidable que celle de l'Allemagne nazie*. Et il se marrait, il se marrait à l'idée que cela dépendait entièrement de lui, que les S.S. ne pouvaient pas lui enlever par la force cette création immatérielle de son esprit, qu'il dépendait de lui de consentir à la livrer ou de reconnaître qu'elle n'existait pas. (Gary [1980] 2010: 209; emphasis added)
>
> [One had only to look at him: he was jubilant. [...] he at least was refusing to give up, and observed us with those small, stubborn, mocking eyes of his, *prisoner to a power far more formidable than that of Nazi Germany*. And he was obviously delighted at the idea that the thing depended entirely on him, that the S.S. were unable to take away from him by force that invisible creation of his mind, that it rested with him alone to consent to hand it over or to recognize that it did not exist. ([1958] 1964: 165; emphasis added)]

Robert's power over his companions and over his enemies is extremely strong. Robert's imagination and the recognition of his imaginative power lead him to consider his imprisonment and the power of his enemies as something laughable: humour developed through imagination is the key to Robert's survival. There is a direct correlation between imprisonment and humour; the tighter and harder the imprisonment becomes, the more powerful Robert's creations and humoristic attitude become. In his one meter ten by one meter fifty cell, he comes up with the image of free elephants that will have an incredible impact on the morale of the Block K men and on the creation of Morel's myth.

Interestingly, Morel describes Robert's imagination as a new prison (he is 'prisoner to a power far more formidable than that of Nazi Germany'), but a prison that assumes positive characteristics. The episode leads to a complete reversal between truth and fiction, a common Garyan theme, and even to the recognition that the criterion of truth is utterly useless with what concerns the power of the imagination as resistance. As Robert told them when explaining the necessity of remaining decorous in front of the woman, what counts is the 'as if', not the reality of what is being performed: 'Vous allez essayer de vous conduire devant elle comme si vous étiez des hommes. Je dis bien "comme si" – c'est la seule chose qui compte (207)' ['You'll try and behave in front of her as if you were men. I say "as if" – it's the only thing that matters' ([1958] 1964: 163)]. Just after Robert's refusal to hand over the woman – to admit the fictionality of his creation in front of the authorities – the narration directly states the meaninglessness of this criterion of truth in Robert's form of resistance: 'L'officier venait se briser les dents contre la fidélité de l'homme à sa convention: peu importait qu'elle fût vraie ou fausse pourvu qu'elle nous illuminât de dignité' (210) ['He had just broken his teeth against man's loyalty to his own convention, and whether it was true or false mattered little provided our human face caught the light of its dignity' ([1958] 1964: 166)]. Gary emphasizes both Robert's exceptionality and the bonding between the men of Block K. Robert's position as the leader and centre of the block is made clear from the start: 'Il était le noyau irréductible de notre block, celui autour de qui tous les "politiques" venaient se grouper instinctivement' (206) ['He was the irreducible core of our block; all the political prisoners grouped instinctively around him' ([1958] 1964: 162)]. At the same time, the impact of his creations on other individuals, and most of all on the collective, is central in the story. The collective subsumed in the term 'Block K' assumes the characteristics of an individual and develops a personality throughout the episode. After the introduction of the woman, for example, the morale of this entity, presented in a personification, experiences a drastic change: 'À partir de ce moment-là, il se passa une chose vraiment extraordinaire: le moral du block K remonta soudain de plusieurs crans' (207) ['From that moment a quite extraordinary thing happened: the morale of Block K rose suddenly by several points' ([1958] 1964: 164)]. Shifts from the individual to the collective take place on several occasions, like in the following passage: 'Il [le commandant] était à la merci de Robert. Il dépendait de *sa* bonne volonté. Il n'y avait pas de force, il n'y avait pas de soldats, il n'y avait pas d'armes capables d'expulser du *block* cette fiction-là: on ne pouvait rien contre elle sans *notre* consentement' (Gary

[1980] 2010: 210; emphasis added) ['He [the Nazi commander] had placed himself at Robert's mercy. He was dependent on *Robert's* pleasure. There was no force, there were no soldiers, there were no weapons capable of making that fiction leave the *block*. Nothing could happen to it without *our* consent' ([1958] 1964: 16; emphasis added)]. The change in determiners, from 'sa' (his) to 'notre' (our), emphasizes both Robert's power as creator and the subsequent power of the prisoners' collectivity in the face of adversity.

Even if the collective aspect is emphasized, some dissenting voices can be heard, and some prisoners remain unable to totally adhere to Robert's creations. They lack the capacity to understand the meaninglessness of distinguishing common truth from fiction in this context of resistance to imprisonment. Morel as narrator describes this capacity as a form of wisdom possessed for example by Habib: 'Ceux d'entre eux qui comprenaient avaient des ricanements cyniques et des regards amusés, indulgents, de sages, d'hommes pleins d'expérience, de réalistes qui savent s'arranger et vivre en bonne intelligence avec leur condition, avec la vie –, des regards d'Habib' (Gary [1980] 2010: 209) ['Those of them who understood gave us cynical grins and amused, indulgent glances of men of sense, men full of experience, hard-boiled realists who had learned to adapt themselves and live on good terms with life, glances like Habib's' ([1958] 1964: 165)]. Habib fully shares Robert's refusal of the tragic attitude and perceives everything in a similar light. His reaction to the Duparc story is on every occasion one of hilarity (205), of 'rire bon enfant' (Gary [1980] 2010: 213) ['tremendous good-natured laugh' ([1958] 1964: 168)]. And even if Morel is shocked by Duparc's actions after the war, he is still able to understand Habib's perception of the story: '"Ça n'a en effet rien de tragique", dit-il, "et je suppose qu'ils ont raison de rire de nous"' (206) ['"There's nothing really tragic about it", he said slowly and quietly, "and I suppose Habib is right to laugh at my anger and shock"' ([1958] 1964: 162)].

Thus, resisting imprisonment through humour is at stake not only for Robert but also for Colonel Babcock, Ostrach, Habib and, at times, Morel. However, the idealistic aspect that marks the humour developed in the camps takes on a greater importance for Morel than for Robert. And more importantly, this idealism is literalized. Morel tries to literally abolish the distance between Robert's creations and his own life. Morel's relationship with Minna can be read as the literalization of Robert's relationship with the invented woman in the camps. Similarly, Morel gives the image of the free elephants a concrete existence by fighting against the plantation owners who kill elephants. Two rejoinders from Morel and Duparc's discussion when they meet again illustrate the contrast between their attitudes:

'Toi! bégaya-t-il. S'il y a un homme qui devrait être avec nous, à défendre les éléphants, c'est toi! Et tu es le premier à les abattre parce qu'ils piétinent ton champ!' Duparc le fixait avec hébétement, la mâchoire pendante. 'Ils piétinent ma plantation, répétait-il, ils m'ont causé un million de perte l'année dernière, ils saccagent les potagers de mes paysans, régulièrement ... J'ai bien le droit de me défendre! Et si tu veux me faire croire qu'il s'agit d'éléphants là-dedans ... Tu n'as qu'à regarder avec qui tu t'es acoquiné!' 'Ça, rigola Habib, c'était pour moi.' (Gary [1980] 2010: 213)

['You' he stuttered. 'You! If there's any man who ought to be on our side, defending the elephants, it's you! And you're the first to kill them just because they trample your field!' Duparc stared at him dully, and his jaw dropped. 'They were ruining my plantation', he shouted. 'They cost me three million francs last year; and they destroy my natives' gardens regularly. After all, I've the right to defend myself! And if you want to try and make believe that elephants are the real issue ... take a good look at your lieutenants!'
'That', laughed Habib, 'was meant for me'. ([1958] 1964: 169)]

The main contradiction breaks through in this dialogue: by fighting for the survival of real elephants, Morel is in no way the most practical of the two characters. On the contrary, Duparc's preoccupations are both extremely realistic and extremely constant: from the creation of the imaginary woman to the killing of the elephants wrecking the plantation, Duparc's actions are directed towards the real-life preoccupations of survival and of getting the most out of life. There is therefore only an apparent contradiction between the choices of Robert and those of Duparc, and this is what Habib's intelligent humour enables him to recognize. Duparc's actions are perceived by Morel as a renunciation of the values he expressed in the camps only because Morel fails to see that literal elephants have never been in question for Robert/Duparc. The reason for Morel's misunderstanding is best explained by Saint Denis, the main voice recalling Morel's story. To him, Morel is handicapped by his lack of humour: 'Je faillis éclater de rire, mais quelque chose, en lui, vous donnait envie de le ménager. Peut-être son évident manque d'humour: il m'a souvent paru qu'à partir d'un certain degré de sérieux, de gravité, un homme, dans la vie, est un infirme, on a toujours envie de l'aider à traverser la rue' (127) ['I nearly burst out laughing, but something in him made me want to spare him. Perhaps his obvious lack of humor: it has often seemed to me that above a certain degree of seriousness, of gravity, a man in real life is a cripple – one always wants to help him cross the road' ([1958] 1964: 95)]. Whereas for Robert/Duparc literal elephants have never been in question, for Morel, the animals in their reality have come to symbolize resistance and freedom. The animals also become the starting point of the creation of another myth, this time around Morel himself.

The multiplication of voices

A particular aspect of the composition of the novel reinforces the power of Robert's story and the creation of myths around the novel's protagonists in general: the multiplication and the intertwining of narrative voices. The whole novel is embedded in a dialogue between Saint Denis and Père Tassin, in which Saint Denis recalls what he has learned via many voices 'including their reports of third-level conversations, which of course themselves allude to information obtained from yet more deeply nested hearsay' (Bellos 2010: 239). This construction is crucial in blurring the line between truth and fiction and is one of the main features contributing to myth-creation in the novel. Moreover, this structural characteristic means that elements of the diegesis are likely to be presented repeatedly and through varied points of view: 'The "Russian doll" form of the narration creates innumerable opportunities for information to be given a second time over, to be illuminated by a different point of view or style of speech. Repetition is the hallmark of Gary's writing practice [...]' (Bellos 2010: 239). The retelling of the Duparc episode (205–15) is indeed an expansion of a shorter mention (54–6). In the full episode, Duparc's story is explained first through Morel's point of view as recalled by Minna, then through Habib's, retelling the reunion between Morel and Duparc to the court's audience, and finally back to Morel's point of view through Minna. The multiplication of voices in this episode is thus representative of the novel. It blurs Morel's voice in the midst of a layered mediation and establishes a myth by creating a public figure acting as a double: 'Morel, in being named, judged, and defined by others, undergoes a sort of doubling. He begins to exist "for the public" only from the moment that he becomes a legend; that is, a fictional construction "narrated by others." His double, once it enters into the public domain, takes on an existence of its own, becomes active in spheres independent of Morel himself' (Schoolcraft 2002: 56).

While Morel is generally at the centre of the mythologization in the novel, in the Duparc episode, Robert assumes the proportions of a mythical figure, of a leader laughing in the face of death and horror and leading his companions to salvation through imagination and humour. Not only have Robert's actions lifted his companions' spirits and helped them survive, but they have later on taken new dimensions in many ways. Robert's stance on life exerts a strong influence on Morel. Morel, more than any other character in the novel, is driven by a powerful ideal that he opposes to humanity's vulgarity. His quest transposes in the openness of the Afrique-Équatoriale Française (A.É.F.), the work of imagination that helped Robert and his companions survive Nazi camps. The experience of imprisonment is thus not a benign analepsis to Morel's story but its starting point: 'Morel, nous dit-on, est un survivant des camps allemands. C'est plus qu'un constat anecdotique: c'est bien au camp que tout a commencé, c'est à Dachau que Morel doit sa prise de conscience écologique, quelque incongru que cela paraisse' (Rasson 2008: 145) ['Morel, we are told, is a survivor of German camps. This is more than an anecdotal observation: it is at the camp that everything started, Morel owes his ecological awareness to his experience of Dachau, however incongruous that might seem']. The very form of the ideal defended by Morel is directly related to Robert's creations: the elephants have come to symbolize the possibility of freedom for the human race, and it is in order to save the latter that Morel defends the former.

The idealization of the symbol of the elephants is entangled in Morel's discourse with the literalization of the symbol. As Morel himself explains early in the novel, the recourse to the image of elephants in order to survive has led him to contract a debt not only towards the image, but towards the reality behind it, the elephants themselves. This debt is first evoked in the conversation already mentioned between Morel and Minna. Morel explains as follows:

> Je dois vous dire aussi que j'ai contracté, en captivité, une dette envers les éléphants, dont j'essaye seulement de m'acquitter. C'est un camarade qui avait eu cette idée, après quelques jours de cachot – un mètre dix sur un mètre cinquante – alors qu'il sentait que les murs allaient l'étouffer, il s'était mis à penser aux troupeaux d'éléphants en liberté – et, chaque matin, les Allemands le trouvaient en pleine forme, en train de rigoler: il était devenu increvable. (Gary [1980] 2010: 54–5)

> [I must also say I became indebted, in captivity, to elephants, and I am only trying to acquit myself. It's a comrade who got the idea, after a few days in solitary confinement – in a one meter ten by one meter fifty cell – when he felt that the walls were closing in, he had started to think about herds of free elephants and, every morning, the Germans would find him in top shape, laughing: he had become indestructible. (my translation; this passage is not in the 1958 English edition)]

Morel's long rejoinder (54–6) is filled with oppositions between imprisonment and freedom, as well as between imminent death and the will to live. The lexical field of imprisonment ('captivité'; 'cachot'; 'un mètre dix sur un mètre cinquante'; 'murs'; 'étouffer' ['captivity'; 'solitary confinement'; 'one meter fifty cell'; 'walls'; 'closing in']) is a lot more developed than the one of freedom ('éléphants en liberté' ['free elephants']). This insistence is however counterbalanced by the comrade's (Robert's) will to live and his attitude. The prisoner is 'en pleine forme' both physically and mentally, constantly laughing (at least when observed by the guards). Morel's description of his comrade culminates in his use of the adjective 'increvable', literally 'unburstable'.[9] The word evokes the powerfulness acquired by Robert through his attitude, especially in front of enemies. It literally means that Robert cannot be killed and suggests exterior attempts to 'burst' him. It is more importantly related to Robert being an endless joker able to resist with humour. Morel's description of Robert combines strength and humour, and 'increvable' condenses the association between survival and humour that we also find in Guareschi's 'Non muoio neanche se mia ammazzano!' (Guareschi [1949] 2009: x) ['I won't die, even if they kill me!' ([1949] 1958: 11)].

Humour's role in the episode is thus manifold. Staged as a liberating device within a literal situation of imprisonment, this 'blessed humour' enables the development of two successive myths. Robert's myth – based on hilarity as resistance and on the power of fiction in the face of abusive authority – becomes Morel's founding myth. Most of the novel revolves around the latter, and the Robert/Duparc episode assumes its full importance when considered as the starting point of Morel's own creation. Robert's resisting laughter is of course reinterpreted in Morel's own way, and the characters' two stances are not equivalent – Morel's idealism remaining uncompromised throughout the novel. Still, the common experience of imprisonment and of resistance through humour and fiction renders possible both positions and both lives and is the root of the narrative on freedom that is *Les racines du ciel*.

Vladimir Nabokov: Humour in a comic world

The relationship between political context and fictional imprisonment is not as direct for Nabokov's *Invitation to a Beheading* (1959) as it is for the two other narratives analysed in this chapter. *Invitation* (1935–1936), just like *Bend Sinister* (1947), with which it is often associated, can at least be partly interpreted as a comment on the effects totalitarian regimes have on individual freedom. These effects, however, are not pictured in the same way in both novels, and the temporal gap between their creations is frequently highlighted. As Brian Boyd (1990) explains, *Invitation* was written in the context of increased Nazi propaganda (with Joseph Goebbels as German Minister of Public Enlightenment and Propaganda) and of increased Stalinist control over Soviet writers in particular and the Soviet society in general, but before the full impact of propaganda and control could be perceived: 'the optimistic Nabokov did not foresee all the horrors of the next ten years, and his novel is not a narrowly political one. He could keep his invented world *lightly comic* in a way he could not in the much more grimly political *Bend Sinister*, written one brutal decade later' (411; emphasis added).

Invitation to a Beheading tells the story of Cincinnatus C.'s nineteen days of imprisonment leading up to his beheading. His abstruse crime, described as 'gnostical turpitude' (72), can be understood as 'impenetrability' or incapacity to blend in the social world that surrounds him and wants to dictate how to apprehend life. The clash between freedom in the development of inner life and exterior rules is at the core of the novel. The 'lightly comic' aspect of *Invitation* noted by Boyd might appear to be the reason for including this novel on imprisonment in my corpus, but this is partly misleading. In fact, in the case of *Invitation*, comic and humour do not mix, but generally oppose each other. The novel certainly presents comic scenes and characters. These, however, are almost never associated with self-consciousness or with the protagonist (which amounts to the same thing, since the protagonist is the only being capable of self-consciousness in the novel). The lack of an existing relationship between self-consciousness and the comic does not mean that humour is absent from the novel. In fact, Cincinnatus's 'crime' ('gnostical turpitude') can be read as his ability to develop a humoristic attitude, set up in contrast with the comic attitude of his gaolers. This opposition is set in the various spaces of the novel: the public space in the case of the comic, and the space of the prison cell and interiority in the case of humour. The contrast is reinforced by oppositions between ways of perceiving time and ways of perceiving the self. The comic and humour do not blend at all in the novel, and Cincinnatus's humoristic perception of life sets itself against the collective comic universe of his gaolers. In the end, his humoristic outlook enables him to perceive himself as the prisoner he is and has always been and to create a space of his own by splitting himself in two.

Spaces of Cincinnatus

The oppositions structuring *Invitation to a Beheading* are set up both physically and socially. Cincinnatus's prison cell is enclosed in a fortress that is never fully described, but that is set in stark and almost caricatural contrast with the outside, and particularly with the Tamara Gardens. Located at the top of the city, the fortress dominates the landscape; it 'tower[s] hugely on the crest of a huge cliff, of which it seem[s] to be a monstrous outgrowth' (42) and leaves the Tamara Gardens, associated with calm, love and freedom, in the distance. Within the fortress, the opposition is more social than strictly spatial. Cincinnatus's cell is constantly being invaded by the other characters and is always being observed. However, the novel establishes a distinction between what we could call the 'space of others' and 'Cincinnatus's space', understood as a way of inhabiting or conceiving space.[10] The protagonist possesses this conception of space from the start but develops it further through the experience of imprisonment. Physical imprisonment and imminent death act as wake-up calls for him, allowing him to see that his imprisonment extends to all social spaces and aspects of life: 'What matters is the suggestion that his jail is not confined to the fortress on the hill: he is a prisoner in his home, his society, his language, literary history, material existence' (Toker 1989: 136). Within his cell, Cincinnatus's feeling of imprisonment grows stronger with time, while his space of relative freedom diminishes: 'In the course of time the safe places became ever fewer: the solicitous sunshine of public concern penetrated everywhere, and the peephole in the door was placed in such a way that in the whole cell there was not a single point that the observer on the other side of the door could not pierce with his gaze' (24–5). Constricted by external social forces, the protagonist's space is thus a lot more limited than the prison cell, and assumes the dimension of Cincinnatus's person, and often only of his interiority. In order to frame his own situation, Cincinnatus has to grasp the gap between his world and the world of the jailers: the latter is false, shallow, circular and comic, while his is associated with a quest for truth, depth, a spiral impulse to break circularity and a humoristic understanding of life.

Cincinnatus perceives some of the differences between the two worlds from the start. Addressing Rodrig Ivanovich, director of the prison, the hero expresses his desire to test the 'unsubstantiality of this world of yours' (70). Lacking substance and depth, this world appears to the protagonist as bi-dimensional, as a 'painted life' (92). Its inhabitants are consequently bi-dimensional characters.

Nabokov turns them into masks coming straight out of a circus and possessing no interiority. M'sieur Pierre, Cincinnatus's fellow prisoner who turns out to be his executioner, is cast in the role of the clown. Using Cincinnatus's cell as his main stage, he is associated with both the desire to provoke laughter (e.g. 114–16) and the production of his own laughter (e.g. 158). His laughter is deprived of self-reflexivity and deployed in order to transform Cincinnatus's tragedy into a comedy. By trying to impose a collective comic image onto a personal experience not felt as comic, M'sieur Pierre tries to distract from the inhumanity and the violence of the 'world of others' that has led to Cincinnatus's imprisonment. The coercive process depicted in the novel consists both in the imprisoning act and in the trivialization and 'comicalization' of imprisonment, which Cincinnatus resists.

M'sieur Pierre's use of the tropes of comedy in an attempt to bring Cincinnatus into the collective circle, through laughter, recalls Bergson's theory of the comic. According to Toker,[11] Nabokov represents the 'common', this 'dead-wood encumbrance on the flow of consciousness' (2005: 233) through the lenses of the comic for parodic purposes (233). To Bergson, 'la vie bien vivante ne devrait pas se répéter' (Bergson [1900] 1975: 26) ['a really living life should never repeat itself' ([1900] 1911: 34)] and the comic arises when something 'encumbers' the flow of consciousness and leads to a mechanical reproduction of life. It is therefore no surprise that repetition is key to understanding the artificiality of the characters of the 'world of others'. M'sieur Pierre abundantly uses repetitions in all four Bergsonian categories of comic – bodily, situational, linguistic and character-related. His self-introduction to Cincinnatus accumulates empty questions in a discourse reminiscent of nursery rhymes and theatrical performances (85). Every night, he performs the same routine, invading Cincinnatus's cell and trying to coerce him into friendship by offering to play games (see, for example, 143).[12] Even his jokes are never renewed. Although presented as a joker, he tells only one formal joke in the course of the novel, modifying it slightly when his public is renewed (84, 183–4). In the end, M'sieur Pierre's whole character is marked by the repetition necessitated by his role. The gestures he performs for Cincinnatus are the same he has done for former prisoners and, we suppose, the same he will do for future ones. At the supper with the City's official, for example, M'sieur Pierre conforms as always to the pre-set rules and begs Cincinnatus to follow at least some of the traditional, senseless gestures like the pouring of wine on the heads of executor and executed: 'do not refuse me this, I implore you, this is the way it is done *always, always* ...' (185; emphasis added). The repeated 'always' sums up M'sieur Pierre's character in his compulsion to repeat at linguistic, bodily and situational levels. It is indeed impossible for a character so preoccupied with protocol to break from the system's stability and consistency. By blindly abiding by the rules of an inhuman system, M'sieur Pierre becomes always less of a human and more of a puppet driven by a controlled mechanism.

The comic repetition of *Invitation* differs from the humoristic repetition we find in Guareschi's prison writings. There is no understated 'plus' in M'sieur Pierre's comedy; he does not evolve and does not adjust to his surroundings. His repeated gestures do not lead to A^{+x} (Jardon) but contribute to the intensification of artificiality. What is often overlooked (e.g. by Toker), however, is that comic laughter is not the only form of laughter present in *Invitation*. A more positive laughter occasionally arises, which is associated with the individual and opposed to the 'common'. As in *Les racines du ciel*, in *Invitation*, laughter assumes the two types identified by Lewis. Contrary to Gary's novel, however, the 'blasted' laughter of homogenization is prominent, while the individualized, 'blessed' laughter rarely occurs. Still, it arises when Cincinnatus critically reflects on the comedy being played for him. In so doing, he stresses the dramatic aspect of the show and the superficiality of the act. In a discussion with his mother Cecilia C., he explains:

> 'For I can see perfectly well that you are just as much of a parody as everybody and everything else. And if they treat me to such a clever parody of a mother ...' [...]
> 'I came because I am your mother', she said softly, and Cincinnatus *burst out laughing*: 'No, no, don't let it degenerate into farce. Remember, this is a drama. A little comedy is all right, but still you ought not to walk too far from the station – the drama might leave without you.' (132; emphasis added)

The hero's laughter arises from the discrepancy between what he knows to be the truth and the dumb show that his jailers want him to believe to be reality. Cincinnatus is the only one who perceives the incongruities between external and internal lives, and the only one capable of transforming his inner life. In the context of a narrative of imprisonment, Cincinnatus is not the only prisoner, but the only character conscious of his state of imprisonment, and thus capable of working towards liberation: 'I am not an ordinary – I am the one among you who is alive – Not only are my eyes different, and my hearing, and my sense of taste – not only is my sense of smell like a deer's, my sense of touch like a bat's – but, most important, I have the capacity to conjoin all of this in one point – No, the secret is not revealed yet' (52).

Cincinnatus's capacity to perceive imprisonment can be seen in another instance, when his laughter becomes a sign of his ability to free himself from the imprisonment in the 'world of others'. Occurring after a description of the silence of the cell that insists on the protagonist's condition of prisoner, laughter is an exteriorization of Cincinnatus's realization that he can destroy his condition of imprisonment.

> For a while they were all silent – the earthenware pitcher with water at the bottom that had offered drink to all the prisoners of the world; the walls, with their arms around each other's shoulders like a foursome discussing a square secret in inaudible whispers; the velvet spider, somehow resembling Marthe; the large black books on the table ...
> 'What a misunderstanding' said Cincinnatus *and suddenly burst out laughing.* (32; emphasis added)

Cincinnatus's sudden revelation is signalled by his laughter. The shift from the silence of the exterior world to the sonorous exteriorization of the character's inner understanding leads to a description of the protagonist's self-dissolution:

> He stood up and took off the dressing gown, the skullcap, the slippers. He took off the linen trousers and shirt. He took off his head like a toupee, took off his collarbones like shoulder straps, took off his rib cage like a hauberk. He took off his hips and his legs, he took off his arms like gauntlets and threw them in a corner. What was left of him gradually dissolved, hardly coloring the air. At first Cincinnatus simply reveled in the coolness; then, fully immersed in his secret medium, he began freely and happily to ... (32; original ellipsis)

The reader will not learn what Cincinnatus is about to do, since the exterior world reasserts its presence and its power over him. Thus, a sound breaking the silence of the cell is enough to have the protagonist return to his previous state: 'The iron thunderclap of the bolt resounded, and Cincinnatus instantly grew all he had cast off, the skullcap included' (32–3). The episode occurs early in the novel, at a stage where the 'world of others' still has a strong hold on Cincinnatus. Still, this scene – with its laughter as a sign of understanding – announces the final one, in which Cincinnatus will finally be in full control of 'his secret medium' and will free himself from his imprisonment.

To break away from the 'world of others', Cincinnatus first needs to comprehend its circular nature. This nature is clear to the reader from the start, when the jailer Rodion leads Cincinnatus for a waltz that has them trace a circle past the guard only to go back again in the cell (14). The idea is reinforced a few pages later when Cincinnatus walks out of the fortress and into the city – in a conflation of reality and reverie – and arrives at his house, only to open the door and find himself in his cell (18–20). Later, strolling inside the fortress, in what first seems to him like a linear progression increasing the distance between himself and his cell, Cincinnatus is surprised by Rodion's indication that his cell is just a few steps away (77). Every time, the circularity of his surrounding comes as a shock to Cincinnatus, while appearing perfectly normal to the other characters, who do not even perceive it anymore. In their case, everything that steps out of the circle's perimeter is shocking and unacceptable. This applies to all aspects of Cincinnatus's life: his body, his actions and his discourse, that must all remain within socially acceptable limits. A conversation between Cincinnatus and his lawyer Roman Vissarionovich makes clear that the prisoner's discourse has been contained and has fought against that containment, something Roman cannot bear:

> It is exactly for that tone …
> 'That I am being executed', said Cincinnatus. 'I know that. Go on!'
> 'Let's change the subject, I implore you', cried Roman Vissarionovich. 'Can't you even now remain within legitimate limits? This is really awful. It is beyond my endurance.' (37)

In a letter to his wife Marthe, Cincinnatus also insists on his circular containment and asks for a breach outside of it, unsuccessfully: 'Marthe, in some such circle you and I revolve […]. I do not ask a great deal of you, only break away for an instant and understand that they are murdering me, that we are surrounded by dummies, and that you are a dummy yourself' (142). To break the circle of the 'world of others' becomes Cincinnatus's goal. Learning how to enact and then control a split between different selves allow him to transform the circle into a spiral. In *Speak, memory* ([1967] 1989), Nabokov stresses the positivity of the spiral seen as a liberated circle: 'The spiral is a spiritualized circle. In the spiral form, the circle, uncoiled, unwound, has ceased to be vicious; it has been set free' (275). We can say that if, in the course of the novel, Cincinnatus clearly shows a spiral impulse, it is in the last pages of the novel that the circle is set free.

The Cincinnatuses

Trying to inhabit two different worlds at the same time, Cincinnatus develops the ability to expand from one universe to the other, to keep one part in the 'world of others' and one in his own. This is described by the narrator as the character's 'fleshy incompleteness':

> The subject will now be the precious quality of Cincinnatus; his fleshy incompleteness; the fact that the greater part of him was in a quite different place, while only an insignificant portion of it was wandering, perplexed, here – a poor, vague Cincinnatus, a comparatively stupid Cincinnatus, trusting, feeble and foolish as people are in their sleep. [...] it was as if one side of his being slid into another dimension. (120–1)

On many occasions, the physical Cincinnatus perceived by the other characters is accompanied by a second Cincinnatus, by '(the double, the gangrel, that accompanies each of us – you, and me, and him over there – doing what we would like to do at that very moment, but cannot ...)' (25). Barbara Wyllie observes how the outcome of the novel is made possible by this state: 'the corporeal split that occurs at the end of the novel is dramatized, in fleeting episodes throughout the narrative, as a pre-existing state' (83). Indeed, it is thanks to this pre-existing split that Cincinnatus can choose to leave the 'world of others'. But more significantly, this 'state' is intimately connected with Cincinnatus's capacity to laugh at himself. Cincinnatus's 'fleshy incompleteness' enables him to put into action the rare capacity of self-division discussed by Baudelaire: 'Ce n'est point l'homme qui tombe qui rit de sa propre chute, à moins qu'il ne soit un philosophe, un homme qui ait acquis, par habitude, la force de se dédoubler rapidement et d'assister comme spectateur désintéressé aux phénomènes de son moi. Mais le cas est rare' (Baudelaire [1855] 1962: 251; original emphasis) ['The man who trips would be the last to laugh at his own fall, unless he happened to be a philosopher, one who had acquired by habit a power of rapid self-division and thus of assisting as a disinterested spectator at the phenomena of his own ego. But such cases are rare' (Baudelaire [1855] 1955: 141)]. Having perceived the distance between the two spaces of his self, Cincinnatus can play with the discordance and use it as a cognitive tool to grasp the absurdity of his situation and laugh at it. It is thus because Cincinnatus can split himself that he can perceive humour.

In concordance with Baudelaire, Nabokov positions Cincinnatus as the exceptional being who can both trip and laugh at his own fall. Conversely, and despite the idea that everyone has this type of double ('the double [...] that accompanies each of us'), the other characters of the novel are not accompanied by a double or are unable to perceive it. Cincinnatus, however, can both perceive his inner double and interact with him: 'Then Cincinnatus would take hold of himself, and clutching his own self to his breast, would remove that self to a safe place' (24). The characters of the 'world of others' do not *have* inner doubles, they *are* external doubles of one another. While Cincinnatus splits himself in space, the other characters, and especially Rodion and Roman (or Rod and Rom at the end), fuse together.

The language of juxtaposition is generally used to designate this 'other', parallel Cincinnatus, with typographical signs like parentheses indicating the juxtaposition (see 40, 69). However, the descriptors sometimes shift to a distinction between a 'real' and a 'non-real' Cincinnatus: 'Cincinnatus got up, made a running start and smashed headlong into the wall – the real Cincinnatus, however, remained sitting at the table, staring at the wall, chewing his pencil, and presently shuffled his feet under the table and continued to write, a little less rapidly' (193). In that instance, reality is attributed to the physical Cincinnatus, as perceived in the 'world of others', but this understanding is completely reversed in the conclusion of the novel. Indeed, only at that moment is the splitting of the selves completed:

> One Cincinnatus was counting, but the other Cincinnatus had already stopped heeding the sound of the unnecessary count which was fading away in the distance; and, with a clarity he had never experienced before – at first almost painful, so suddenly did it come, but then suffusing him with joy, he reflected: why am I here? Why am I lying like this? And, having asked himself these simple questions, he answered them by getting up and looking around. (222)

At the end of the novel, Cincinnatus is thus able to use his 'secret medium' (33) to its full capacity. In order to be able to completely split and to live as one of the two parts of himself, though, he will have to make decisions both at the spatial and at the temporal levels. Indeed, the character chooses to inhabit only the 'world of the self', to disregard the 'world of others' as unreal, while choosing a new conception of time that rejects clock time. This new form of time has been hinted at earlier in the novel, when Cincinnatus recalls seeing a man's shadow waiting before it follows the man's movements: 'but here is what I want to express: between his movement and the movement of the laggard shadow – that second, that syncope – here is a rare kind of time in which I live – the pause, the hiatus – when the heart is like a feather ... [...] I'm wrong when I keep repeating that there is no refuge in the world for me. There is! I'll find it!' (53).[13] Opting for the space of the self and the 'time of the hiatus' means rejecting the repetition of the same, the repetition of the comic 'world of others' and affirming the character's humoristic capacity to see things anew.

In his capacity to liberate himself from the space and time of the others, and to develop an understanding of the unreality of his imprisonment, Cincinnatus is comparable to Guareschi's *persona*. The importance of self-reflexivity and the ability to fuse future and present tenses into a perception of the moment recall Guareschi's definition of humour. As Guareschi explained in the Lagers, 'umorista è chi sa retrodatare le sue azioni e le sue sensazioni' (Guareschi [1989] 2011: 64) ['the humorist is one who can backdate their actions and their sensations'], which implies the fusion of different moments in time in the subject's perception. Cincinnatus pushes this conception of time to its extreme in his desire to fuse all moments and all spaces in a point and therefore to make circular movements impossible (and thus imprisonment impossible). Cincinnatus's 'capacity to conjoin all of this in one point' (52) is reinforced by his obsession with spatial centres. The narrator makes it clear that the other characters are unable to identify the centre of spaces, while Cincinnatus naturally perceives it and grasps its importance.[14] The spatial and temporal fusions in turn enable the dissociation of the self, in a similar way for Cincinnatus and for Guareschi's *persona*. Devoid of the comic, which assumes only negative connotations in Nabokov's novel, Cincinnatus's humoristic understanding is expressed by his self-reflexive laughter.

Cincinnatus's space has the potential to unfold into a spiral. And this is indeed what happens in the very last lines of the novel, when Cincinnatus 'made his way in that direction where, to judge by the voices, stood beings akin to him' (223). The experience of imprisonment has made it possible for the character, understood as a section of space, to accumulate energy through this obliged constriction and, in the end, to expand and move in the desired direction. According to Hyde, 'like the "oppressive" forces in Kafka's world, the prison is there because Cincinnatus at bottom *wants* it to be. Of course he changes in the course of the novel' (147; original emphasis). A modification in the conception of the space has to occur before Cincinnatus can free himself, and it is closely related to a modification in the conception of the power of one's imagination. Like Robert in *Les racines du ciel*, imagining his prison cell expanding and exploding under the powerful feet of a herd of elephants, Cincinnatus has the literal and metaphorical walls imprisoning him destroyed, and becomes 'an embodiment of the generic possibilities of human freedom' (Alter 1997: 64).

Humour as impulse

The three narratives analysed in this chapter feature situations of political imprisonment that are negotiated through the use of literary humour. *Diario clandestino 1943-1945*, Guareschi's autobiographical diary of two years in Nazi camps, is, more than a prisoner's humoristic account of his experience, a *humorist*'s perspective on his imprisonment. It is 'la prigionia vista da un umorista' (Guareschi [1949] 2009: xv) ['a humorist's account of his prison' ([1949] 1958: 15)]. Indeed, humour cannot be conceived as a way to merely embellish an experience; it is at the core of the author's conception of life and art and born out of his very experience of imprisonment. That is not to say that style is not essential in the constitution of Guareschian humour. On the contrary, humour as a way of life is made possible through the creation of a specific style, based on falsely logical deductions such as Jonathanisms (Nash 1985: 47), figures of oppositions, euphemisms, a falsely naïve tone and repetitions of words, themes or structures that hide surplus meanings. A key motor of Guareschi's style is its ability to temporarily hide a dysphoric element within a euphoric discourse (Morin 2006: 9). In the Jonathanism introducing the diary, 'Questo "Diario clandestino" è talmente clandestino che non è neppure un diario' (vii) ['This *Secret Diary* is so secret that it isn't a diary at all' ([1949] 1958: 9)], humour is located in the hidden surplus, the idea that it is *more than* a diary, that it will not give an accurate account of the events but will transfer them into a humoristic retelling that will be able to convey *more* than a diary. Humour is the hidden surplus meaning, the 'x' of Jardon's definition of humour as A^{+x} (1988: 145). The existence of the surplus is intimately connected with Guareschi's experience of imprisonment, which 'figuratively split him in two' (Perry 2007: 47). Indeed, as Zupančič puts it, 'when in comedy some (imaginary) Oneness or Unity splits in two, the sum of these two parts never again amounts to the inaugural One; there is a surplus that emerges in this split, and constantly disturbs the One' (2008: 185).

In Romain Gary's novel *Les racines du ciel*, the episode of Second World War imprisonment is at the root of the split between reality and fiction that structures the narrative and that leads to a reversal between the two notions. War camp imprisonment can be conceived as the humoristic hidden surplus, embedded in an analepsis within an analepsis and nested in a tale that blurs the distinction between multiplied narrative voices. The postwar myth emerges out of the literalization of wartime resistant humour, by the displacement from Robert's imaginary elephants as symbols of freedom within confinement to Morel's defence of actual African elephants. Literalizing the humoristic image, Morel makes possible a reversal between truth and fiction that prolongs humour's ability to blur conceptual boundaries.

Finally, in Nabokov's *Invitation to a Beheading*, the surplus of humour is located in Cincinnatus's 'fleshy incompleteness' (120), his ability to exist in more than one dimension, in more than one world. Cincinnatus's self-dissociation is nourished and developed during his nineteen days in a prison cell, which reveal an opposition between the circular, repetitive world of his gaolers and his own way of inhabiting the world. The opposition is strengthened and signalled by the characters' diverse uses of laughter, which fictionalize Lewis's 'blessed' and 'blasted' laughter. The characters of the 'world of others' pertain to the flat realm of the comic, while the prisoner is pictured as a lone humoristic laugher who perceives the existence of a third dimension. Cincinnatus's defensive reaction against the circularity of the 'world of others' leads to the development of a spiral impulse towards enfranchisement, that can only signal the end of the narrative and the end of humour.

In the three narratives, humour leads to the discovery or the creation of 'another space', which gains as much weight in the narratives as the space of imprisonment. This humoristic space 'discloses the potentiality of an entirely different world, of another order, another way of life. It leads men out of the confines of the apparent (false) unity, of the indisputable and stable' (Bakhtin 1984b: 48). Coexisting with the space of imprisonment, it is not a space of freedom, but of resistance, indissociable from the existence of the prison. Guareschi's *persona*, Robert Duparc and Cincinnatus are all 'white resisters' (Lugaresi 2011: 6), resisters within imprisonment. Their humour resists the univocality of imprisonment, hence the splitting of the selves, of time, of space and of the word that occurs in their narratives. The temporal, spatial and thematic dissociations of the narratives are embodied in the linguistic capacity of literary humour to divide and to cumulate layers of meaning at the same time. By creating a tension between the frame of the prison and impulses towards liberation, the narratives thus set the oscillation of humour in motion. As the case of Cincinnatus shows, the impulse of humour arises from a capacity to perceive one's imprisonment in spaces which were not conceived as such at first. Cincinnatus is not the only prisoner, but the only character who understands that he is. *Invitation to a Beheading* extends the understanding of imprisonment from a physical situation to a social condition. It is in the latter sense that I understand the notion in Chapter 3, that discusses social entrapment in pre-set roles and the ambivalence of the mask, with its liberating and imprisoning potential.

3

Social Entrapment: Humoristic Characters vs. the World

The fool, the rogue and the clown

In humoristic narratives, the focus on the relationship between the self and the other is often formulated thanks to the notion of imprisonment. Moving away from representations of characters who are prisoners in cells or war camps, this chapter considers the social position of characters as seen through the eyes of the characters themselves. As a feeling of entrapment in one or many roles or positions imposed from outside of oneself and perceived as major impediments to be oneself, social imprisonment is eminently subjective. Identifying what constitutes social imprisonment for a given subject cannot be done without access to that subject's own perspective. In addition, humour defined in the restricted sense, and in opposition to the more social comic, is a primarily individual phenomenon. As Freud has underlined, it takes place within the self and does not need a public. For these reasons, the three works studied in this chapter – *Uno, nessuno e centomila*, *Snooty Baronet* and *Les clowns lyriques* – are chosen for the particular insight they give into the character's self-representations. Their recourse to first-person narration or their use of forms of direct speech such as inserted monologues is representative of the focus of humoristic narratives on the character's individuality.

To look at the clash between individual perspective and social demands, I focus on three individuals who voice the perception of their own entrapment through the use of humour. I first discuss the trajectory of Vitangelo Moscarda, the protagonist of Pirandello's last novel, *Uno, nessuno e centomila* (1926). An epiphanic discovery in the first lines of the novel shatters Moscarda's perception of himself and of social relationships. I look at his attempt to destroy all the social masks imposed upon him and strip himself of social impositions, an endeavour that leads him straight to a homeless shelter where he spends the rest of his life. Whether the choice of this shelter constitutes a means to entirely flee society and find freedom in a spatial enclosure is discussed with the help of both Pirandello's and Lewis's theories, to show his radical choice in different lights.

I then turn to Lewis's *Snooty Baronet* (1932), a puzzling first-person narrative in which the character of the 'Baronet' (Sir Michael Kell-Imrie) also attempts to destroy images of himself that are circulating in his social milieu. The narration, however, is the character's attempt at creating his own social image to launch into the world. The playfulness and unreliability of this character-narrator complicate the reading of the conflict between the protagonist and the other characters. In the end, Snooty's narration becomes a violent weapon to seek self-assertion through the annihilation of others.

Finally, I look at La Marne, one of the many protagonists of Gary's *Les clowns lyriques* (1979). Within the variegated cast of the novel, La Marne strikes the reader as the emblematic lyrical clown, making use of a number of masks that give him both the freedom not to be trapped in a single identity, and the frustration of being trapped in those masks and the social positionings that come with them. This conflict is most apparent in a long monologue by La Marne, set in an entr'acte episode during the Nice carnival. I read this episode and the positioning of La Marne in parallel with Bakhtin's notion of the 'chronotope of the entr'acte' and highlight the role of that particular socio-temporal setting on the character's negotiation of his social role.

In the three cases, the conflict between the individual and the group is shaped by the image of the mask. It helps to frame the protagonists' concerns about their social place and can be an ambivalent tool containing a high potential for creativity and freedom, while risking becoming yet another prison. It is a humoristic figure par excellence, which connects the different theories of humour of my theoretical framework. Bakhtin's 'The Functions of the Rogue, Clown and Fool in the Novel', a section of 'Forms of Time and of the Chronotope in the Novel. Notes toward a Historical Poetics', captures in a nutshell the three types of characters studied. Moscarda the fool,[1] Snooty the rogue and La Marne the clown are confronted with the fact that they are socially identified with their perceived roles. Their identification with these masks is both a curse and a blessing and is deeply ambivalent. Indeed, it is first and foremost a social stamp, imposed from outside. Moscarda, for example, can only be considered a fool for those characters who do not have access to his internal process – the reader should be aware that he is posited as an enlightened character. The internal Moscarda and the external one (within the diegesis), thus, constitute two sides of the same coin, and this duality and ambivalence mark the humoristic character to his core.

I study the figure of the mask in relation to the enunciative strategies of the three works. *Uno, nessuno e centomila,* Pirandello's last novel, is narrated by its protagonist, Vitangelo Moscarda, and *Snooty Baronet* is Lewis's only first-person narrative, a feature that the novel itself thematizes. Gary's *Les clowns lyriques* uses third-person narration and is emblematic of Gary's polyphonic novels, alternating between three contrasting couples of characters and, by association, three different styles, and mixing up the voices and points of view. In the three cases, I focus on the lone humoristic character's difficulty living according to normalizing social rules. I show how humour is posited as a tool to negotiate the position of the individual with regard to those rules. Humour as a response to social entrapment might give the individual the freedom not to abide by those social, political and literary rules, but it is also a process of enlightenment that reinforces one's consciousness of the power of those rules.

Moscarda's trajectory: From social entrapment to spatial confinement

For Pirandello, masks are one of the multiple forms that entrap the fluidity of a human being. The reflection on the problems and powers of masks spans Pirandello's career. His last novel, *Uno, nessuno e centomila,* published in instalments in 1925 in the magazine 'La Fiera letteraria' and as a whole in 1926, presents Pirandello's protagonist who will go the furthest in the destruction of social constructs. Vitangelo Moscarda undertakes a radical self-transformation in his attempt to get rid of the prisons of roles, names, body and acts, up to the point of embracing a life in a homeless shelter[2] where one can be guided by the flow of life and recreate one's self at every moment.

The destruction of masks to live 'freely' needs to be preceded by the recognition of masks. Moscarda's path very closely recalls the two-step process of *umorismo*, where the 'perception of the opposite' is the necessary first step leading to the 'feeling of the opposite'. Moscarda's trajectory from a 'comic' to a 'humoristic' character is also a passage from a 'perception of the opposite' to a 'feeling of the opposite'. This transition leads Moscarda to his ultimate choice of confinement in a shelter ('ospizio') that can be read either as a consequence of or as a way out of the instability of humour.

Incipit: Perception of the opposite

Uno, nessuno e centomila opens up *in medias res*, with a short dialogue that could well have come out of one of Pirandello's plays, before shifting a few lines later to a narrative expansion of the same scene, this time contextualized in the protagonist's life story. The dialogue between Moscarda and his wife Dida leads to an epiphanic realization on the part of Moscarda, which sets the whole plot in motion. The sequence is the following: Moscarda discovers, thanks to his wife and his reflection in a mirror, that his nose is askew. This leads to the revelation, still thanks to Dida, that every particular part of his body is somewhat askew, which in turn leads to the conclusion that he cannot perceive his own body as others can.

The brief opening scene is crucial to the understanding of the transformation to take place. The whole dialogued incipit reads as follows:

> –Che fai?–mia moglie mi domandò, vedendomi insolitamente indugiare davanti allo specchio.
> –Niente,–le risposi,–mi guardo qua, dentro il naso, in questa narice. Premendo, avverto un certo dolorino.
> Mia moglie sorrise e disse:
> –Credevo ti guardassi da che parte ti pende.
> Mi voltai come un cane a cui qualcuno avesse pestato la coda:
> –Mi pende? A me? Il naso?
> E mia moglie, placidamente:
> –Ma sì, caro. Guárdatelo bene: ti pende verso destra. (739)

> ['What are you doing?' my wife asked, seeing me linger, unusually, in front of the mirror.
> 'Nothing', I replied. 'Just looking at myself, at my nose, here, inside this nostril. When I press it, I feel a little pain.'
> My wife smiled and said: 'I thought you were looking to see which way it tilts'.
> I wheeled around like a dog whose tail has been steeped on.
> 'Tilts? My nose?'
> And my wife said, serenely: 'Of course, dear. Take a good look. It tilts to the right.' (3)[3]]

The scene embeds multiple reflections. Moscarda is reflected in a mirror that doubles him and that will enable the development of his self-consciousness. This reflection is however further mediated: the first words of the scene (and of the novel) are uttered by Dida, Moscarda's wife, enquiring about his behaviour. Moscarda as narrator provides us with important information about the role and place of the mirror scene in his life: he is unusually taking his time in front of the mirror, hence the interest of his wife. As the narrative makes clear later, Moscarda has not been particularly conscious of his bodily or social self up to that moment in his life. Following the others' expectations for him, he has never particularly taken the time to decide what to do with his life. In the mirror scene, the key input about himself still comes from someone else, and Dida even has to insist before Moscarda acknowledges the physical defect she noticed: 'Ma sì, caro. Guárdatelo bene: ti pende verso destra.' ['Of course, dear. Take a good look. It tilts to the right.'] Dida expressly encourages Moscarda to look at himself from outside, insisting that he 'take a good look' at the nose reflected in the mirror in order to notice a slight imbalance that cannot be perceived from inside.

However, if Dida acts as mediator between Moscarda and the mirror, the mirror is also a mediator between Dida's world and Moscarda's, and the presence of Moscarda in front of that mirror is crucial. The stage needs to be set in order for Dida to come up with the remark that will deeply strike Moscarda. There needs to be some reason for him to do something different from his habits, and to linger in front of the mirror, and this reason is mentioned in passing: he has felt a certain little pain in his nose. Physical pain is the starting point of Moscarda's transformation. The pain will soon transform into metaphysical pain, something that the closing remark of the first chapter of Book I already announces:

> Cominciò da questo il mio male. Quel male che doveva ridurmi in breve in condizioni di spirito e di corpo così misere e disperate che certo ne sarei morto o impazzito, ove in esso medesimo non avessi trovato (come dirò) il rimedio che doveva guarirmene. (742)

> [This was the beginning of my sickness. The sickness that would quickly reduce me to conditions of spirit and body so wretched and desperate that I would surely have died of them or gone mad, if I had not found in the sickness itself (as I will tell) the remedy that was to cure me of it. (5)]

Pain, in its capacity to arouse bodily awareness, plays a pivotal role in the development of the 'perception of the opposite'. It is also important to stress that the pain is associated with the nose, a key element of humoristic writing,[4] in part thanks to its capacity to conjoin the external and the internal, and to become the symbol of the external perception others have of us. In this case, the nose is the externalized representation of the protagonist's feeling of entrapment and the entry point of the humoristic narrative.

Bodily awareness is thus at the origin of the protagonist's inquiry about himself. Pain arouses Moscarda's desire for self-observation, which in turn leads to the realization of his bodily asymmetry. For Pirandello, imperfection and asymmetry possess a capacity of revelation: they enable the character to move from perceiving a being in its absolute totality, to perceiving it as a relative entity to be deconstructed in its many components. Bodily asymmetry is indeed a feature of other Pirandellian protagonists, most notably Mattia Pascal with his strabismus. To Paola Daniela Giovanelli, strabismus is a symbol of dissonance and rebellion in front of the established order (76). It literalizes the capacity to relativize in the very body of the character, who can see the same object from two different perspectives (Giovanelli 1997: 76). While for Mattia Pascal asymmetry is related to the organ that observes, for Moscarda, asymmetry pertains to the most visible organ of the face, that can hardly be observed by oneself. Hence the crucial roles of the mirror and of Dida in facilitating Moscarda's 'perception of the opposite' between his point of view and others' perception of him.

However, the incipit does not stop at the asymmetry of the nose. Dida's remark is continued in the following paragraphs, passing from nose to eyebrows, ears, hands, legs and knees, in a movement from top to bottom and from the most to the least evident. Moscarda's asymmetrical body, or rather the insistence on these asymmetries in the incipit (since we are dealing, on the whole, with slight physical asymmetries that are common in any human body), becomes a sum of potential dissonances that will be actualized throughout the novel. Only thanks to the awareness of his physical defect can Moscarda start to relativize his own body and his own identity, and to see it fragmented – into one hundred thousand images – as if through the eyes of others looking at him from outside. After the mirror scene, Moscarda is on his way towards transforming his first 'perception' of a discrepancy with regard to his social image, into an unsettling 'feeling' of that discrepancy. From this point onwards, the novel creates constant ruptures from observations to feelings of discrepancies that, according to Pirandello, explain the discontinuous form of humoristic narratives (Pirandello [1920] 1992: 40, 43, 150).

'Il punto vivo': Moscarda vs. Gengè

Moscarda's discovery that his vision of himself does not correspond to the idea others have of him leads to his desire to destroy the various social *personae* others have built for him. His quest for freedom implies the destruction of all constraining forms – of social roles, names, acts and of his own body. In terms of the evolution of the narrative, the destruction of social masks becomes the central aspect. Moscarda deplores that up until that moment in his life, he has not been conscious of the masks created for him and has not tried to construct a version of himself that would correspond to his own vision: 'Purtroppo non avevo mai saputo dare una qualche forma alla mia vita' (780) ['Unfortunately, I had never been able to give any sort of form to my life' (43)]. Before being able to create a competing version of himself for others, he has to destroy the versions already in circulation, particularly the 'usurer' and 'Gengè'.

The attempted destruction starts with the 'usurer' image, 'che risiede mille volte sfaccettata nella testa dei suoi concittadini' (Gioanola 1997: 90) ['located, cut into one thousand facets, in the heads of his fellow-citizens']. Despite its multifaceted aspect, Moscarda supposes that a sufficiently striking action could change the perspective of most people at once. He decides to take back the right of lodging of a poor man (Marco di Dio) in one of the premises owned by the Moscarda family, in order to give him back a better lodging and a monetary donation for the installation of a laboratory and to prove his generosity and thoughtfulness. However, in his desire to turn around public opinion in an instant, Moscarda does not take into account the external perception which such apparently sudden changes might provoke, and his plan backfires. Rather than destroying the image of usurer, the crowd creates a new image of Moscarda as a usurer-turned-madman, a fool who has not understood the social rules of the game.

While Moscarda-as-usurer is a widespread public *persona*, 'Gengè', 'che risiede nella testa di sua moglie' (Gioanola 1997: 90) ['located in his wife's head'], is at the border between his public and his private life. The name, and the mental creation associated with it, is summoned by Dida in the couple's house, but also travels within the small town when Dida talks about her husband to her friends or acquaintances. The destruction of Gengè must then take place in a setting that combines the public and the private. It culminates in Book V, Chapter 8, 'Il punto vivo', during a conversation between Moscarda, Dida and Sebastiano Quantorzo, one of the two friends who take care of the bank after the death of Moscarda's father. The setting reinforces the place of Gengè as a semi-public semi-private figure. The episode takes place in the Moscarda's private home, in the goal of clarifying the future of the bank, and stages two characters who play roles both in Moscarda's private life and in the future of his business.

For Dida and Quantorzo, who have not been struck like Moscarda by the 'perception of the opposite' or at least who have not transformed this perception into feeling thanks to reflection, the conversation simply has three interlocutors. However, for the *umorista* in the making, the characters participating in the conversation are equal in number to the square number of participants, since each of them is perceived by three people (himself and the two others). This mathematical multiplication of selves is further complicated by the impossibility for Moscarda, at this stage of the story, to internally form an image of himself. Indeed, Moscarda refers to himself as 'nessuno' ['no one'] and explains that 'io–per me stesso–ormai non contavo più' (847) ['I – for myself – no longer counted' (107)]. In 'Moltiplicazione e sottrazione' ['Multiplication and subtraction'] (Book V, Chapter 6), Moscarda lists the eight people he considers take part in the conversation:

1. Dida, com'era per sé;
2. Dida, com'era per me;
3. Dida, com'era per Quantorzo;
4. Quantorzo, com'era per sé;
5. Quantorzo, com'era per Dida;
6. Quantorzo, com'era per me;
7. Il caro Gengè di Dida;
8. Il caro Vitangelo di Quantorzo.

S'apparecchiava in quel salotto, fra quegli otto che si credevano tre, una bella conversazione. (847–8)

[1) Dida, as she was for herself;
2) Dida, as she was for me;
3) Dida, as she was for Quantorzo;
4) Quantorzo, as he was for himself;
5) Quantorzo, as he was for Dida;
6) Quantorzo, as he was for me;
7) Dida's dear Gengè;
8) Quantorzo's dear Vitangelo.

In that living room, among those eight who thought they were three, a fine conversation began. (108)]

In the course of the conversation, Gengè and 'il caro Vitangelo' (the nickname given by Quantorzo) become the exemplars of the imprisoning masks. They are depicted as puppets, as empty figures entirely stripped of will or power. Having explained his desire to sell the bank, Moscarda is put down as a child who does not know what is right for him and acts silly. The whole conversation hinges on Moscarda's capacity to have his desires listened to and acted upon by his interlocutors. To do so, he has to get rid of the 'nota e cara sciochezza del suo [Dida's] Gengè' (855) ['the familiar, dear foolishness of her Gengè' (114)].

Moscarda's own desires also gain force during the conversation, which becomes the space where his internal sense of self can be regained. Frustrated by Dida and Quantorzo's reactions to his requests, Moscarda is shocked by Dida's laughter, which seems to condemn him to be an insignificant husband anyone can reprimand and control.

> Ebbene, da quella risata mi sentii ferire all'improvviso come non mi sarei mai aspettato che potesse accadermi in quel momento, nell'animo con cui un po' m'ero messo e un po' lasciato andare a quella discussione: ferire addentro in un punto vivo di me che non avrei saputo dire né che né dove fosse; tanto finora m'era apparso chiaro ch'io alla presenza di quei due, io come io, non ci fossi e ci fossero invece il 'Gengè' dell'una e il 'caro Vitangelo' dell'altro; nei quali non potevo sentirmi vivo. (855)
>
> [Well, I felt suddenly wounded by that laughter, in a way I would never have expected at that moment, in my spirit, which had participated in that argument a bit, and a bit had relaxed. I was wounded inside, to the quick, though I couldn't have said what or where that quick was, since it had seemed so clear to me till then that I, in the presence of those two, I as myself, was absent; present, on the contrary, were the 'Gengè' of one and the 'dear Vitangelo' of the other, in whom I didn't feel I lived. (114–15)]

As in the incipit, pain plays a key role in the evolution of Moscarda. Gengè and 'il caro Vitangelo' cannot be directly wounded as they possess no reality of their own. Pain, therefore, can only be felt by a self that goes beyond the masks created by the others. Moscarda, who at this moment in the narrative feels devoid of a sense of self, is reawakened by emotional pain. The conversation, starting with 'quegli otto che si credevano tre' (848) ['those eight who thought they were three'] actually ends with the participation of a ninth actor: Moscarda as perceived and felt by Moscarda. The birth of this new sense of self in turn gives more confidence to Moscarda about his desires. The last section of 'Il punto vivo' shows him as an aggressive, confident man – something that however reinforces the perception of him as a madman by the other characters, who fail to understand the motivations behind his requests. The conversation ends when Moscarda, having violently pushed back Dida in her armchair, makes explicit his desire to see the puppet Gengè destroyed: 'Finiscila tu, col tuo Gengè che non sono io, non sono io, non sono io! Basta con codesta marionetta! Voglio quello che voglio; e come voglio sarà fatto!' (858) ['No, you stop this. I'm not your Gengè! I'm not! I'm not! Enough of that marionette! I will have what I will have: and as I will, it shall be done!' (118)].

Moscarda's newly acquired strength is also demonstrated by his use of laughter, which drastically contrasts with Dida's. During the same conversation, Moscarda senses doubt in the faces of his interlocutors and reacts in the following way:

> Scoppiai a ridere; ma né l'uno [Quantorzo] né l'altra [Dida] ne indovinarono la ragione; fui tentato di gridargliela in faccia, scrollandoli: 'Ma vedete? vedete? e come potete essere allora così sicuri se da un minuto all'altro una minima impressione basta a farvi dubitare di voi stessi e degli altri?' (853)
>
> [I burst out laughing; but neither one of them guessed the reason; I was tempted to shout it in their face, shaking them: 'Why, can't you see? Can't you see? And how can you be so confident when, in the space of a minute, a slight impression is enough to make you doubt yourselves and the others?' (113)]

This laughter highlights the precariousness of certainties. It becomes a signal of the character's consciousness. It is, as Lewis has expressed, 'the climax in the tragedy of seeing, hearing and smelling self-consciously' (1927: 236). Dida's laughter aims to reassert a faith in the continuity of one's being: to her and to Quantorzo, Moscarda must be coherent with himself, that is with what they know of him and of his past actions. Trying to fit Moscarda back within the stable and comforting walls of Gengè's personality, Dida's laughter can be read as a Lewisian 'blasted' laughter, or a Bergsonian comic corrective laughter aiming to reinsert the individual within the social circle. Moscarda's burst of laughter, however, illustrates the Lewisian 'blessed' (and 'humoristic') laughter that runs against social reintegration. It is also an expression of Moscarda's newly acquired positionality as a fool figure (or 'usurer-turned-madman'). Like other fools, as well as clowns and rogues, Moscarda is 'laughed at by others, and [himself] as well. [His] laughter bears the stamp of the public square where the folk gather' (Bakhtin 1981: 159–60). Indeed, the private conversation between Moscarda, Dida and Quantorzo illustrates on a small scale the social movement of desired inclusion and the contrasting desire of self-exclusion that respond to each other in the narrative. The clash between these two forces, illustrated by the two types of laughter of the preceding section, creates the oscillatory movement of humour that leads to the creation of the excluded figure of Moscarda-as-a-fool. However, from Moscarda's personal standpoint, he can be read both as a Bakhtinian fool and as a laughing observer or 'metaphysical satirist', expressing their discovery of human imprisonment in forms, through laughter. The unfolding of the novel deepens the schism between the other characters' perception of Moscarda, and his self-understanding, that is, the schism between a comic perspective and a humoristic one.

Both the public scene of the usurer-turned-madman and the husband-puppet-turned-madman highlight how others fail to understand Moscarda's motivations and to follow the unfolding of his reflection on identity. Moscarda's behaviour is not consistent for an outsider. His progression, just like the novel's progression, is built on swift alternations of contrary attitudes or reflections, which do not find a balanced outcome in the eyes of the other characters, or the readers. It is exactly for that reason that Moscarda is the epitome of a humoristic character: he is not logical, he is not consistent, nor predictable. His main project is to deconstruct all that seemed unified. As Pirandello explains in *L'umorismo*, the humorist deliberately foregrounds the characters' incongruities: 'egli [l'umorista] non compone di quegli elementi un carattere; ma scompone il carattere nei suoi elementi; e mentre quegli [il poeta] cura di coglierlo coerente in ogni atto, questi si diverte a rappresentarlo nelle sue incongruenze' (Pirandello [1920] 1992: 152) ['[the humorist] will decompose the character into his elements and while the epic or dramatic poet takes pains to picture him as coherent in every action, the humorist enjoys representing him in his incongruities' ([1920] 1974: 143)]. Moscarda is decomposed into a plurality of facets throughout the narrative, and structural devices like the fragmentation into eight books and dozens of small chapters, or the use of enumeration and 'multiplication tables', reflect the protagonist's fragmented identity.

The shelter as possible space of freedom and the transfer of imprisonment

The fragmentation of identity through *umorismo* leaves Moscarda with the impossibility of living in a world of constructed selves. The destruction of his social *personae* leads him to seek a place outside of his former social environment. Indeed, Moscarda's attempt (and whether it is a successful or a failed one is debatable) to free himself from the imposition of social roles and masks leads him to the choice of the shelter as an enclosed space in which to live for the rest of his life, at the outskirts, both literally and metaphorically, of society. The movement is one from an imposed form of social imprisonment to a chosen form of a more literal imprisonment, where the self is let free. To Pirandello, Moscarda's transformation highlights the positive and constructive aspect of his literary production:

> Avrebbe dovuto essere il proemio della mia produzione teatrale e ne sarà, invece, quasi un riepilogo. È il romanzo della scomposizione della personalità. Esso giunge alle conclusioni più estreme, alle conseguenze più lontane. Spero che apparirà in esso, più chiaro di quel che non sia apparso finora, il lato positivo del mio pensiero. Ciò che, infatti, predomina agli occhi di tutti è il solo lato negativo: appaio come un diavolo distruttore, che toglie la terra di sotto i piedi della gente. E invece! Non consiglio forse dove i piedi si debba posare quando di sotto i piedi tiro via la terra? (Pirandello [1922a] 2006: 1153)
>
> [It should have been the preface of my theatrical production and it will be, instead, almost an epilogue. It is the novel of the decomposition of the personality. It arrives at the most extreme conclusions, the most distant consequences. I hope that in it will appear, clearer than it has appeared until now, the positive side of my reflection. What, in fact, predominates in everyone's eyes is only the negative side: I appear like a destructive devil that removes the ground under the people's feet. But on the contrary! Do I not advise where to lay one's feet when under the feet I remove the ground?]

It is true that the 'lato positivo' ['positive side'] is at the least nuanced, if not contested, by a number of stylistic elements in the narration. Moscarda's choice is abrupt and very quickly explained. His agency is also mitigated by the formula that introduces his explanation: 'Si venne alla decisione che io avrei dato un esemplare e solennissimo esempio di pentimento e d'abnegazione, facendo dono di tutto, anche della casa e d'ogni altro mio avere, per fondare con quanto mi sarebbe toccato dalla liquidazione della banca un ospizio di mendicità [...] e che io stesso vi avrei preso stanza' (899) ['We reached the decision that I would set an exemplary and solemn example of repentance and self-sacrifice, donating everything, even my house and any other possessions of mine, along with what would come to me from the liquidation of the bank, to establish a home for the destitute [...] and I myself would take a room in the home' (158)]. The passive form and the indistinct pronoun 'si' in 'si venne alla decisione' [literally 'the decision was made'] indicate that Moscarda has not been the sole agent behind the choice of the shelter. Yet, as it is part of Moscarda's choice to relinquish his right to make any decision affecting his life, the matter of whether or not this is a choice remains ambiguous. It is clear however that the rejection of social masks goes hand in hand for the protagonist with the rejection of conventional social spaces. The shelter forms 'an other space' or heterotopia, defined by Foucault as 'sortes d'utopies effectivement réalisées dans lesquelles les emplacements réels, tous les autres emplacements réels que l'on peut trouver à l'intérieur de la culture sont à la fois représentés, contestés et inversés' (Foucault 1994: 755) ['a kind of effectively enacted utopia in which the real sites, all the other real sites that can be found within the culture, are simultaneously represented, contested, and inverted' (Foucault 1986: 24)]. Moscarda's choice enacts 'the fool's time-honored privilege not to participate in life' (Bakhtin 1981: 161). By adopting 'the fool's unselfish simplicity and his healthy failure to understand' (162), that is, by the standards of his social milieu, Moscarda opts for 'the mode of existence of a man who is in life, but not of it, life's perpetual spy and reflector' (161).

The passages describing the shelter focus on the exterior and natural setting, where the only communication with other social spaces is the sound of bells heard in the distance: 'L'ospizio sorge in campagna, in un luogo amenissimo. Io esco ogni mattina, all'alba, perché ora voglio serbare lo spirito così, fresco d'alba, con tutte le cose come appena si scoprono, che sanno ancora del crudo della notte, prima che il sole ne secchi il respiro umido e le abbagli' (901) ['The home stands in the country, in a lovely spot. I go out every morning, at dawn, because now I want to keep my spirit like this, fresh with dawn, with all things as they are first discovered, that still smack of the raw night, before the sun dries their moist respiration and dazzles them' (160)]. The feeling of freedom and the amenable nature of the place coexist with its enclosed structure, another important feature of heterotopias, which 'supposent toujours un système d'ouverture et de fermeture qui, à la fois, les isole et les rend pénétrables' (Foucault 1994: 760) ['always presuppose a system of opening and closing that both isolates them and makes them penetrable' (Foucault 1986: 26)]. Moscarda has relinquished the possibility of exiting the boundaries of the shelter and its enclosure, and its fixed spatiality is essential to his new humoristic consciousness. Indeed, Pirandello's *umorismo*, defined earlier as a shift from stability to instability, leaves the humoristic character in a state of unrest that is hard to bear. The humoristic character lives on unstable grounds, outside of the social circle, in a fight against reintegration. Thus, the choice of the shelter can be read as a way out, possibly the only way out, of humour. Despite the insistence within the narrative on the role of internal self-reflexivity, the novel ends with the total exteriorization of Moscarda: 'Sono quest'albero. Albero, nuvola; domani libro o vento: il libro che leggo, il vento che bevo. Tutto fuori, vagabondo' (901) ['I am this tree. Tree, cloud; tomorrow book or wind: the book I read, the wind I drink. All outside, wandering' (159–60)].

Moscarda's humoristic transformation and his use of 'blessed' laughter point at the role of humour in highlighting human entrapment and at the impossibility of being set free from it. The recognition of his entrapment in social roles and of the impossibility of escaping from this constitutive limitation leads Moscarda to choose the form of confinement that will least entrap his conscience into set 'forms'. It would be hard to picture the choice of the shelter as an unmitigated liberation made possible through humour. However, humour has made possible the discovery of Moscarda's own tragic condition, and the transmutation of this entrapment into a chosen configuration of imprisonment. This trajectory recalls, but in a reverse way, the choice of Guareschi's *persona*. For Guareschi, imprisonment is the starting point of humour, while for Moscarda, humour is the cause leading to spatial imprisonment as a way out of the instability of humoristic self-reflexivity.

Snooty's battle: The literary mask to fight them all

The instability of the humoristic character that led to Moscarda's choice of permanent physical enclosure is also central in Lewis's 1932 novel *Snooty Baronet*. However, contrary to Moscarda, Snooty's interior quest is always mediated by an opaque process of narration which is built as a weapon. Snooty is writing, as he puts it, 'to vindicate [his] name' (102), and to fight against other 'versions' of himself that are circulating in his social milieu. Snooty's tale is not as earnest as Moscarda's. Like Moscarda, Snooty is oppressed by the social images of him which he would like to destroy. However, rather than trying to strip himself from these social masks, Snooty uses a choice weapon to fight against existing images: that weapon is his tale. Snooty is a humoristic character in a different way from Moscarda. He is not a laughing observer or a metaphysical satirist, but a humoristic writer, building his own incoherent character-image and eluding the possibility of framing himself in a single, coherent whole.

Humoristic narration is Snooty's reaction to his feeling of entrapment. The structural humour of the novel – Snooty's clever word-play, the situational comedy, the swift alternation of contraries, the construction of a new incoherent mask – is the protagonist's attempt to break the prison of forms, and especially the imprisoning social forms in which he is trapped. I will therefore focus on Snooty's choice of the medium of writing in relation to his feeling of entrapment, and especially on a passage that thematizes the recourse to writing as a means to express one's singularity.

Sir Michael Kell-Imrie, a.k.a. Snooty Baronet, First World War veteran, arrives in London from New York at the beginning of the novel. In London, he meets his literary agent, Captain Humphrey Cooper Carter ('Humph'), who convinces him to undertake a research trip to Persia to write a new behaviourist book. Humph plans this trip as a publicity stunt, with a mock attack from Persian bandits that would certainly be relayed by the media. Kell-Imrie, for his part, brings his annoying lover Valerie Ritter on the trip, in the hope that she will get involved with Humph and that he could be rid of both of them at once. After a sojourn in the South of France where Kell-Imrie witnesses the death of his close friend Rob McPhail, the 'hero' arrives in Persia and contradicts Humph's plan by – at least according to what he tells the reader – shooting Humph himself in the mock attack. This act is pictured as logical and explainable by behaviourism. Kell-Imrie then leaves Valerie, suffering from smallpox, in Persia. Back in England, he sets out to write the book we are reading as a response to Valerie's circulating version of the events (she is now also back in England) where she asserts that he has not killed Humph.

In the first half of 'Chapter III – Humph', the narrator recalls the process that led him to conceive of himself as a trapped beast, a single strong individual in perpetual fight against the mass of undefined – and therefore, in Lewis's scheme, dangerous – people. This section also unfolds, as if in passing, the narrator's first reasons for writing and the evolution of his modes of writing, years before the story told in *Snooty Baronet* starts. Although the narrator's justifications for writing this particular book are interspersed at other key points of the novel (esp. 102–3), Chapter III acts both as a summary of the narrator's literary progress and as a statement on his poetics. The conception of the trapped self and the need to write are intimately connected in the narrative. Indeed, the protagonist's isolation and entrapment in other characters' schemes spark the need to write, and to write the narrative we are reading in its particular form. Snooty's humoristic narration is therefore a device triggered by and delving into the feeling of social and metaphysical imprisonment of the modernist character, a device designed to highlight the absurdity inherent in human life. In concordance with Lewis's theories, the use of structural humour in the narrative is not meant to free the character from imprisonment, but rather to collide with it and resist it.

The lone beast vs. the Ahabs of this world

Sir Michael Kell-Imrie, similarly to Moscarda, passes through a series of moments of illumination before conceiving of himself as socially trapped and needing to fight against his entrapment. Chronologically, the first key moment the narrator identifies as the one that 'tipped the scales' (60), both in the literal and the figurative way, is his catch of 'an amazingly large fish' (60) on a fishing trip, ten years before the story we are reading. The event is later recalled in the printed media and has an important impact on the constitution of one of Kell-Imrie's social masks, the very 'Snooty Baronet' that will give the book its title. Kell-Imrie's first books led him to be nicknamed 'the Douanier', through a comparison with the French painter Le Douanier Rousseau, an association loathed by the narrator. When Kell-Imrie obtains his title of baron, the first moniker is replaced by the new 'Baronet', which in turn becomes the 'sinister Baronet' who 'some years ago [...] landed a fish of such dimensions that it required a crane to lift it into the upper museum gallery' (67). More immediately in the narrative, the summary of the fish episode at the beginning of Chapter III leads to the development of a causal relationship between seafaring, literature and the feeling of imprisonment. Indeed, the narrator expands on the image of the 'catch of a fish' to explain both his realization of his isolated social position and the development of his literary career.

The first string of expansion of the fish image associates the narrator and the trapped animal. It is announced by a statement at the same time isolated and highlighted by parentheses: '(I am a sort of caged beast myself. I have been winged)' (61). The comment is set apart in terms of both temporality and importance, through the use of typographical signs and the shift from present to past. As is often the case in Kell-Imrie's narration, the parentheses give the statement the status of metacommentary by the narrator on his narrative. In this case, the use of both the present and the present perfect opens and highlights the different temporal levels of the novel.[5] Seemingly pertaining only to a comparison with the fish 'that tipped the scales' on a first reading, the statement is incorporated into a much larger scheme of associations a few paragraphs below when the narrator introduces his discovery of *Moby Dick*. The narration then expands the image of the 'caged beast' and draws on a series of oppositions between the free wild beast and the human hunter, between oppressed and oppressor. In a Pirandellian humoristic way, the narrator's thoughts on the subject quickly shift between an aspect and its contrary: 'All the while I felt strong and *free*. Yet I knew henceforth I had been in some strange manner *entrapped*' (61; emphasis added).

The epiphanic realization of the narrator's entrapment must be read in light of Lewis's polemics against the masses. Robert T. Chapman situates the *Moby Dick* episode in the line of the early Lewisian theme of the One and the Many, and explains the narrator's development of 'a plot against Mankind' (Lewis [1932] 1984: 63) as a consequence of this Lewisian premise: 'In this novel, Lewis uses *Moby Dick* as an archetype of this struggle [of the one against the many] and Snooty's response to Melville's tale suggests his own deeply held antagonism towards the mass of humanity' (Chapman 1973: 114). As for Robert Duparc in *Les racines du ciel*, the grandeur and loneliness of a wild animal become a symbol for the oppressed to resist the oppressor. In *Les racines du ciel*, the imagined elephants are both the tool to survive and the starting point of Morel's mythical story. Similarly, in *Snooty Baronet*, the reading of *Moby Dick* enables the narrator to formulate his vision of the world as an opposition between a lonely beast and a mass of negligible people, though powerful through their sheer number. The opposition between the man imprisoned in solitary confinement – and by extension the group of prisoners of Block K – and the Nazi perpetrators that we find in Gary's novel is radicalized in *Snooty Baronet*. Indeed, it now almost entirely isolates the narrator from the rest of mankind. Even if Kell-Imrie mentions that he would 'never attack, upon that point [he] was firmly decided, any man [he] could respect' (63), and that 'those who have submitted to elaborate training or enjoyed its advantages, or those rare figures possessed of original intellect, those [he] never touch[es]' (64), this applies to very few people, and does not allow to conceptualize any coalition, brotherhood or any kind of group that would be connoted positively, as they are in Gary. Other worthy individuals are left in peace in their own isolation, in their own narratives (and Rob McPhail's death surely encloses his story forever in the narrator's perspective), and any group of more than two people immediately becomes a 'mass'. The narrator's self-perpetrated isolation is radical when compared with the one of a character like Robert Duparc who pictures the elephants as a group of lone beasts set against mankind and encourages his fellow prisoners to imagine them with him. No such coalition around an idea or value is possible in *Snooty*.

The Lewisian logic of the battle between the One and the Many sheds light on episodes that first seem incomprehensible or illogical, such as Snooty's behaviour with Val Ritter and Humph. The 'farcical events' and the 'Chaplinesque comedy' would be driven by 'a plea for the inviolability of the free spirit; the right of large mammals to go in peace. In the light of Snooty's idiosyncratic morality, the imagery of the chase – Val and Humph are always "hunting" for Snooty – provides the rationale behind his own "lone-beast" violence' (Chapman 1973: 115). The menace that threatens the narrator's freedom justifies the apparently non-motivated structure of the narrator's actions and retelling thereof. The narrator elects the book as a place where he can 'mark down and pursue, selected for the purpose, members of those ape-like congeries' (Lewis [1932] 1984: 64) in order to show his 'victims' for what they are: 'lifeless puppets' that menace any creatures 'who seemed destined to advance to a higher perfection of living, or who had Infinity in their glances' (64). Despite his appropriate reading of the narrator's motivations, Chapman goes on to conclude that 'the symbolic triumph of the One over the Many is, in its realization, so bizarre that it cannot be taken seriously. The whole affair – indeed, the whole novel – is extremely witty intellectual "play"' (115), and thus fails to explain the narrative 'awkwardness' of the book. The association between entrapment and comedy that Chapman perceived needs to be interpreted at the level of humoristic narration in order not to remain 'bizarre' and 'un-serious'. The mode of narration is in fact indebted to the narrator's drive towards freedom.

Fighting imprisonment through humoristic fiction

Once again, the trapped fish metaphor is a pertinent starting point to understand Kell-Imrie's narrative. The second string of fish images associates the trapped fish with the process of narration itself and with literature in general. The parenthetical statement on imprisonment – '(I am a sort of caged beast myself. I have been winged)' (61) – is actually set in the midst of an explanation of Kell-Imrie's literary development, where the narrator identifies the starting point of his literary career and traces its evolution, from writing a diary, to newspaper articles, to his first 'naturalist' book:

> Sedentary occupations I frankly detest – unless you call seagoing sedentary, I except that. (I am a sort of caged beast myself. I have been winged.) But I am very introspective. Consequently, I contracted the habit of keeping a diary. (All this is how my life as a writer started.) From that I passed, almost imperceptibly, to enlarging, in the form of newspaper articles, any experience of interest in scottish [*sic*][6] sport magazines. From that it was but a step, I suppose, to making

up into a book such matters as I considered might be of scientific value. My first book dealt with the Big Game of the Great Deeps. I was purely a naturalist. (61)

The passage gives a hint at the narrator's particular linguistic logic. In typical Snootian fashion, the narrator stretches causal links between propositions, overusing adverbs of purpose such as 'but' and 'consequently'. The logical link between detesting sedentary occupations and being introspective is not a direct opposition, as the use of 'but' might have us think. Kell-Imrie's narration is rich with 'common types of logical malpractice' like 'the false syllogism, the mismanagement of because and therefore, confusions in the scope of all, some, many, most: etc, the attribution of positive reference to a negative sign' (Nash 1985: 112). In the Lewis passage just quoted, the narrator plays with the evasive 'all this', opening yet another metacommentary. Read in light of the following development on *Moby Dick*, we can understand 'all this' to evoke not only what precedes (being introspective; writing a diary), but also what follows, his illumination with regard to his social position as a 'lone beast'.

Understanding the particularities of Kell-Imrie's linguistic logic helps to grasp his general logical conclusions, which follow similar patterns. In the famous passage of the automaton, where the protagonist compares himself to a hatter's dummy in a shop window (130–9), Kell-Imrie's mental process can be summarized in the form of the following flawed syllogism: the automaton is like me; the automaton is not real/is a puppet; therefore (and according to behaviourist principles), I am not real/I am a puppet. The perfect logic of the statement can of course be criticized, since the premise, 'The automaton is like me', is not exactly true. In accordance with the behaviourist doctrine, it fails to take into account Kell-Imrie's own internal experience. A similar progression, albeit not as clear-cut, can be perceived in the *Moby Dick* episode: in Moby Dick, the lone beast is set against the masses; I am a lone beast like the whale; therefore, I am against the masses. Once again, the fake logical structure can be dismantled, since it is grounded on the association the narrator draws between Ahab and the masses: 'But I saw Captain A. as the spear-head of the Herd. He stood for Numbers' (63). Nevertheless, this structure seems to convince Kell-Imrie of the validity of his conclusions.

The narrator's flawed logic opens up the question of the relationship between humour and the absurd. In 'The Meaning of the Wild Body', Lewis identifies the capacity to perceive absurdity as the root of philosophy, and therefore of his eventual theory of external satire: 'This sense of the absurdity, or, if you like, the madness of our life, is at the root of every true philosophy' (244). *Snooty*

Baronet illustrates the 'exaltation of the absurd' (Lafourcade 1982: 412) of the Lewisian thought of the 1920s–1930s by making the act of narration a part of the universalized absurdity of life: 'Concomitantly, and more significantly, the debunking extends to the whole idea of the novel as a dramatic representation of significant human action' (Pritchard 1968: 114). At the same time, *Snooty* problematizes this 'exaltation of the absurd'. As Lafourcade explains, the general theoretical vision of the absurd 'operates however on the level of logic, for it takes a logical man to perceive the absurd – a situation congenial to the mechanical paradoxes of Lewis's dualism' (1982: 413). Contrary to the separation between Wild Bodies and laughing observers, Kell-Imrie is an ambiguous narrator that we can neither relate back to any of the two types of Lewisian puppets, nor understand as a compromise of the dualistic vision. He is his own creature. Moreover, Kell-Imrie's logic, flawed though it is, leads to the same conclusions about the absurdity of life as Lewis's 'logical' conclusions in his essays (see *Men Without Art* and *Satire and Fiction*). Kell-Imrie's humoristic narration plays with the flawed syllogism and the semblance of logic to appear as a coherent construction, while making sure that his choices cannot be logically explained, and that the character remains illogical and incoherent.

In *Snooty Baronet*, humour is not circumscribed inside the diegesis. Rather, it is behind the very configuration of the narrative and the way in which the protagonist is constructed throughout the novel. Lafourcade connects it to the 'great Anglo-Saxon tradition of Nonsense' initiated by Laurence Sterne's *The Life and Opinions of Tristram Shandy, Gentleman* and highlights the similarity between both novels, which 'produce a coherence of the incoherent involving, roughly, the same Carrollian pack of cards – time/space, action/fixity, the body/death, the inside/the outside, solipsism/les autres, subject/object, desire/trauma, natures/puppets, the organic/the mechanical, parody/identity, freedom/contingency, thought/stimulus, rationality/the absurd, language/incommunicability, fiction/reality, art and life (to make it thirty-two) – haphazardly dealt and whimsically arranged by the persona-ed "First Person Singular"' (Lafourcade 1984: 255). In a larger European context, the construction by oppositions is in line with Pirandello's claim that the apparent 'disorganized' structure of works of humour is caused by their quick associations and movements between opposite concepts, movements that are caused by the role of active reflection:

> È stato tante volte notato che le opere umoristiche sono scomposte, interrotte, intramezzate di continue digressioni. […] Questa scompostezza, queste digressioni, queste variazioni non derivano già dal bizzarro arbitrio o dal

capriccio degli scrittori, ma sono appunto necessaria e inovviabile conseguenza del turbamento e delle interruzioni del movimento organatore delle immagini per opera della riflessione attiva, la quale suscita un'associazione per contrari: le imagini cioè, anziché associate per similazione o contiguità, si presentano in contrasto: ogni immagine, ogni gruppo d'immagini desta e richiama le contrarie, che naturalmente dividono lo spirito, il quale, irrequieto, s'ostina a trovare o a stabilir tra loro le relazioni più impensate. (Pirandello [1920] 1992: 128-9)

[It has often been observed that humoristic works are disorganized, disconnected, interrupted by constant digressions. [...] The disorganisation, the digressions and divergencies do not derive from the writer's eccentricities or personal whim, but are precisely the necessary and inevitable consequence of the disturbance and disruption which are produced in the organizing movement of the images through the work of the active reflection, which evokes an association through contraries: in other words, the images, instead of being linked through similarity or juxtaposition, are presented in conflict: each image, each group of images evokes and attracts contrary ones, and these naturally divide the spirit which, in its restlessness, is obstinately determined to find or establish the most astonishing relationships between these images. ([1920] 1974: 119)]

The role of humour in this case is to deal with the instability of the spirit caused by an active reflection that divides the psyche. The scission of the psyche as a cause of humour is made explicit by Pirandello's or Freud's theories. In fiction, it can take the form of a Moscarda, divided between one hundred thousand images of himself that he cannot reconcile, but it can also be embodied by the association of two characters that form together a representation of the polarization of the psyche. We will see this to be the case in both Gary's *Les clowns lyriques* (Chapter 3) and *La danse de Gengis Cohn* (Chapter 4).

Fredric Jameson has shown how Lewisian narratives often feature this polarized representation, such as the pair of Satters and Pullman of *The Childermass* ([1928a] 1965), which differs from other types of literary couples.[7] Jameson develops his understanding of Lewisian pairs around the notion of the 'agon'. He dissociates it from a Hegelian Master-Slave dialectics (60) and depicts it as a vicious circle that cannot lead to a synthesis, in an oscillatory process recalling Pirandello's *umorismo*. Jameson also borrows Samuel Beckett's notion of 'pseudo-couple' (from Beckett's novel *L'innommable*) to pinpoint the situation of a pair of characters who form a unity:

Yet this is a very different relational category from the conventional pairing of lovers or partners, of siblings or rivals; we need a different word to convey the symbiotic 'unity' of this new 'collective' subject, both reduplicated and divided all at once. It is therefore useful to borrow Samuel Beckett's term for similar character relationships in his own work, and to designate as the *pseudo-couple* all those peculiar and as yet imperfectly studied pairs in literary history which reach well beyond the twin 'heroes' of *The Childermass* [...] all the way back to Faust and Mephistopheles, and beyond them, to *Don Quixote*. (58; original emphasis)

Snooty Baronet also presents a form of coupling, but in a more twisted way. In other Lewisian narratives, the pseudo-couple, embodied by two fictional characters (Tarr and Kreisler in *Tarr* ([1928b] 2010), Pullman and Satters in *The Childermass*, and his categories of Wild Bodies and laughing observers), is presented by a third-person narrator positioned outside of their dynamics. In *Snooty*, the creation of a book to be read by the internal, fictional readers allows for the superposition of two 'Snooties': Kell-Imrie as a writer and character of Wyndham Lewis, and Kell-Imrie as the protagonist of his own narrative. The first-person narration creates a mise en abyme of literary creation and displaces the scission of the psyche from two characters to two levels of representation of one character. Kell-Imrie is 'both reduplicated and divided all at once' (Jameson 1979: 58). This unique feature – and *Snooty Baronet* has a unique place in Lewis's creation by being its only first-person narrative – is a direct consequence of Kell-Imrie's preoccupation with the control of his image by other social actors. Written to create his own image, his narrative sets itself against the imprisoning images others have created for him and that pervade the story: the Douanier and the Baronet.

Mask creation and the 'annihilation of enemies'

The narrator's attempt to destroy or control the Douanier and the Baronet images recalls Moscarda's attempted destruction of the usurer image, of Gengè and of the 'caro Vitangelo'. Their trajectories are even similar at first, with epiphanic moments by way of reflection, first mediated by a mirror and his wife in the case of Moscarda, and by a literary work in the case of Kell-Imrie (*Moby Dick*). The unfolding of their thought (Moscarda) and their writing (Kell-Imrie) also follow comparable structures. Yet the similarities end there, and Moscarda's and Kell-Imrie's fates are almost diametrically opposed, in spite of a shared isolating effect.

Moscarda's fixation on the destruction of all masks in order to be set free leads him to the realization that the annihilation of his social being is the only possible way to go. Hence his ascetic and isolating choice of the shelter. Kell-Imrie's solution, on the other hand, is not spatially static: 'Sedentary occupations I frankly detest' (61). It is rather combative. He chooses to fight back against the social creation of imprisoning images through the self-construction of a new literary mask designed to supersede all others.[8] Kell-Imrie's 'Snootian' creation is 'the rogue's cheerful deceit' that opposes and exposes the conventionality of the circulating versions of the Douanier or Baronet (Bakhtin 1981: 162). Both Kell-Imrie's starting point (the reading of *Moby Dick*) and end point (the creation of the book we are reading) are literary. They are also both violent. Snooty highlights this feature of *Moby Dick*: 'The book had a great vogue after the war, because it was violent I think (certainly not its beauty). It was an epic of a great "Kill"' (61). Later, recalling the critic who was to set the Douanier trend, the narrator exclaims 'I could have shot him!' (65). From then on, his writing will be designed to 'shoot' the creators of imposed images like the Douanier or the Baronet. Only the self-imposed, self-created image is valorized. It is pictured as the only one that can be controlled by its creator.

The violence of Snooty's narration is closely related to his desire to assert himself as an entity separated from its social structures. In newly translated additions to *Rabelais and His World*, Bakhtin insists on the opposition between worlds of fiction based on the interconnectedness of characters, and others where self-assertion prevails, and where individuality 'protest[s]' (Bakhtin 2014: 525). 'Self-assertion', Bakhtin proposes, 'is inseparable from the annihilation of enemies – exaltation is inseparable from diminishing all other people' (527). Through his narration, Snooty asserts his freedom to create the figure he chooses for himself and thus to diminish the impact of others' voices. Not unlike Nabokov's Cincinnatus C. who destroys all other characters around him in order to be able to assert his own individuality, Snooty is driven by a desire for entire control over his self that requires the destruction of any other competing version. Indeed, the last chapter of the novel reveals the existence of other versions of his tale – especially Valerie Ritter's (see 252) – that Snooty wants to cover up. Snooty's reaction to his feeling of social entrapment is a non-carnivalesque, annihilating and self-asserting use of the mask. That 'self-assertion is inseparable from the annihilation of enemies' is a more explicit and more violent expression of an idea otherwise present in Bakhtin's notion of monologism. Snooty attempts to stifle the voices of the other. However, the narrative construction of his tale lets those voices filter through his *attempt at monologizing* his discourse. His fight also brings to mind Dostoevskian characters who 'all do furious battle with such definitions [secondhand definitions of man] of their personality in the mouths of other people. They all acutely sense their own inner unfinalizability, their capacity to outgrow, as it were, from within and to render *untrue* any externalizing and finalizing definition of them' (Bakhtin 1984a: 59; original emphasis). Thus, Snooty's endeavour, even with its monologizing impulse, opposes the finalization of man. The following character to be considered does not seek to annihilate the other characters that contribute to giving him his particular social position. La Marne, one of Gary's clowns, rather considers the other as a necessary element in the framing of his own freedom, recalling Bakhtin's ideas on the 'I' and the 'thou' in 'From Notes Made in 1970–71'.

La Marne/Bebdern: The ambivalent surface of the clown mask

In Romain Gary's work, the relationship between the One and the Many can be both antagonistic and complementary. Once again, the Group-Individual relationship is expressed via the figure of the mask. Moscarda's first impulse was to seek to destroy social images, framed as negative and oppressive constructs. Snooty's creation of his own literary mask is antagonistic: it is a response to already existing masks with which his creation competes. Both characters act in reaction to existing images. Gary's La Marne is framed differently. His use of masks is pictured first and foremost as a personal creative impulse; not a reaction, but an action. The mask as action possesses an ambivalent power closely connected to the particular temporal and social positions available to a masked character, as Bakhtin shows in his study of the masks of clown, fool and rogue in 'Forms of Time and of the Chronotope in the Novel'.

The relationship of Gary's writing to a carnivalesque universe, which is most striking to readers of Bakhtin, has been recently established in Garyan criticism. Yves Baudelle (2005) has demonstrated the pertinence of analysing Gary's fiction through the prism of Bakhtinian ideas, highlighting the presence of many carnivalesque traits in Gary, notably the spirit of relativism and ambivalence; the role of polyphony, dialogism and multilingualism; the rejection of the single-tone; and the presence of stylistic hybridity and parodic inversions.[9] Gary's carnivalesque impulse is best seen at play in the figures of the 'lyrical clowns',[10] who incarnate the ambivalence of the clown mask, its extreme potential for freedom yet at the cost of personal annihilation. La Marne, the epitome of the 'lyrical clowns', locates this ambivalence in the 'chronotope of the entr'acte'

Bakhtin identifies as intrinsically connected with the existence of the mask of the clown (Bakhtin 1981: 163). The spatio-temporal localization of La Marne within the novel's frame is crucial in understanding his social interactions and the cohabitation between a freeing impulse and his entrapment in particular roles.

The carnivals

Les clowns lyriques[11] follows the stories of three main couples of characters. It alternates between lyrical sections that tell of the love story of Ann Garantier and Jacques Rainier, and parodic ones, that deal mostly with the characters of Willie Bauché (Ann's husband and impresario) and La Marne (Jacques's best friend).[12] While the episodes featuring La Marne are pervaded by a carnivalesque atmosphere, the love story of Ann and Jacques is mostly lyrical and serious in tone. From the moment of the meeting of the lovers, the novel mainly alternates between two settings, casts and tones, between the lyrical and the clownish. This strict duality is however complicated by the intrusion of a third couple of characters, Soprano – hired by Willie officially to kill Jacques, but in actuality to kill Willie himself – and his acolyte Le Baron, who appears in at least half a dozen of Gary's novels and never utters a word. The intersecting stories emanate from the carnival as setting, mode of behaviour and individualized universe.

The novel plays with the tradition of the carnival in both explicit and implicit ways. The layers are multiple. There is, first, the city carnival. The novel is set in Nice, in the South of France, over the course of ten days during the February carnival. The celebration is crucial in the story. It is thanks to the crowd of the street carnival that Jacques Rainier, a Compagnon de la Libération, and Ann Garantier, a Hollywood actress, meet. The February carnival is juxtaposed with other forms of social behaviour described by the narrator as carnivals and circuses, such as the Hollywood film industry and capitalist bourgeois society in general. Indeed, the title of the second version of the book is taken from a citation attributed to Maxim Gorki, constantly rehashed in the novel, comparing the capitalist society to a circus: '*Les clowns lyriques qui font leur numéro humanitaire dans l'arène du cirque capitaliste*' (Gary 1979: 27; original emphasis) ['The lyrical clowns who perform their act in the arena of the capitalist circus'].

There is another form of carnival, less expected because it is individual.[13] It is the carnival that certain characters of the story carry with them no matter where they go. One character in particular embodies it: La Marne. He has no first name, and his name is a pseudonym. The reader does not have access to previous names or identities.[14] La Marne first appears in Chapter II, alongside Jacques Rainier, his longtime friend and comrade-in-arms. He is introduced separately from Jacques in the following chapter, where an analepsis presents their meeting in the military following the French Liberation, about a decade before the novel's action. After the encounter between Ann and Jacques, La Marne, finding his union with Jacques disrupted, has to seek a new place in the distribution of characters. He thus transfers to the other main universe of the novel, gravitating around Willie, Ann's deserted husband. This moment of transition is crucial in that it helps to see what particular traits are carried along by the character, and what new localization is available to him. Chapter XII shows this moment of transition, where the carnival literally enters Willie's hotel room in the person of La Marne, renaming himself for this occasion as 'comte de Bebdern' (96). The choice of a fake noble name hints at the reversal between lower stratum and higher stratum of society, typical of the folk carnival or festival, and more particularly at the crowning of the clown figure in the time of the carnival (Bakhtin 1984b: 81, 197, 219, 370). While the carnival in the streets of Nice makes possible the encounter of Jacques and Ann, the personal carnival of the lyrical clowns emerges from the meeting of La Marne/Bebdern and Willie Bauché in temporary and circumscribed conditions (Bakhtin 1984b: 89).

La Marne's meeting with Willie and Garantier (Ann's father, who hangs around Willie) is first presented as a blackmailing scene, since La Marne indicates he could 'sell' Ann's infidelity story with Jacques to the multiple journalists hunting the famous Hollywood couple. However, it soon becomes clear that La Marne is not after money or mediatized fame. What he seeks in Willie's hotel room is more likely a stage and a stage companion to replace Jacques for the duration of his escape with Ann. This interlude is an exacerbation of, rather than a change from, his previous attitude, and 'Bebdern' is pictured not as a different being, but as a somewhat caricatured La Marne. While Willie and Garantier address him as Bebdern, the narrator refers to him both as La Marne and as Bebdern. I will refer to him as 'La Marne/Bebdern' to encompass both (that is an understatement) of his identities.

Theatre world

La Marne/Bebdern's intrusion in Willie's hotel room makes clear that the character inhabits a unique universe, which he brings with him wherever he goes. Bakhtin's idea that 'the rogue, the clown and the fool create around themselves their own special little world, their own chronotope' (Bakhtin 1981: 159) is seen at play thanks to the spatial transfer from the streets of Nice to the hotel room. The movement also changes La Marne/Bebdern's social position, as he moves from Jacques's side, as a seemingly permanent sidekick of the stable and idealistic Jacques, to perform in front of Willie and Garantier on the stage of the rich man's hotel room. The performative aspect of his appearance sheds light on the type of universe surrounding him, namely what Bakhtin calls the 'chronotope of theatrical space' or 'chronotope of the entr'acte' (Bakhtin 1981: 163), pertaining to the larger category of the 'intervalic' [sic] chronotope (166). La Marne/Bebdern enters Willie's room at the beginning of what will be a ten-day 'entr'acte', an intermission in the lives of Jacques and La Marne/Bebdern. The two friends, regardless of the power of Ann and Jacques's love, depart at the end of the novel to fight in the Korean War, as they had planned from the start. The whole novel, except the last two pages, presents this entr'acte to the reader. The entrance of La Marne/Bebdern and his following performance must be placed in the context of this 'novel-as-entr'acte'.

The notion of entr'acte relativizes the freedom that La Marne/Bebdern might find in his performance. As Bakhtin has noted, the freedom gained during carnival is by definition relative and ephemeral (Bakhtin 1984b: 89). Even if Bakhtin highlights the power of a freedom so concentrated – 'The very brevity of this freedom increased its fantastic nature and utopian radicalism' (Bakhtin 1984b: 89) – it is nevertheless circumscribed to an extremely limited time and social space. Furthermore, Chapter XII, the intrusion of La Marne/Bebdern in the hotel room, constitutes a form of 'entr'acte' within the 'novel-as-entr'acte', a buffoon performance for the sake of Willie and Garantier, and of La Marne/Bebdern himself. It is set as a theatrical performance from the moment of La Marne's appearance. Willie and Garantier have been discussing Ann's escape and Willie's inability to admit his pain, when the then-named La Marne comes in:

> Le groom violet de l'hôtel ouvrit la porte et ce que Willie vit d'abord, fut un chapeau pressé sur le cœur, dans un geste de piété, et le personnage entra ainsi comme dans une cathédrale. Il était très petit et portait les traces d'une ancienne joliesse olivâtre que le temps avait boursouflée et ridée et jaunie, si bien qu'il évoquait un peu l'image de quelque eunuque habillé à l'européenne et jeté par une révolution loin de son harem natal. (Gary 1979: 94)
>
> [The purple page-boy opened the door, and what Willie saw first was a hat squeezed against the heart in a gesture of piety; the man came in like that, as though entering a cathedral. He was very small, and still had traces of a cherubic

prettiness, which time had swollen and raddled and yellowed to an extreme, so that he evoked the image of some eunuch put into European clothes and flung, by a revolution, far from the harem of his birth. (Gary [1953] 1976: 97)]

The sacrality of the entrance, which is echoed in La Marne/Bebdern's long prayer-monologue a few pages later, affects the perception of the character's size and position. La Marne/Bebdern is not only physically small, he is also positioned at the bottom of the scale, or at the margins (as a displaced element, outside of his normal habitat), as a negligible element of the social sphere. His reaction when entering the space of prestige of Willie's room is to revere what he sees – or to appear to do so. This impression of negligibility is immediately confirmed by the first exchange between the characters:

> –Qu'est-ce que c'est que cette façon de vous introduire ici? gronda Willie. Qui êtes-vous, d'abord?
> La Marne s'inclina, la tête rentrée peureusement dans les épaules. Suppliant:
> –Une silhouette, une simple silhouette, bégaya-t-il, avec empressement. Très rapidement esquissée et sans aucune prétention … (Gary 1979: 94)

> ['How the hell did you get in here?' [Willie] growled. 'Who are you, anyway?'
> The man bowed, his head retracted timorously into his shoulders. Beseeching:
> 'A silhouette, a mere silhouette', he stammered eagerly, 'Very rapidly sketched and without the slightest pretension …' ([1953] 1976: 97)]

La Marne/Bebdern's physical attitude and first rejoinder insist on his smallness and marginality. The character is entering a sphere where he does not belong. By so doing, he brings his own universe of theatre and mask, signalled from the start by the description of his face as a deformed and exaggerated human face ('boursouflée', 'ridée', 'jaunie' ['swollen', 'raddled', 'yellowed']), and by the change in the writing style. His first line in the 'hotel room scene' is introduced by a 'Suppliant:' ['Beseeching:'] that mimics a stage direction. From now on in this chapter, the narrator alternates between a more novelistic narration, using simple past and imperfect, and a form of theatrical discourse with stage directions, such as 'Immensément cochon:' (Gary 1979: 98) ['Slyly, and with a piggish grin:' ([1953] 1976: 101)] or the numerous 'À part:' (Gary 1979: 95, 96, 97, 109) ['Asides' ([1953] 1976: 98, 99, 100, 110)]. The asides, a feature of this chapter, introduce a dynamic effect, emphasizing the character's theatricality.

La Marne/Bebdern's goal with this visit to Willie has everything to do with the notion of role. His first short monologue, right after his entrance, contrasts his role prior to that moment and the change he is hoping for:

La vie, jusqu'à présent, ne m'a jamais donné l'occasion d'une réplique, elle ne m'a jamais honoré d'une situation... Toujours en marge, toujours un figurant, obligé de me contenter d'une muette apparition, jouant les simples utilités... obligé de me contenter de la vie des autres, de vivre par procuration, par le trou de la serrure... Vierge, si Monsieur me permet de préciser... Vierge et expert-comptable, par-dessus le marché... Voyant toujours tout de l'extérieur, sans pouvoir mettre le doigt sur rien... C'est pour la première fois que, grâce à un concours de circonstances favorables... Je me trouvais au bar, lorsque Mlle Garantier... (Gary 1979: 94)

[Life, up to now, has never seen fit to give me a cue, to honour me with a scene of my own... Always in the wings, at best a walk-on, obliged to settle for mute appearances, playing the most minor parts... obliged to content myself with other people's lives, living by proxy, through the keyhole... Virgin, if Monsieur will allow me to be thus precise... Virgin and chartered accountant to boot. Always an outsider... Viewing all from without, unable to become a part of anything... Now, for the first time, able to put my foot in, thanks to a combination of favourable circumstances... I found myself at the bar, when Mademoiselle Garantier... ([1953] 1976: 97–8)]

By giving voice to La Marne in this moment of transition, the novel allows us to understand his self-conception as a character trapped in the role of sidekick who has no story of his own. For the 'being' of the masked characters 'coincides with their role, and outside this role they simply do not exist' (Bakhtin 1981: 159). La Marne/Bebdern's introductory speech thus seems to reveal a self-conception of entrapment in one's role and a desire to exist outside this role, not unlike a Moscarda or a Snooty. The absence of Jacques becomes a motivation to try on a new role, to be an active participant and get involved in the lives of the Hollywood stars. La Marne/Bebdern is indeed given a more active role from this moment, a more prominent place in the novel and a lot of discursive space to voice his story and his ideas.

The superficial character

La Marne/Bebdern's externality and position at the margin is related to his intrusion in Willie's private life and his threat to expose the latter to the public square. For Bakhtin, this is exactly the rogue, clown and fool's role:

They re-establish the public nature of the human figure: the entire being of characters such as these is, after all, utterly on the surface; everything is brought out on to the square, so to speak; their entire function consists in externalizing things (true enough, it is not their own being they externalize, but a reflected, alien being – however, that is all they have). This creates that distinctive means for externalizing a human being, via parodic laughter. (Bakhtin 1981: 159–60)

La Marne/Bebdern seems to be only a surface for the reader. He is, literally, a superficial character. A 'silhouette […] [t]rès rapidement esquissée' (Gary 1979: 94), he 'mesure un mètre cinquante-cinq d'un côté – rien de l'autre' (97) ['mere silhouette […] [v]ery rapidly sketched' ([1953] 1976: 97), he 'measure[s] five feet two on one side, nothing on the other' (100)]. His discourse parodically plays with the notion of the surface, and he seems both to live on the surface and not to be able to live on the surface. A crucial moment of his self-expression, and one of the most theatrical ones, is a long monologue framed in the form of a prayer addressed both to a god-like paternal figure and to Willie. The monologue is an ode to simplicity, a prayer asking to be freed from idealism, pictured as a dangerous purity based on an impersonal collectivity.

The rhetoric of the monologue hints at the character's difficulty with remaining on the surface associated with his role of clown, by paradoxically insisting on the value of the surface. La Marne/Bebdern reclaims and values superficiality and condemns the evil of depth and height, be it introspection or idealism:

> Ô Vous qui avez créé les abîmes et le Kilimandjaro, rendez-nous enfin l'usage du superficiel! Sauvez-nous du hara-kiri de l'introspection! Libérez-nous des traités hautement sérieux et du narcissisme, prenez l'homme et dénouez-le! Il s'est entortillé en un nœud tellement inextricable que, de tous les côtés, on veut le couper sous prétexte de le libérer! (Gary 1979: 102)

> [Oh You, Who have created unfathomable depths and Kilimanjaro, give us at last the use of the superficial! Save us from the hara-kiri of introspection! Liberate us from highly serious treatises and from wisecracking and from seriousness; take man and untie him. He is tangled in a knot so inextricable that people come from all sides to cut him to pieces, on the pretext of liberating him. ([1953] 1976: 104)]

Like the Bakhtinian clown figure, La Marne/Bebdern rejects the 'other-worldly vertical axis' (Bakhtin 1981: 166) in favour of the surface of everyday life. Elevation can come through a better understanding and use of humanity and of the human body. In a reversal typical of Gary's writing, superficiality becomes the only way to attain a form of elevation:

> Notre Père qui êtes au ciel, pria-t-il. Permettez-nous de nous élever! Permettez-nous d'accéder à la surface, rendez-nous superficiels! Donnez-nous un

millimètre de profondeur, permettez-nous enfin d'être simples comme bonjour! (Gary 1979: 101)

['Our Father which art in heaven', he prayed. 'Grant that we may attain superficiality! Deliver us from depth, let us surface, like all breathing things! Deliver us from submersion. Take the thinking reed and grant it a complete and serene lack of understanding'. ([1953] 1976: 103)]

True human superficiality, that would anchor us in the world and help us live more adequately within it, is not yet mastered by the human being. Idealism, collective ideologies, seriousness or narcissism have pushed the human being out of his boundaries in a way that dramatically limits his happiness: 'Laissez-nous petits et aimables! Arrêtez tout et vérifiez soigneusement nos mesures: nous sommes sortis de nos dimensions! Nous sommes devenus trop grands pour notre petitesse!' (Gary 1979: 102) ['Leave us small and friendly. Stop everything and check our sizes carefully: have we grown out of our dimensions? Have we become too large for our smallness?' ([1953] 1976: 104)]. Chiasmic reversals abound in the monologue, the main of which might be that giving clear boundaries to the human figure can become a way to liberate it, to free it from the constriction of idealism.

In that light, the surface of the mask becomes La Marne/Bebdern's ideal. The character seems to inhabit that surface in this particular episode, and to play the clown figure to the best of his abilities within the frame of the hotel room and the time of the carnival. La Marne/Bebdern nevertheless goes back to his former position and chooses Jacques and the Korean War. La Marne/Bebdern's act thus remains a prayer, an entreaty. 'Libérez-nous', 'Donnez-nous', 'Rendez-nous', 'Laissez-nous' ['Deliver us', 'Give us', 'Grant us', 'Liberate us', 'Leave us'] point at the character's incapacity to entirely live on the surface. His supplication indicates that, despite what he tries to be in front of Willie, he has clearly not attained superficiality, that is, got rid of ideals. The character is desperately trying to be only superficial and to live up to the standard of the mask of the clown, but partly fails. His address to his creator and his imploring to 'arrêtez tout et vérifiez soigneusement nos mesures' (Gary 1979: 102) ['stop everything and check our sizes carefully' ([1953] 1976: 104)] highlight the author's attempt to make of this character a 'limited' character, and a counterpoint for the idealist Jacques, who has clearly 'grown out of his dimensions'; La Marne/Bebdern's desire to live on the surface is inseparable from the idealism and depth of the characters with which he is paired.

Pairs and parasites

The use of a character to balance another one and the association of characters in pairs highlight a core concern of Gary's writing: the role of duos. The most important aspect of the monologue might be La Marne/Bebdern's call to fraternity, in opposition to collectivity. The quest for fraternity is one of the driving forces of the novel and is personified in La Marne/Bebdern as a form of parasite calling for a close other. Despite the blackmailing threat, which he never actually carries out, La Marne/Bebdern is not after a role of parasite in the strictly economic sense, but rather of a form of social parasitism. He is looking for a new host to replace Jacques during his absence.

Contrary to Bakhtin's notion of carnival as a collectivity in which the individualities are annulled (for a time), Gary's carnival is based on the collective's most essential expression: the pair. His collective of two, a fraternity on a small scale and in a concrete sense, counters the grand-scale collectivities that obliterate close human relationships and that are generally associated in Gary's work with totalitarianism. Gary's carnival cannot actually be shared by a whole collectivity but becomes the prerogative of a few 'initiés', a 'fraternité des mimes inspirés' (Gary 1979: 105) ['fraternity of inspired mimes' ([1953] 1976: 106)]. Rather than be seen as a doubling (a reproduction) or as an addition, the fraternal pair of characters can be pictured as a scission, which recalls the Freudian split of the self and the pseudo-couple. As Gary explains in *Pour Sganarelle*, the duo is a tool he constantly uses in his writing:

> Il va sans dire que le procédé de fendre l'homme pour en faire deux personnages en conflit a été inventé par Cervantes et que je me bornerai à l'utiliser d'une autre façon, ce que je n'ai jamais cessé de faire dans mes romans, et qui explique pourquoi, depuis *Tulipe*, tous mes personnages 'dominants' ont toujours été assistés par un contradicteur. (248)

> [It goes without saying that the process of splitting man in two to make two characters in conflict out of it has been invented by Cervantes, and that I will restrict myself to use it another way, something I have always done in my novels, and that explains why, since *Tulipe*, all my 'dominant' characters are assisted by an opponent.]

In *Les clowns lyriques*, the lyricism and the clownishness find their perfect embodiment in the pair Rainier – La Marne, but many other pairs are constituted throughout the novel to complicate the first, rather blunt figure of opposition (Willie – Ann; Jacques – Ann; Willie – Garantier; Willie – La Marne; Soprano – Le Baron).

In his monologue, La Marne/Bebdern insists on the importance of the pair, be it of brothers or of lovers. Love, in this sense, becomes one of the incarnations of the desired 'fraternity' and counters the grandiosity of idealism. Imploring the father-godly figure he has created for the sake of his monologue, La Marne/Bebdern expresses the close relation between the positive smallness of the human and the ideal group of the pair, in opposition to 'clusters' of humans: 'Ô Vous, pour qui l'amour n'est que le petit besoin des hommes, laissez-nous à notre petit besoin! Laissez-nous par couples, empêchez les grappes! Rendez-nous le goût des duos!' (Gary 1979: 103) ['Oh You, for Whom earthly love is only a small mundane need, leave us to our small need! Leave us in couples, and not in clusters. Give us a taste for duets' ([1953] 1976: 104–5)]. The staging of the monologue also shows La Marne/Bebdern's attempt to create duos. One of his goals is to recreate a fraternal (or parasitic) pair with Willie, something that actually happens, for the time of the carnival, in the following chapters, since Willie recognizes and shares this need. Reflecting on his encounter with 'Bebdern', he understands the essentiality of the other in his mode of living:

> Il [Willie] avait, en dehors de tous les dons dont la nature l'avait comblé, celui de se mouvoir à la surface[15] de lui-même, en évitant de crouler à travers la très mince et craquante carapace dont il s'était couvert. Cela finissait par ressembler à une sorte de patinage artistique, de ballet d'une perpétuelle *commedia dell'arte*, une improvisation dont l'enjeu était d'éviter à tout prix la confrontation, avec le petit garçon terrifié, abandonné depuis trente ans dans le noir et qui n'avait même plus le droit d'appeler maman.
>
> Mais cette *commedia* exigeait avant tout des partenaires, il ne fallait surtout pas rester seul, et l'apparition inattendue de Bebdern avait été à cet égard un véritable don du ciel. (Gary 1979: 121; original emphasis)[16]

[Willie had, apart from all the gifts nature had bestowed upon him, the gift of moving with supreme ease on his own surface, never tumbling through the very thin, brittle shell that covered him. It resembled a kind of *commedia dell'arte* ballet, where the object was to avoid at all costs a confrontation with the little boy forgotten in the dark for thirty years, who no longer had the right to call mamma. Most of all it was important not to be alone, which was why Willie always dragged other lyric clowns along with him. ([1953] 1976: 123)]

Willie's reflection highlights the role of the carnival and of parody in fighting cosmic fear, and especially the role of the collective, here in its most essential form of the pair. The mask of clown, in this regard, points to a deeper authenticity of human relationships hidden behind the appearance of the superficial: 'Le corps libéré par le masque marque paradoxalement l'authentique contact avec l'autre, l'authentique élément subjectif. [...] À la fois artifice et vraie nature de l'individu, *persona*, le masque, donne à voir le visage et donne à entendre la personne. Il indique une dimension étrange mêlant le comique, la parodie et le tragique.' (Laufer 2005: 47) [The body liberated by the mask paradoxically signals the authentic contact with the other, the authentic subjective element. [...] At the same time artifice and true nature of the individual, *persona*, the mask, enables to see the face and to hear the person. He indicates a strange dimension mixing the comic, parody and the tragic.] Reversing Sartre's famous 'l'enfer, c'est les Autres' (Sartre [1947] 2000: 93), Gary asserts that 'La liberté, c'est l'autre' (Gary 2005: 274). Parasitism, in this context, is a positive relationship that is not opposed to the possibility of individual freedom. Contrary to Snooty, La Marne is perfectly conscious of the impossibility of asserting himself as an entity separate from the other social beings around him. For La Marne, isolation is not an expression of freedom, but of fragility. As Holquist puts it, 'the dialogic subject, existing only in a world of consciousness, is free to perceive others not as a constraint, but as a possibility: others are neither hell nor heaven, but the necessary condition for both' (Holquist 1990: xxxviii).

La Marne/Bebdern's newborn relationship with Willie comes to an end after the entr'acte, and the relative freedom (Bakhtin 1984b: 89) granted to La Marne to take on the new identity of Bebdern and the more active place of the instigator of the action with Willie ceases with the carnival. When the 'entr'acte' of the Nice carnival ends, La Marne/Bebdern goes back to his original companion, and follows him to fight in Korea, and they both eventually get killed in Indochina. The ending of the narrative is extremely abrupt: after more than two hundred pages narrating a dozen days, the last two pages go over months and laconically depict the death of the two acolytes. Fighting in Korea is depicted as a heavily symbolic choice. At the beginning of the novel, the narrator mentions in passing that Jacques has a hard time getting accepted as a volunteer because of his missing arm, but is accepted for his 'symbolic' and 'legendary' value as former fighter in the Spanish Civil War, member of the French Resistance and Compagnon de la Libération (24). Jacques's choice is also explained by his difficulty to 'rompre avec soi-même, c'est-à-dire avec le besoin de justice et de liberté pour les autres' (25) ['break up with himself, that is to say with the need for justice and freedom for others']. He is shown relinquishing his love for the sake of a fight for others' freedom. *The Colours of the Day*'s epigraph, Lovelace's 'To Lucasta, On Going to the Wars', announces Jacques's choice of war above love.

With this conclusion, the opposition between the duo and the anonymous collectivity is annulled, as the pair gets included within a bigger ideological and literal fight. In the economy of Gary's polyphonic novel, the chronotope of the entr'acte and the freedom it gives to La Marne/Bebdern are framed within a lyrical tale that emphasizes the choice of the ideal. The assertion of freedom through the enactment of the role of clown and of various identities thus seems to lose its power in light of this integration within the framework of the ideal. It is as if the would-be-two-dimensional character was not actually trapped by its 'surface' but by the three-dimensional world of Jacques and of ideological fights. The last two pages would show La Marne's definitive inclusion in that three-dimensional world.

However, the character's positioning in the ending does not allow for such a tragic interpretation: 'La Marne était tombé à côté de son ami, accroché à sa manche vide. Son visage avait cet air de sombre satisfaction de quelqu'un qui avait toujours dit que ça allait finir comme ça' (Gary 1979: 253) ['As for La Marne, he had fallen beside his friend, holding on to his sleeve. His face had the air of sombre satisfaction of someone who had always said it would end this way' ([1953] 1976: 271)]. La Marne's presence alongside Jacques does not reintegrate the two-dimensional character within the ideal world. The clown figure is not 'integrated' but 'added', almost 'pasted' to the picture of the desired idealism. He constitutes a reminder that humans have 'grown out of their dimensions', a tender parodic criticism of the idealistic Jacques, and an embodiment of the chronotope of the entr'acte. And as such, La Marne's existence within his mask and his chronotope seems to mock the very notion of the social entrapment of characters. A co-dependent character cannot truly be trapped. He cannot truly be free either. A Moscardian or a Snootian conception of imprisonment and freedom hardly applies for the lyrical clown.

La Marne's existence is 'a reflection of some other's mode of being – and even then, not a direct reflection' (Bakhtin 1981: 159). It is a deformed, parodic reflection that paradoxically criticizes and asserts Jacques's ideals. In his 'Note de l'auteur' for the French edition of *Les clowns*, Gary explains: 'Depuis que j'écris, l'ironie et l'humour ont toujours été pour moi une mise à l'essai de l'authenticité des valeurs, une épreuve par le feu à laquelle un croyant soumet sa foi essentielle, afin qu'elle en sorte plus souriante, plus sûre d'elle-même, plus souveraine' (Gary 1979: 9) ['Since I started writing, irony and humour have always been for me a means of testing the authenticity of values, a trial by fire to which a believer subjects his essential faith, so that it may come out of it brighter, surer of itself, more sovereign']. While for Huston (1995: 56–7), this assertion cannot be taken at face value, since faith has not survived the trial by fire, for me, the values and the faith are neither made stronger nor destroyed by the parodic trial. They are rather both shattered and recreated, and what comes out of the Garyan use of humour is the movement of their destruction and their recreation: the humoristic oscillation.

The shelter, the book and the hotel room

The three individuals studied in the chapter adopt radical positions in their humoristic negotiation of the difficulty of living collectively. Moscarda rejects society altogether and chooses isolation; Snooty violently tries to repel competing tales and characters by imposing his own version of himself; and La Marne/Bebdern both critiques and embodies the mask of the clown and its parasitic positioning, even if that means dying for the ideal of the other. In the three cases, humour is the process that leads to radical choices.

Moscarda's transformation can be read both as an exemplification of Pirandello's *umorismo*, or, according to a Lewisian framework, as a process of enlightenment with regard to one's own constitutive entrapment. Humour enables the positive cognitive process of becoming self-conscious but leads to such instability for the character and its narration that the choice of physical enclosure seems like the only way to 'conclude' the narrative. Like the Dostoevskian hero of the underground, Moscarda's 'consciousness of self lives by its unfinalizability, by its unclosedness and its indeterminancy' (Bakhtin 1984a: 53). Moscarda's trajectory is framed by the initial recognition of social entrapment and the final deliberate choice of spatial imprisonment in the shelter. Spatial imprisonment thus comes back in our study, as an end point rather than a starting point. Similarly, Snooty sets up an enclosed space in his attempt to combat the circulating social images of him; the space of his narration. Moscarda, Snooty and La Marne/Bebdern alike convey their stories in their own words. However, only Snooty's tale becomes an enclosed object circulating in society and trapping him in a new fixed image, albeit as humoristically contradictory as possible. Snooty's attempt to free himself from social entrapment leads him to a possibly worse form of entrapment. Conversely, La Marne/Bebdern's consciousness of the need for the other in the constitution of the 'I' does not make of him a trapped character, but an enlightened one. La Marne/Bebdern's character is seen at play in the enclosed space of the hotel room that enables him to stage a new self in front of a new public, within the chronotope of the entr'acte. La Marne's new mask of Bebdern reasserts the lyrical clown's need of a host in order to be able to position oneself as clown.

The opposition between the collective and the individual thus opens up on another preoccupation of the novels: the figure of the double and the pairs of characters. It is the absent term of the title *Uno, nessuno e centomila* that seemingly emphasizes the absence, the unity and the collective, but where the tropes of the double, of doubling, of reflection, of clashes of contraries are actually crucial aspects of Moscarda's epiphany and trajectory.[17] In *Snooty Baronet*, the famous automaton scene and the *Moby Dick* reflection emphasize Snooty's need to become conscious of an otherness that is nevertheless a reflection of the self, in order to position his own subjectivity in the social group. Through his identification with the whale, Snooty, who seemingly emphasizes the need for isolation, actually asserts the need for the other – in this case, the image of another that helps to frame one's uniqueness. For Bakhtin, the impossibility of self-observation leads to the 'absolute need for the other':

> one can speak of a human being's absolute need for the other, for the other's seeing, remembering, gathering, and unifying self-activity – the only self-activity capable of producing his outwardly finished personality. This outward personality could not exist, if the other did not create it: aesthetic memory is productive – it gives birth, for the first time, to the outward human being on a new plane of being. (Bakhtin 1990: 35–6)

The same has happened to Moscarda in front of his mirror, since one's own reflection cannot truly lead to self-observation and the creation of a coherent external image of oneself. Both Moscarda's and Snooty's responses to the discovery of the impossibility of defining one's self without recourse to an external point of view are antagonistic. Both refuse to participate in a dialogical movement of co-creation of one's image. This is where La Marne offers a contrasting response. The necessity for the other is most explicit in *Les clowns lyriques*, and La Marne is conscious of this necessity from the starting point. His actions are motivated by his understanding of the need for the co-creation of one's image in partnership with another character. La Marne's take is also Bakhtinian in that it goes against 'the current fashion for theories of alienation', asserting that the discrepancy between two perspectives 'is no cause for despair. On the contrary, in a happy paradox, unbridgeability does not disqualify or disable us in our need for others but heightens and refines that need [Gogotishvili 1992: 117] [...] Personality [...] can always define itself creatively against another personality' (Emerson 1997: 199).

4

Humour in the Cells: Configurations of the Body as Prison

Material and immaterial prisoners in dialogue

Following the prison (Chapter 2) and the mask (Chapter 3), this chapter looks at the body as a third site of confinement for the humoristic character. The narratives discussed conceive the body as a space: a space of imprisonment provoking the production of narrative humour, and ultimately a narrative space where the negotiation of imprisonment can take place, through humour. The intersection of humour and imprisonment is framed through three configurations of bodily imprisonment. First, Gary's *La danse de Gengis Cohn* (1967) pictures an immaterial character trapped in the material body of another character. The Jewish *dybbuk* Gengis Cohn inhabits former Nazi officer Otto Schatz's psyche, depicted in the novel as a physical location surrounding Cohn. Cohn desires to escape this enclosure but understands that his relationship with his host has made his survival possible. The relationship between the two characters, first shown as a straightforward container-contained dynamic, is muddled by the narrative. Both characters are presented in turn as the other's ventriloquist, until a third voice, that of their creator, appears at the end of the novel and complicates this reading. The humoristic narration of the novel enables the reversibility of the characters' positions and creates an oscillation between the character's immortality and death.

The notion of the victim haunted by another's presence comes back in the guise of Albert Albinus, the protagonist of Nabokov's *Laughter in the Dark* (1932 in Russian; 1938 in English). Albinus's increasing imprisonment within his own body is encouraged by the attitude of his lover Margot and of her own lover Axel Rex. The latter, a joker figure in the narrative deck of cards, is instrumental in helping the wheel of fortune reverse the characters' positions. Rex influences Albinus's decisions and trajectory, promoting and revelling in the downward movement of Albinus's life. In the novel, humour arises within the diegesis at the expense of Albinus, and his imprisonment (both social and bodily) is perceived in light of Rex's love for a 'good laugh' that leaves Albinus in the dark.

Finally, we go back to the first character discussed in this book, Guareschi's autobiographical *persona*, to see how a character can contain within himself a representation of his own past self, who wears his bodily envelope as a shell both imprisoning his past and letting it pierce through the cracks. While Chapter 2 focused on Guareschi's political imprisonment in war camps, this chapter looks at the individual body conceived as a prison. I analyse two configurations of the duality of the self spanning Guareschi's writings from the 1940s to the 1960s: companion selves and synecdochical selves. The dialogue between selves trapped in the frame of the body enables the creation of a type of humour that insists on the continuity between different forms of entrapment, reasserting the necessity of grasping imprisonment along a continuum to comprehend its relationship with humour.

Humour in the subconscious ghetto in *La danse de Gengis Cohn*

The second book of the Frère Océan [Brother Ocean] trilogy,[1] *La danse de Gengis Cohn* (1967), features the disembodied character Gengis Cohn, pseudonym of Moïché Cohn, a Jewish comic performer killed by the Nazis during the Second World War. Cohn is a *dybbuk*,[2] a Jewish spirit that possesses the body of the former SS officer Otto Schatz, the man who gave the order to kill Cohn in 1944. The novel is set twenty-two years after Cohn's death. Schatz is now Police Commissioner in the city of Licht, and he investigates the disappearance and death of dozens of men, all found half naked with an uncanny expression of pleasure on their faces.

Schatz and Cohn's relationship is first depicted as one of container and contained, or possessed and possessing, but is complicated until it becomes increasingly hard to say who inhabits whom, and whose voice is heard when. The undecidability and untenability of the relationship play a key role in the development of the novel's humour. Chapter XIX, 'L'un dans l'autre',[3] constitutes a crucial moment of transition in the development of this relationship. It occupies a central position in the novel (it opens the second of three sections) and emphasizes the importance of questioning the two characters' subject-positions. It also acts as a watershed between the spatial settings of the novel. The preceding half mostly takes place in Schatz's office, while the latter half, set in the forêt de Geist, develops an allegorical story involving the characters of Lily (representing Humanity), Florian (Death), Le Baron and Le Comte (Aristocracy), among others. Most importantly, from Chapter XX onwards, the relationship between Cohn and Schatz becomes a secondary feature as their intimate cohabitation is ruptured and the two characters pursue relatively distinct endeavours in the forêt de Geist. After this turning point, the sporadic intrusion of a third narrative voice also changes the nature of the relationship depicted before, until it takes over the narration in the last pages of the book.

Ventriloquism as a context of imprisonment trapping the voices of Cohn, Schatz and their creator enables the creation of humour around personal and collective horror. The relationship of ventriloquism is first made possible by the spatialization of Schatz's subconscious,[4] which becomes Cohn's prison. However, both Cohn and Schatz – who considers himself a prisoner of his *dybbuk* – negotiate their respective imprisonment through the various levels of humour at play in the narrative. The pair become a narrative incarnation of the Freudian split self, which enables the creation of humour within imprisonment, while the humoristic narration muddies the waters and overturns the subject-positions, creating in the end an oscillation between the death of the character and his immortality.

Reading Gary's novel through a Freudian framework raises a certain number of problems. As I showed in my analysis of *Les clowns lyriques*, Garyan characters more often than not assert their existence as surfaces that have no depth. Gary repeatedly exposes the psychoanalytic belief in the depth of the human mind as a fallacy, as in Chapter XLVIII of *Pour Sganarelle*, 'La faillite des théories abyssales de l'homme' (384–9) ['the failure of the abyssal theories of man']. To Gary, Freud's emphasis on the vertical vector neglects the importance of the individual's surroundings. Freud 'tend à séparer l'histoire de l'Histoire' (385) ['tends to separate the story from History'], with devastating consequences:

> si toute ma famille a été brûlée dans un four crématoire par les nazis, mon psychisme n'en est pas marqué: mon inconscient ne s'en aperçoit pas. C'est essentiellement une doctrine d'un milieu privilégié, des malheurs exquis: le choc délicat, minime, intime, la fêlure, y prend infiniment plus d'importance que trente millions de morts, la *nursery* marque plus que l'Apocalypse. (385; original emphasis)

[if all my family has been burned in a crematory oven by the Nazis, my psyche does not bear the imprint of it: my unconscious does not notice it. It is essentially a doctrine of privilege, of exquisite misfortunes: the delicate, minimal, intimate shock, the crack, takes on infinitely more importance than thirty million deaths, the nursery leaves a bigger mark than the Apocalypse.]

In terms of literary development, Gary argues that the emphasis of the 'theories of the abyss' on individual exceptionality leads to the expulsion of the character from the novel (as in Le Nouveau Roman), and to 'l'absence de tout caractère humain dominant, de sa généralité et de son universalité, de son caractère le plus lumineux et le plus heureux, rejeté comme incapable de signifier la profondeur de l'être' (388) ['the absence of any dominant human feature, of its generality and its universality, of its brightest and happiest feature, cast-off as incapable of signifying the depth of being'].

Gary does not reject the concept of the unconscious, but he insists on the importance of the relationship it has with the culture at large: 'Je choisis plutôt comme romancier le conscient collectif de la culture et son lent travail, ses dépôts, son action sur l'inconscient' (385) ['As a novelist, I rather choose the collective conscious of culture and its slow work, its sediments, its action on the unconscious']. Reading Schatz and Cohn as split selves will show how the Freudian theory of humour, developed at the level of the individual psyche, can shed light on the relationship of humour with literary creation in general and how, in Garyan terms, Cohn and Schatz's interaction is not limited to the vertical axis but is connected to the 'horizontal' surface of culture.[5]

The spatialization of the subconscious: A tale of two ghettos

Chapter XIX describes the effect of Ennoctal, a chemical injected to Schatz by medical staff after a mental breakdown that seems to be caused by the investigation he is leading. The exhilarating power of the drug comes close to killing Cohn for a second time, erasing his existence from Schatz's subconscious. Cohn, however, fights from within his host's psyche, hoping for a survival that necessitates Schatz's presence while trying to escape from his parasitical situation.

The short chapter is divided into five sections, created by line breaks. The sections alternate between Cohn's and Schatz's voices. In the opening section, Cohn describes Schatz's subconscious as a room he inhabits. It is the first thorough depiction of the space he lives in and it creates a striking contrast between Schatz's external and internal spaces. In the opening chapter of the novel, Schatz is pictured as someone obsessed by cleanliness, constantly washing his hands:

> Le bureau est très propre, mon ami est obsédé par la propreté. Il se lave les mains continuellement: c'est nerveux. Il s'est même fait installer un petit lavabo, sous le portrait officiel du président Luebke. Il se lève toutes les dix minutes pour aller faire ses ablutions. Il emploie à cet effet une poudre spéciale. Jamais le savon. Schatzchen a pour le savon une véritable phobie. On ne sait jamais à qui on a affaire, dit-il. (Gary [1967] 1995: 14)
>
> [The office is very clean, my friend is obsessed by cleanliness. He washes his hands continuously: it's nervous. He has even had a little sink installed, under the official portrait of President Luebke. He gets up every ten minutes to perform his ablutions. He uses to this end a special powder. Never soap. Schatzchen has a real phobia of soap. You never know who you're dealing with, he says.[6]]

Schatz's subconscious space, on the other hand, is neglected and dirty. It is a 'taudis' ['hovel'], a 'poubelle' ['trash can'], filled with 'immondices' ['refuse']. As often happens in Gary's work, the dirt is ideological, composed of Nazi slogans, swastikas and anti-Semitic graffiti. The description culminates with a simile between the subconscious space and the sewers, the most neglected space of the most important European ghetto destroyed by the Nazis: 'À côté du subconscient de Schatz, les égouts du ghetto de Varsovie, c'était un palais pour princesses de légende' (158) ['Compared to Schatz's subconscious, the sewers of the Warsaw ghetto were a palace for princesses from legend']. The comparison with external, physical dirt emphasizes Cohn's critique: Schatz's immaterial subconscious is ideologically dirtier than any possible material setting. Conversely, the Jewish ghetto – even its sewers – can be read as a space of ideological cleanliness.

The simile also presents Schatz's subconscious as another 'ghetto' for Cohn, where he sometimes feels at home, particularly at the beginning of the novel, but which becomes increasingly constraining. In the first sentence of the novel, 'Je suis chez moi, ici.' (9) ['I am home, here'] (9), 'ici' ['here'] encompasses Germany, Licht (the German town), and Schatz. In 'L'un dans l'autre', however, Schatz's subconscious space is described by means of an abundant negative isotopy of confinement: 'Pas de lumière, pas d'air, un plafond bas, des murs qui se referment sur vous de tous les côtés [...]' (158) ['No light, no air, a low ceiling, walls that close on you from all sides [...]']. Moreover, Cohn exclaims 'C'est une chose merveilleuse d'être enfin chez moi' (157) ['It is a marvellous thing to finally be home'] only after having been expelled from Schatz, thus re-signifying 'home' as a place outside of his German host.

Despite its decay, Schatz's mental space is not entirely forgotten, and Gary does not only focus on a historical past. The 'dirt' of the contemporary German society gets included bit by bit in the German's psyche, adding to the accumulated mess of Schatz's inner space:

> Personne ne vient balayer, là-dedans, au contraire, on en rajoute: tous les jours quelqu'un vient y déverser des ordures nouvelles. Si ce ne sont pas les néo-nazis, et leur presse, ce sont toutes sortes de détritus historiques, des vieilleries puantes d'un autre âge, avec des taches ignobles de sang et de Dieu sait quoi [...] (158)

> [No one ever comes to sweep in there, on the contrary, they add some more: every day someone comes to dump new filth in. When it's not the neo-Nazis and their papers, it's all sort of historical litter, stinking old-fashioned stuff of another age, with awful stains of blood or God-knows-what [...]]

The subconscious space is not impenetrable, since society's new dirt can enter it quite easily. But there is no movement the other way around. The subconscious is only able to absorb, accumulate and blur. The claustrophobic sensation of the *dybbuk* can therefore only augment with time, and Cohn's situation, two decades after his death, is increasingly untenable. Buried in the accumulated dirt of the subconscious, Cohn attempts, through his narrative, to reclaim a space of his own. One of his strategies is to render conscious what has been subconscious by having Schatz bring into action Cohn's suggestions from within his subconscious. Cohn revels when he manages to have Schatz formulate aloud his own ideas or act according to his own desire, as for example when Schatz is surprised by his landlady while offering kosher food to the invisible Cohn during Hanukkah – something Cohn describes as 'un incident particulièrement amusant' (16) ['a particularly amusing incident'].

Cohn's will to bring his existence to consciousness and Schatz's desire to repress that very existence establish an oscillation in the narrative, a tension between two opposite drives. Yet the distinction between the two drives is also questioned. In Chapter XIX, Cohn is not the only one fighting against his extinction, since Schatz also plays an active role in Cohn's survival.

Humour's ambiguity: The horror of laughing at horror

Reclaiming the space of the Jewish victim within the German host goes hand in hand with reclaiming a space for humour and ambiguity in the narrative. Humour is a feature of Cohn as a character and as the novel's narrator. We know from the start that Cohn used to be a Jewish comedian whose humour was hard-hitting: 'Les critiques faisaient quelques réserves sur mon humour: ils le trouvaient un peu excessif, un peu agressif, cruel' (12) ['Critics expressed reservations about my humour: they found it a little excessive, a little aggressive, cruel'].[7] The habit of humour is so deeply entrenched in the character that his last gesture before being killed is to show his butt to Schatz while shouting 'Kisch mir in tokhès!' (33) ['Kiss my ass!' in Yiddish]. Cohn's presence within Schatz hinges on this humoristic outburst. It explains why Cohn in particular has struck Schatz's subconscious to the extent of haunting him for more than two decades. This vulgar gesture even leads to a complete reversal of the logic of the Shoah: 'le tour de force opéré par le héros consiste précisément à renverser la norme éthique criminelle qui régit la procédure génocidaire. Pour y parvenir, Gengis Cohn oppose à l'obscénité institutionnalisée par la SS – faire participer les victimes à leur propre mise à mort – une des injures les plus obscènes associant la scatologie à la sexualité.' (Rinn 2009: 85) ['The feat operated by the hero consists precisely in reversing the criminal ethical norm that rules the genocidal procedure. To achieve this, Gengis Cohn opposes to the obscenity institutionalized by the SS – to involve victims in their own killing – one of the most obscene insults associating scatology and sexuality.'] Humour thus lies at the origin of the relationship between Schatz and Cohn and is constantly deployed to maintain their relationship.

Thanks to the first-person narration, Cohn's production of humour is generally made possible both at Schatz's expense, such as in the case of his celebration of Jewish rites described above, and in complicity with him. The alternation of voices in 'L'un dans l'autre' also enables the creation of humour at Cohn's own expense. In the chapter, Cohn's laughter is first presented as the chemical and inevitable consequence of the injection of Ennoctal, which produces a 'douce hilarité' (157) ['gentle hilarity']. This hilarity is of course physically expressed by Schatz's body, since Cohn has no body of his own. But Schatz's is a derivative laughter, a reaction to Cohn's initial laughter:

> L'idée qu'on faisait une piqûre à Cohn, comme au bon vieux temps, pour nous débarrasser de sa présence, et que ce petit malin de Juif tellement méfiant ne se méfiait de rien et devait croire que c'était seulement sa vocation qui se manifestait à nouveau, son atavisme comique, était irrésistible. Il faisait hi, hi, hi! et je faisais ho, ho, ho! et le côté désopilant de la situation s'ajoutant à l'effet hilarant de l'Ennoctal, tout cela faisant boule de neige, en quelque sorte, je ne pouvais plus m'arrêter. Il riait à rendre l'âme, cet enfant de pute, et c'était exactement ce qui était en train de lui arriver. (159)

[The idea that they were giving Cohn a shot like in the good old days, to get us rid of his presence, and that this suspicious smarty-pants of a Jew was not suspecting anything and must have thought that it was only his vocation that expressed itself again, his comic atavism, was irresistible. He was doing hee, hee, hee! and I was doing ho ho ho! and the hysterically funny side of the situation adding itself to the hilarious effect of the Ennoctal, all this snowballed in some way and I couldn't stop anymore. He was laughing to give up the ghost, this son-of-a-bitch, and it was exactly what was happening to him.]

Schatz's commentary on Cohn's 'comic atavism' sheds a new light on the role of humour, and particularly Jewish humour, in the novel. Indeed, Cohn's habit of humour is pictured as a possible cause for the erasure of memory, since dismissing the horror through the production of laughter leads him to forget the possibility of his imminent destruction. In Schatz's comment, the compulsion of humour is in direct contrast with the capacity to be suspicious that is needed to defy oppression. In this particular case, only something strong enough to fight against the erasure of memory, the mention of the word 'gas' by a doctor, enables Cohn to fight against his own erasure:

Ça m'a sauvé la vie. Il y a des mots qu'on ne dit pas deux fois à un Juif, et le mot 'gaz' est de ceux-là. J'étais déjà, sans le savoir, très affaibli par l'action instantanée de la piqûre, je pouffais, je ne pouvais plus m'arrêter, tout en étant dans mon état d'euphorie, je me réjouissais de tout coeur à l'idée que j'allais enfin être débarrassé de Schatz [...]. J'avais complètement oublié que sans lui je disparaîtrais, je cesserais d'être individuellement perceptible, dans la masse anonyme des statistiques [...]. (160)

[It saved my life. There are words you don't say twice to a Jew and the word 'gas' is one of them. I was already, without knowing it, very weakened by the instantaneous action of the injection, I was bursting out with laughter, I couldn't stop myself, while being vaguely conscious that I was erasing myself, but in my state of euphoria, I was rejoicing wholeheartedly thinking that I would finally be rid of Schatz [...]. I had totally forgotten that without him I would disappear, I would cease to be individually perceptible in the anonymous mass of statistics [...].]

The word 'gas' wakes Cohn from his apathy by recalling the Nazis' use of gas as a weapon of mass murder. The word also enables the return to a creative use of humour by Cohn as narrator, that is added to the physical expression of laughter. Cohn's first words when he recovers his understanding become an occasion for word play. His use of the expression 'on ne dit pas deux fois' ['words you don't say twice'] takes on a literal meaning when associated with the infamous word 'gas' – the word can literally not be said twice to a Jew since it refers to a weapon that has caused death. In this context, the expression 'on ne dit pas deux fois' becomes a semantic syllepsis, combining a figurative and a literal meaning. It is doubled by the presence of situational irony, since the weapon that killed in the past now becomes the tool that saves.

Regaining his ability to produce tendentious and rebellious humour, Cohn also reflects on the possible dangers and the horror of humour. On the following page, Cohn's voice comments on the presence of laughter in their 'situation', expressing that 'l'effet hilarant de cette piqûre, c'est quelque chose de tout à fait effrayant' (161) ['the hilarious effect of this injection, it's something absolutely terrifying']. Anaesthetic laughter (Lewis's 'blasted' humour) and rebellious laughter (Lewis's 'blessed' humour) co-exist once more in Gary's narration, as was the case in *Les racines du ciel*. In *La danse de Gengis Cohn*, Cohn's physical laughter, produced by the Ennoctal, is exemplary of a blasted humour that makes one forget one's pains or struggles. On the other side, Cohn's reaction when he hears the word 'gas', that is, the creation of word play and the impulse towards rebellion, illustrates Lewis's positively connoted blessed humour. In both cases, the power of humour – power of erasure or of rebellion – exists in relation to memory. Whereas Cohn's vulgar humour at the moment of his death was an act of rebellion that enabled the remembrance of the horror of the Shoah, the imposed laughter of the Ennoctal induces hilarity in order to erase memory, both for Schatz and for Cohn. The Ennoctal, read as an image for the external control exerted on collective and individual memory, is a horrifying device. Accordingly, the laughter it induces adds to the horror of the situation, to the horror of laughing at horror. After laughing at one another's failure to grasp the situation, Cohn and Schatz then mutually comprehend the horrifying aspect of laughing at horror itself.

In the end, however, Cohn has the upper hand, thanks to his strategy of the 'piège israélien' (163) ['Israeli trap']. By insinuating to Schatz that not impeding his erasure would amount to taking part in his death a second time and thus be the target of Israeli criticism (162), Cohn makes sure that he is saved by the man who killed him. 'Le côté désopilant de la situation' (159) ['the hysterically funny side of the situation'] that Schatz perceived as Cohn's lack of understanding of the situation is now reversed, as Schatz is manipulated by Cohn. Cohn regains a certain amount of freedom by inciting Schatz to turn his subconscious thoughts into conscious action, running from the ambulance to the forêt de Geist. The language of the *dybbuk* as Cohn-in-Schatz is also reversed. The last section of the chapter goes back to Cohn's voice and shows Schatz-in-Cohn's ejection from the Jewish character: 'Ouf. Ça va un peu mieux. Il dort maintenant, écroulé dans les fourrés. J'ai eu raison de lui souffler cette idée de piège israélien, au dernier moment. Il a eu peur et ça m'a tiré d'affaire. Je respire. Je me suis débarrassé de Schatz. Je suis dénazifié' (163) ['Phew. It's a little bit better. He's sleeping now, collapsed in the thickets. I was right to direct him at the last moment with the Israeli trap idea. He got scared and that got me out of it. I can breathe. I got rid of Schatz. I am denazified'].

The ventriloquist(s)

In these last lines of the chapter, Cohn explicitly takes on the traits of the ventriloquist, whose voice inhabits the other's body. The voice of the *dybbuk* is made concrete through the use of words that denote its physicality. The exhalation 'Ouf' ['Phew'] that opens the section, and the emphasis on breathing in the shortest sentence – 'Je respire.' ['I can breathe.'] – concretize Cohn's presence despite his lack of bodily form. The use of the verb 'souffler', signifying both 'to breathe' and 'to prompt' (as in a theatre), also adds to the denotation of breath and to the description of the power of Cohn's voice as the voice of a ventriloquist. As Luc Rasson remarks, the *dybbuk* is indeed a 'maître ventriloque' ('master ventriloquist') (Gary [1967] 1995: 124; Rasson 2008: 146), and 'la ventriloquie est le phénomène garyen par excellence dans la mesure où elle est créatrice d'identité […]. Ce phénomène d'indivision énonciative relève sans doute de ce que Gary dans *Vie et Mort d'Émile Ajar* appelle "la plus vieille tentation protéenne de l'homme: celle de la multiplicité".' (Rasson 2008: 146) ['ventriloquism is the ultimate Garyan phenomenon inasmuch as it is a creator of identity […]. This phenomenon of enunciative indivision probably falls in what Gary, in *Vie et mort d'Émile Ajar*, calls "the oldest protean temptation of man: the one of multiplicity"']. Gary's 'temptation of multiplicity' is closely connected with the conditions of emergence of humour. In relation to Freud's theory of humour, ventriloquism can be read not only as a cohabitation of identities but also as a literary incarnation of the split self. The passage of *Pour Sganarelle* in which Gary explains his predilection for the process of splitting man into two to create pairs of characters confirms the validity of this hypothesis.

Considering Schatz and Cohn as two parts of a same narrative voice – one self split in two, or two entities playing in turn the roles of the ventriloquist and the marionette – explains how humour is constructed in the novel. The split self is what makes humour on the subject of the Shoah possible at all. In light of Freud's theory and of Gary's predilection, Cohn and Schatz can be read as representations of psychic entities that interact with one another. In 'L'un dans l'autre', the horror of Cohn's possible extinction, a second death, is treated through jest just like the super-ego treats the traumas of the external world through jest to assert the ego's invulnerability:

> We obtain a dynamic explanation of the humorous attitude, therefore, if we assume that it consists in the humorist's having withdrawn the psychical accent from his ego and having transposed it on to his super-ego. The super-ego, thus inflated, the ego can appear tiny and all its interests trivial; and, with this new distribution of energy, it may become an easy matter for the super-ego to suppress the ego's possibilities of reacting. (Freud [1927] 1961: 164)[8]

As we have seen, however, Schatz is also able to produce humour at Cohn's expense, and no strict association between Cohn and the super-ego and Schatz and the ego can be made. The Freudian framework suggests that a representation of individual and collective trauma through humour would rely on a split self. Yet Freud's distinctions are complicated by narratives like Gary's. It is also crucial that in Gary's narrative the treatment of horror through humour does not erase the emotions related to horror, as Freud would have it: 'the essence of humour is that one spares oneself the affects to which the situation would naturally give rise and dismisses the possibility of such expressions of emotion with a jest' (Freud [1927] 1961: 162). Pierre Bayard has noted how Gary's 'verve comique n'atténue pas l'horreur des situations évoquées, et, au premier rang, de la Shoah' (1990: 83) [Gary's 'comic eloquence does not alleviate the horror of the situations evoked and, in the first place, of the Shoah'].

Nevertheless, the reading of Schatz and Cohn as a Freudian split self helps to shed light on the unfolding of the novel, and particularly on the intrusion of a third narrative voice, that is first alluded to about twenty pages after 'L'un dans l'autre' (180), and then sporadically throughout the second and third parts of the novel. This voice, that will be called Romain only in the last pages of the novel, is a representation of the *persona* of the writer, who thematizes himself within his own creation. The twice-split narration thus destabilizes Cohn's first-person narration from within. The Russian doll structure of Chapter XIX, with Cohn revealing Schatz, who in turn reveals Cohn again, is complicated by the appearance of Romain's voice. The porosity between Schatz and Cohn's consciousnesses is redefined by their inclusion within this third consciousness. The split self thus takes on new meanings: the narrative voice of the ending (the 'I' of Romain Gary's *persona*) is represented in the process of creating a narrative where his own psyche takes the double form of Schatz and Cohn, and is even further multiplied into a series of allegorical characters that cohabit in the forêt de Geist, this representation of the 'spirit' as a natural setting.

The perception of the characters of Cohn and Schatz as a single identity narratively developed as two also explains the imbrication and the reversibility of the positionings of victim and perpetrator. The cohabitation of identities erases the distinctions between the Jew and the ex-Nazi and makes possible the complete reversibility of their roles, something made particularly clear at the end of the novel:

> Dans les dernières pages, nous voyons Cohn métamorphosé en GI massacrant des civils vietnamiens et appelant à l'aide Schatz dont l'expérience militaire pourrait lui être utile. Certes, ce n'est qu'un cauchemar mais la suggestion est claire: les places ne sont pas distribuées une fois pour toutes, la victime peut se reconvertir en bourreau. Ainsi la critique du totalitarisme implique un refus du stéréotype, un rejet des identités fermées – la victime, le bourreau – même dans le contexte d'Auschwitz. (Rasson 2008: 147)

> [In the last pages, we see Cohn morphed into a GI slaughtering Vietnamese civilians and calling to his help Schatz's military experience. To be sure, it is only a nightmare, but the suggestion is clear: the roles are not distributed once and for all, the victim can transform into the persecutor. In this way the critique of totalitarianism implies a refusal of stereotype, a rejection of closed identities – the victim, the persecutor – even in the context of Auschwitz.[9]]

The positioning and even the existence of the *dybbuk* as ventriloquist are also transformed by the infiltration of the voice of the creator's *persona*. Cohn-as-character is now pictured as the puppet whose voice is being prompted by the author-ventriloquist. Still, Cohn's position as first-person narrator not only ensures that the voice of the author-ventriloquist is constantly mediated through Cohn's, but also enables Cohn to formulate criticism against his own positioning – something he increasingly does until the end of the novel.

Cohn's imprisonment in his creator's psyche becomes increasingly oppressive, and he even starts wishing for his own extinction, while noting the impossibility to distinguish his prison from his existence: 'J'avais complètement oublié où j'étais. Ce type-là est une vraie ordure et son subconscient, c'est un nid de vipères. C'est bon, j'ai compris. Je n'y resterai pas une seconde de plus. Mais je ne suis plus sûr de rien. Je ne sais même plus si c'est moi qui pense ou si c'est lui. (322) ['I had totally forgotten where I was. This guy is a real scumbag and his subconscious is a viper's nest. It's ok, I understand. I won't stay here a second more. But I am not sure of anything anymore. I don't even know if it's me who's thinking or if it's him']. As in 'L'un dans l'autre', then, Cohn understands that leaving his creator's psyche would lead to his disappearance, and thus oscillates between his desire to be free and his will to exist. The only possible 'liberation' for the character now appears to be the finalization of his literary incarnation: 'Il n'y a plus de doute: ce sont mes derniers instants. [...] Je ne sais pas encore comment ils vont s'y prendre: je suppose qu'ils vont faire de moi un livre, comme toujours, lorsqu'ils cherchent à se débarrasser de quelque chose qui leur est resté sur l'estomac.' (324) ['There is no possible doubt left: these are my last moments. [...] I don't know yet how they will manage: I guess they will transform me into a book, as always when they want to get rid of something they cannot stomach'].

Understanding that his disappearance, that is the transformation of his life story into a work of art, is now inevitable, Cohn comments on the mode of narration of the story:

> Je me tords. Je n'essaie même pas de me défendre. Si ce type veut me balayer, avec tout le reste, du moment que c'est dans un éclat de rire, je suis d'accord. Finalement, plus j'y pense, et plus je suis convaincu d'une chose. Foutus pour foutus, éclater de rire, c'est encore la meilleure façon d'éclater. (334)
>
> [I'm rolling about laughing. I'm not even trying to defend myself. If this guy wants to sweep me away, with everything else, as long as it is in a burst of laughter, I agree. Finally, the more I think about it, the more I am convinced of something. If we're screwed anyway, bursting out laughing is still the best way to burst.]

To die, or in the case of a character, to morph into a work of art, through humour: this is exactly what Cohn's creator-ventriloquist is attempting to do. In the final section of the novel, creation risks destroying Cohn's specificity, since it incorporates him into a boundless fraternity and transforms his personal pain into literature. However, Cohn asserts that the transformation of personal (and collective) suffering through humour remains the most acceptable means to do so.

As the 'I' of Cohn-as-narrator is gradually replaced by the 'I' of Gary's *persona* (literally appearing on page 348, six pages before the end), it might seem that Cohn has indeed been killed again and that his voice has been muted. Yet Cohn-as-character comes back in the last paragraphs, described both by the new narrator and in a conversation between Lily and Florian (an allegory of Death). In the last lines of the novel, Florian comments on Cohn's existence: 'C'est seulement ton Juif, ma chérie. Toujours le même. Il s'est encore tiré d'affaire, ce salaud-là. Enfin, je n'y peux rien. Increvable. Viens, ma chérie. Il ne dérange personne' (353) ['It's only your Jew, my darling. Always the same. He got himself out of it again, this bastard. Anyway, I can't do anything about it. Indestructible. Come, my darling. He's not bothering anyone']. Reminiscent of Jesus Christ, Cohn walks away bearing his cross, alive in the reader's psyche after having fought for his existence within his author's mind. He is the result of the creative struggle thematized before our eyes. The residue of humour is thus this 'increvable', and Cohn is both 'killed' and immortalized by the narrativization of the immortal figure of the Jew. Like in *Les racines du ciel*, where Robert Ducamp becomes 'increvable' through his use of humour (see *Les racines du ciel* 54–5 and my discussion in Chapter 2), Gengis Cohn's figure cannot truly be destroyed by Death/Florian, who even admits his powerlessness. He is so 'increvable' that he will come back in Tahiti in the following novel of the trilogy, *La tête coupable* ([1968] 1994), under other guises but with the same pseudonym.[10] By his creation, Gary affirms in the same breath his faith in the perpetual existence of the character, and the ambiguous role humour plays in this renewed creation.

Laughter in the Dark: The game of humour

The pair of the victim and the perpetrator is present again in Nabokov's *Laughter in the Dark*,[11] in a less clearly defined manner than it was in *La danse de Gengis Cohn*. In the same way as Gary, the pairing of contrasting characters is typical of Nabokov. Julian Connolly remarks that the two main characters of the novel, Albert Albinus and Axel Rex, constitute 'a characteristic Nabokovian pair – the predator and the prey' (1992: 248).[12] The novel's protagonist, Albert Albinus, is first presented as a 'victim' of love. The middle-aged Berlin art critic falls in love with Margot, a young cinema usher and aspiring actress. His love for Margot, who becomes his mistress but does not love him, brings his downfall, as Albinus loses his wife Elisabeth and his daughter Irma (who dies), his sight, and eventually his money and his life. More importantly, the action of fate is combined with the other characters' power over Albinus's life, over his personal choices, his imagined universe and his very body. One character in particular is instrumental in encouraging Albinus's downward trajectory. Indeed, throughout the novel, Albinus becomes unknowingly controlled by decisions made between Margot and her own lover, the caricaturist Axel Rex. The latter's power to limit Albinus's agency and to superimpose a fictive universe of his own making onto Albinus's world is enabled by his very particular definition of caricature and humour, which I will discuss at length.

The distribution of the power to create humour is even more uneven in Nabokov's novel than it was in Gary's. While both Cohn and Schatz create humour at the other's expense, in Nabokov, Rex is the only one endowed with the power of humoristic creation, and the power to foster the other's entrapment. The opposition between Rex's cruel humour and Albinus's credulity in love is accompanied by a parallel opposition between the capacity and the incapacity to see. In the novel, the power of humour goes hand in hand with the power to perceive that which is external to oneself. Rex, the humoristic character, is also the enlightened character, and Albinus's oppression through humour is directly proportional to his loss of vision. Rex's capacity to control Albinus's surroundings and interpretations thereof precludes Albinus from direct access to reality, thus limiting his sphere of action to his individual body.

Rex's mediation of Albinus's world through humour creates a new situation of imprisonment for the modernist character: the entrapment of a character within his own body through the agency of another's humour. The power of Rex's conception of humour over Albinus's trajectory towards confinement within his own body means that humour can also be a source of imprisonment. The direction of humour and the temporal framework differ from the other works studied so far. In *Laughter in the Dark*, imprisonment does not predate humour. And humour is not directed only towards the self; it is also used as a tool to imprison others. Although they share some common traits, Rex's humour is different from the comic of Rodion, Rodrig or M'sieur Pierre in *Invitation to a Beheading*. Maurice Couturier stresses this distinction when he notes that the reader can include himself in part of Rex's laughter, but not in M'sieur Pierre's laughter (1993: 296). Although I agree with Couturier in that regard, my approach differs in that I do not discuss the presence of humour from a reader's point of view, but from an intradiegetic one. I am looking at constitutive traits that make Rex a humoristic character. Rex's humour and M'sieur Pierre's laughter are both oppressive and directed towards a vulnerable other, but, as I will show, Rex's humour is also self-reflexive, and does not aim at reintegrating anyone in a social group.

Detail is always welcome

The first paragraph of *Laughter in the Dark* announces the novel's narrative arc in a nutshell: 'Once upon a time there lived in Berlin, Germany, a man called Albinus. He was rich, respectable, happy; one day he abandoned his wife for the sake of a youthful mistress; he loved; was not loved; and his life ended in disaster' (7). This short mise en abyme of the whole novel reads as a parody of a fairy tale, setting up an expectation that it immediately contests. The vague temporal framework of the iconic formula 'once upon a time' clashes with the degree of precision of the location of the story. There is a complete absence of the mystery a fairy tale might suggest, and the character's trajectory is depicted as a matter-of-fact succession of events, rather than as a quest to be undertaken. The opening also suggests the repetition of a conventional plot, which will be obvious to the reader but will not be perceived as such by the clueless Albinus.

Having so concisely revealed the protagonist's story, the narrator sets out to explain the pertinence of expanding the short summary into a novel: 'This is the whole of the story and we might have left it at that had there not been profit and pleasure in the telling; and although there is plenty of space on a gravestone to contain, bound in moss, the abridged version of a man's life, detail is always welcome' (7). This could be said of any story, but what is the particular quality of the profit and pleasure to be gained from being told of Albinus's downfall? The readers could perhaps profit from the depiction of the character's failures by learning how to avoid them or obtain pleasure by distancing themselves from the character's hardships. The latter aspect calls to mind superiority theories of humour, which are usually traced back to Hobbes's idea that 'the passion of laughter is nothing else but *sudden glory* arising from some sudden *conception* of some *eminency* in ourselves, by *comparison* with the *infirmity* of others, or with our own formerly' (Hobbes [1650] 1839–1845: 46; original emphasis). Indeed, Couturier has noted a parallel between Hobbes's superiority theory and laughter in Nabokov's works (1993: 303).[13] This conception aligns with what we later learn of Rex, that he derives a particular pleasure from the hardships of others:

> It amused him immensely to see life made to look silly, as it slid helplessly into caricature. He despised practical jokes: he liked them to happen by themselves with perchance now and then just that little touch on his part which would send the wheel running downhill. [...] The art of caricature, as Rex understood it, was thus based (apart from its synthetic, fooled-again nature) on the contrast between cruelty on one side and credulity on the other. (143)

The narrator's commentary on the expansion of the incipit into an entire novel can be read as a comment on the reception of Albinus's story within the diegesis, by the character whose external perception will have the most power on Albinus. Despite Rex's comment on the syntheticism of caricature, and thus on caricature as a result, the movement towards caricature by small degrees is key to his appreciation of the end result. Watching Albinus 'slid[ing] helplessly' can be posited as the source of the pleasure of the story, if not for the reader, certainly for the intradiegetic onlooker. Toker relates this desire for detail to Schopenhauer's notion of comedy:

> 'The life of every individual,' says Schopenhauer, 'viewed as a whole and in general, and when only its most significant features are emphasized, is really a tragedy; but gone through in detail it has the character of a comedy.' [Schopenhauer [1819] 1969: 322] The 'detail' in question is exactly what, according to the second paragraph of *Laughter in the Dark*, 'is always welcome'. (Toker 1989: 120)

Rex's interest in the unfolding of Albinus's adventure seems to align with the Schopenhauerian definition. However, I will show that Rex's definition of humour and of caricature is in fact the opposite of Schopenhauer's. To Rex, the 'synthetic' image of one's life is the most 'comic' in the Schopenhauerian sense.

The importance of the other characters' perspective is also key to getting a more complete picture of the roots of Albinus's failures, and the nature of the enclosure in which he is gradually trapped. Margot, love and Albinus's own agency are only part of the picture. Small specific actions of peripheral characters or, as Rex puts it, 'little touch[es] on [their] part' have more impact on Albinus's decisions than what he actually perceives, to the extent that his decisions are almost always mediated by other characters. In the incipit, the narrator presents Albinus's idea to 'animate' colour drawings, but immediately rectifies that the idea 'was not quite his own, as it had been suggested by a phrase in Conrad (not the famous Pole, but Udo Conrad who wrote the *Memoirs of a Forgetful Man* [...])' (7). The source of the revelation having been exposed, the narrator explains that Albinus's appropriation of Conrad's idea is not passive, as he actively 'ma[kes] it his own by liking it, playing with it, letting it grow upon him' (7–8). Yet, the movement of the idea from Conrad to Albinus hints at a crucial opposition between the capacity to generate new ideas and the vicarious use of ideas. The writer Conrad and the caricaturist Rex are opposed to the art critic Albinus, since the former have an immediate connection to art and creation, while the latter's is always mediated, or parasitical.[14] Albinus's experience of life is filtered through his knowledge of the Old Masters: 'As an art critic and picture expert he had often amused himself by having this or that Old Master sign landscapes and faces which he, Albinus, came across in real life: it turned his existence into a fine picture gallery – delightful fakes, all of them' (7–8). In that sense, Albinus is the Masters' slave, relying on them to experience the beauty of the world surrounding him. While Conrad's or Rex's creations are posited as real, Albinus's use of art is deemed fake, because of its mediated nature.

The joker's 'little touch'

Rex's pivotal role in Albinus's trajectory stems from the opposition between the creator and the consumer of art. Albinus first contacts Rex to ask him to implement his idea of producing 'colored animated drawings', moving pictures that would animate well-known paintings on screen (8–10). After having won Albinus's trust, Rex uses his visible position alongside Albinus to maintain a hidden role (as Margot's lover) and to use Albinus in various ways. Rex's financial gains from his association with Albinus are significant, but the pleasure he derives from his clever tricks is even greater. The root of Rex's actions is to be found in his philosophy of humour:

> It amused him immensely to see life made to look silly, as it slid helplessly into caricature. He despised practical jokes: he liked them to happen by themselves with perchance now and then just that little touch on his part which would send the wheel running downhill. He loved to fool people; and the less trouble the process entailed, the more the joke pleased him. And at the same time this dangerous man was, with pencil in hand, a very fine artist indeed.
>
> Uncle alone in the house with the children said he'd dress up to amuse them. After a long wait, as he did not appear, they went down and saw a masked man putting the table silver into a bag. 'Oh, Uncle', they cried in delight. 'Yes, isn't my make-up good?' said Uncle, taking his mask off. Thus goes the Hegelian syllogism of humor. Thesis: Uncle made himself up as a burglar (a laugh for the children); antithesis: it *was* a burglar (a laugh for the reader); synthesis: it still was Uncle (fooling the reader). This was the super-humor Rex liked to put into his work; and this, he claimed, was quite new. [...]
>
> The art of caricature, as Rex understood it, was thus based (apart from its synthetic, fooled-again nature) on the contrast between cruelty on one side and credulity on the other. (143–4; original emphasis)

The first element to note regarding this conception of humour is the downward movement it implies. To Rex, life becomes amusing when it 'slid[es]' into caricature, when a story unfolds as a 'wheel run[s] downhill'. Rex's participation in the creation of humour involves identifying this movement in life and exerting minimal pressure at key moments, and this is exactly what he endeavours to do to Albinus. Albinus's life has already started going downhill after his falling in love with Margot. Rex witnesses the movement on its way. However, Albinus's 'entrapment' in love is not a joking matter prior to Rex's intervention. His 'little touch' is an addition to a state of affairs that already exists but that has not yet been touched by an artist's hand.

Rex's intervention is actually an artistic one. Despite the remark that 'this dangerous man was, *with pencil in hand*, a very fine artist indeed' (emphasis added), it is clear that Rex is a 'very fine artist' even without a pencil in his hand, and that his talent at caricature translates into life. His suggestive powers and ability to convince enable him to impose his creative vision of the world onto the other characters, be it in oppressive ways (with Albinus) or not (with Margot). A key scene in that regard takes place in Switzerland, when Margot introduces Albinus to the house prepared for his recovery after the car accident leaves him blind: 'Margot described all the colors to him – the blue wallpaper, the yellow blinds – but, egged on by Rex, she changed all the colors. The fact that the blind man was obliged to picture his little world in the hues prescribed by Rex afforded the latter exquisite amusement' (260–1). The idea of Rex providing colours for Albinus is not new. Albinus had insisted on the importance of Rex's ability to precisely reproduce colours to realize his idea of 'colored animated drawings' (8). In the Swiss chalet, Rex's invisible input in Albinus's mental creations becomes one of those 'little touch[es]' that encourages life to be sillier for the creator (Rex) and the spectator of humour (Margot). In so doing, the production of humour reduces Albinus to a passive state, stripping him of his agency. As is often the case in passages using internal focalization from Rex's point of view, Albinus is not even named anymore, but simply designated as 'the blind man'.

So far, Rex's humour with regard to Albinus seems to align with the Bergsonian comic. To Toker, 'Albinus is a perfect illustration of what Bergson described as a potentially comic character, one whose emotion is a parasitic growth, rigid and disconnected from the rest of the soul' (1989: 118).[15] However, there is a crucial dimension of Bergson's comic that is absent from *Laughter in the Dark*, and from Rex's attitude: the social dimension, and as its correlate, the notion that laughter can have the social role of a corrective. This dimension was present in *Invitation to a Beheading*. In *Laughter*, however, the invisibility of Rex's laughter strips it from the possibility of having any corrective impact on the character who is laughed at. Bergsonian laughter is both expressed socially and expressed for society. To be the case, this laughter needs to be overt. Rex's laughter is not. Even the illogical and oppressive characters of *Invitation to a Beheading* believed that their vision of society could be communicated to their prisoner, who could then accept or refuse to participate in their collective world, either conform or die. This possibility to choose knowingly is not offered to Albinus.

Rex's humour is devoid of perfectibility. It assesses a state of affairs without presuming that this state should or could be otherwise. Couturier stresses the non-didactic and non-perfectible qualities of Nabokov's laughter, picturing it as a 'rire dionysiaque qui ne cherche à corriger personne et qui ne vise en aucune manière à donner de leçons' (1993: 290) ['Dionysian laughter that does not aim to correct anyone and that does not aim in any way to give lessons']. In that regard, Rex's mentality resonates a lot more with a Lewisian framework than with a Bergsonian one. Lewisian laughter is 'useless' and 'impersonal': 'any master of humour is an essential artist; even Dickens is no exception. For it is the character of uselessness and impersonality which is found in laughter (the anarchist emotion concerned in the comic habit of mind) that makes a man an "artist". So when he begins living on his laughter, even in spite of himself a man becomes an artist' (Lewis 1927: 239). The assessment of the absurdity of human life (through the observation of others and through self-observation) is the end point of this vision of humour, and its value is detached from the potential impact it can have. Rex's positioning in the novel is akin to the position of Lewis's laughing observer, 'a fanciful wandering figure', 'the showman to whom the antics and solemn gambols of these wild children [the Wild Bodies] are to be a source of strange delight' (Lewis 1927: 232). Watching Albinus's sufferings as a joke, Rex concludes that not only Albinus's life is such a joke, but that human distress in general is set up as a staged comedy:

> He watched with interest the sufferings of Albinus (in his opinion an oaf with simple passions and a solid, too solid, knowlege [sic] of painting), who thought, poor man, that he had touched the very depths of human distress; whereas Rex reflected – with a sense of pleasant anticipation – that, far from being the limit, it was merely the first item in the program of a roaring comedy at which he, Rex, had been reserved a place in the stage manager's private box. (182–3)

Even though the focus of Rex's observation is Albinus, his humour can also be directed towards himself. It is not devoid of self-reflexivity, as the association with a Bergsonian comic would imply. Rex's ability to 't[ake] life lightly' (183) enables him to laugh at ridiculousness in his own life too.

Rex as observer of the absurdity of life can also take on a more active role, furthering an ongoing impulse to exaggerate the natural movement of life, exactly as he would on paper in his caricatures. The movement of exaggeration is also complemented by a movement of inversion. In the passage from page 143, the movement of humour described by Rex is not solely descending. The image of the wheel also evokes the wheel of fortune, which has the capacity to invert positions. Rex's 'little touch' is not so little – thanks to his intervention in the story, the wheel of fortune inverts the positions not only of Albinus and Rex, but also of Margot, Elizabeth and Irma.[16] The movement of inversion of the wheel of fortune and Rex's role in encouraging that movement point to the significance of chance and of games in the novel. In Chapter 18, just before explaining Rex's definition of humour, the narrator stresses the importance of card games, and especially poker, in Rex's life[17]:

> Having cultivated a penchant for bluff since his tenderest age, no wonder his favorite card-game was poker! He played it whenever he could get partners; and he played it in his *dreams*: with historical characters or some distant cousin of his, long dead, whom in *real life* he never remembered, or with people who – in *real life* again – would have flatly refused to be in the same room with him. In that *dream* he took up, stacked together, and lifted close to his eyes the five dealt to him, saw with pleasure the joker in cap and bells, and, as he pressed out with a cautious thumb one top corner and then another, he found by degrees that he had five jokers. (141; emphasis added)

The chiasmic movement from dreams to life and life to dreams mimics the revolving movement of the wheel of fortune. More significantly, the passage stresses the need for partners in the game of poker, be they real or fictive, consenting or not. It is clear that the passive, non-consenting Albinus is made to play the same type of game, in real life, which Rex plays in the dream. The game of humour, as Rex understands it, requires a partner such as Albinus, just like a laughing observer needs a Wild Body in the Lewisian framework.

The passage on poker also emphasizes the role of the joker, and even exaggerates it. The character in 'cap and bells' is emblematic of the intersection of humour and games. As a fool or a trickster, the joker is a game changer, able to invert a player's position from one extreme to another. The joker is hidden in the deck of cards just like Rex is concealed from Albinus's life. In the Swiss chalet, Rex enjoys playing the fool next to the blind man, making 'droll gestures' (253) for Margot's amusement, or standing naked in the house (276), visible to spectators but not to his game partner. In that sense, Rex becomes the joker in the author's deck of cards. Rex's absence from Albinus's life in the first third of the novel does not diminish his impact. His existence outside the narrative, initially hidden from the readers as well, creates a structural parallelism with his existence in the darkness that surrounds Albinus for the latter part of the book. Just as in Rex's dream where the jokers are slowly revealed, Rex's presence is also unveiled by two other players: Udo Conrad, who unknowingly exposes Margot and Rex's relationship to Albinus (222), and Paul, Albinus's brother-in-law, who comes to Switzerland to bring Albinus back to Berlin (277).

Connolly reads this passage as the end of Rex's 'reign', signalling his failure to recognize the limits of his 'directorial' impulses and to acknowledge his role as puppet (121–4). Yet, Rex does not claim to have the level of control of a director. On the contrary, he insists on the smallness of his impact and on his position as observer, while using his power as strategically as possible. His role of observer is particularly clear at the Swiss chalet, where his direct interventions with Albinus are sparse and his main 'interaction' with him consists in 'watching [Albinus's] movements' (258). Rex is attracted both by the details of Albinus's movements and by the overall arc of his trajectory. He does not claim to be the author or the stage manager of the unfolding comedy, but to occupy a position adjacent to the one of stage manager, at a distance from the scene. Even more importantly, when acting as puppet, Rex knows that he is acting like one. Welcoming Margot on her arrival at the Swiss villa with the blind Albinus, he uses the window of the house as a puppet theatre: 'Rex, meanwhile, leaned out of the window and made droll gestures of greeting to Margot: he pressed his hand to his heart and flung out his arms jerkily – it was a capital imitation of Punch – all this of course in dumb show […]' (253). Connolly remarks that a similar scene had occurred with Albinus earlier in the novel: 'Albinus too is depicted in the novel framed by a window and making pantomime gestures; this occurs when he searches for Margot after learning that she has deceived him with Rex' (Connolly 1992: 248; Nabokov [1938] 1960: 223). But whereas Rex is a conscious agent of his dumb show, Albinus is an unconscious actor of the pantomime. Rex and Albinus might both be puppets, but Albinus is incapable of acknowledging it. Like in the Lewisian framework, both the laughing observer and the Wild Body are their creator's 'puppets' (Lewis 1927: 232), but the laughing observer is aware of being one, and thus of being a thing.

The self-consciousness of laughing observers enables them to identify the rules of the game they are part of, and to tamper with them. In the dream poker game, Rex is depicted as a character who has the power to fool others and to change rules, multiplying the number of jokers as he sees fit. In that sense, he can also be read as a figure who is given licence to play with social rules and with social positionings, recalling the Bakhtinian fool figure. The novel plays with associations between the fool and the king, and the possible inversion of their positions. Games can be read as 'a condensed formula of life and of the historic process: fortune, misfortune, gain and loss, crowning and uncrowning [...] dr[awing] the players out of the bounds of everyday life, liberat[ing] them from usual laws and regulations, and replac[ing] established conventions by other lighter conventionalities' (Bakhtin 1984b: 235). In his dream, Rex is playing with King Henry the Eighth, brought back to life for the duration of the game. But even outside the specific game environment, Rex considers his relationship with Albinus to be a game with two players. The onomastic choices and the narrative arc of the novel point at the reversal of Albinus and Rex as players that would switch positions during a game. Albinus, the blind fool, moves from the highest social position – 'He was rich, respectable, happy' (7) – to the lowest, unloved, unhappy, poor, betrayed. Rex arrives in Albinus's life as a somewhat poor artist and reclaims the role of Margot's lover from Albinus while using the man's financial resources to regain an economic standing. Rex is the fool who wishes to take the King's place, and his name 'Rex' insists on the king-like qualities he aims to attain. However, unlike in Bakhtin's vision of the carnival, there is no collective witnessing or endorsement of Albinus's uncrowning. Even if we consider Margot or Paul as witnesses of the reversal of roles, the exchange is not framed within a game whose rules would be shared by all players. Whereas the carnival fool and king are not permanently trapped within their roles, in *Laughter in the Dark*, the reversal of roles also implies Albinus's definitive enclosure within the prison of his body. Indeed, Albinus's literal blindness introduces a new element that impedes him turning back the wheel of fortune and regaining his former position. He has lost his social status and his role as Margot's lover – two aspects that could potentially be regained – but he has also been denied the possibility to perceive the world on the same footing as the other player(s) of the game. His blindness to the rules of the game as well as his physical blindness trap him in a new role and position he does not even perceive. Unlike in the Bakhtinian framework where the collective emphasis implies the sacrifice of any individual perspective, Nabokov's approach, focused on individual upward and downward trajectories and on the successes and failures of each character, allows for Rex's individual perspective to take precedence over Albinus's.

Love is blind; humour has 20/20 vision

Contrary to the bodies of Bakhtinian characters, Albinus's body is thus closed, unable to connect with the outside. His incapacity to communicate is present from the start but the joker's humoristic endeavours encourage a movement towards full enclosure within Albinus's self, to the extent that Rex becomes 'the lens admitting only as much of the real world as Albinus is allowed to see' (Hyde 1977: 71).[18] In the novel, the power of bodies and the absence thereof is expressed through sight. The possibility of seeing conditions the degree of freedom and the power of the characters, while the perception of nuances of colours is an indicator of the characters' agency. The emphasis on colours is accentuated in the 1938 version by onomastic changes. Kretschmar of the 1932 version becomes Albinus in 1938. Albinus 'the white' contains all the colours within himself, but only through the intervention of a prism can they be revealed. When Rex pushes Margot to alter the colours of Albinus's world, he uses her as one such prism. Albinus becomes both a prison enclosing the colours of the world and the white canvas on which Rex can produce his artistic vision. As Hyde puts it, 'his art being that of the caricaturist', Rex 'needs material like Albinus' (1977: 69). Through humoristic processes, Albinus's body is objectified; its limitations are highlighted and used by the other characters to shape the life they desire.

The possibility to do so derives from Albinus's lack of awareness of his surroundings, but also from his lack of bodily awareness. The consciousness that is necessary to create humour and that Rex possesses contrasts with Albinus's disregard for his own materiality. The distinction between laughing observers and Wild Bodies relies precisely on the formers' bodily awareness, and the latters' lack thereof. More precisely, laughing observers perceive the comic because they can see themselves and their fellow human beings for what they truly are: things behaving as persons (Lewis 1927: 246). As the novel progresses, Rex never loses the sense of his materiality, while Albinus is increasingly enclosed within his materiality, until the almost inevitable completion of his enclosure, 'bound in moss' (7) within his body. A stylistic shift on the last page of the novel accentuates this movement. While the incipit played with the codes of the fairy tale, the explicit uses formal aspects of the dramatic genre that introduce a break in the fluid narration of the novel. The two last paragraphs, immediately following the description of Albinus's death by gunshot, are stage directions explicitly introduced as such – 'Stage-directions for last silent scene: door – wide open. Table – thrust away from it' (292) – that go on for a dozen lines. These mock stage directions, as well as the mention 'the end', make explicit the processes of fictional creation and Albinus's existence as a character. Albinus as a puppet of Rex is now pictured as his creator's puppet, in a process that recalls the ending of *La danse de Gengis Cohn*. Albinus's author does not appear explicitly as the figure of the author does in Gary's novel or in other Nabokov novels such as *Bend Sinister*, but the actions of the creator are revealed through the intrusion of the dramatic form in the novelistic fluidity. The stylistic shift also allows the narrator to further externalize the novelistic character and emphasizes Albinus's materiality. In the end, Albinus, who is not even named anymore, is pictured as a doll being put to rest, a physical body equal to the objects that surround it (292). The explicit is thus the culmination of Albinus's entrapment in his body. Albinus has been gradually unable to connect his subjective perception to the external world, to the point of being entirely expelled from this world created for him by others and the stage directions 'tactfully make the point that with the extinction of his point of view there is no novel' (Hyde 1977: 72). The enterprise of the novel depended on Albinus's human point of view and cannot exist without him.

The final scene evacuates Albinus's subjective and flawed self-perception from the novel, to focus only on what can be seen if one backs up and looks at the scene from an external point of view. The directions switch back and forth between what is visible (the colours of the clothes, the presence of a lady's glove, a colored label from 'Rouginard') and what is invisible ('automatic pistol not visible', the miniatures that have been removed, a porcelain piece that has been displaced). The distanciation from the scene also shows the entirety of a body at a glance, thus forming a 'synthetic' image. The final stylistic shifts actualize both elements of Rex's definition of caricature: its synthetic nature and the contrast between cruelty and credulity. The cruelty of Albinus's death is directly related to his credulity throughout the novel. His death is also cruel as a result of its ridiculousness and its lack of dignity. Once again, the ridiculous aspect of Albinus's death exemplifies Rex's reflection on the matter:

> 'Death', he had said on another occasion, 'seems to be merely a bad habit, which nature is at present powerless to overcome. I once had a friend – a beautiful boy full of life, with the face of an angel and the muscles of a panther. He cut himself while opening a tin of preserved peaches – you know, the large, soft, slippery kind that plap in the mouth and slither down. He died a few days later of blood poisoning. Fatuous, isn't it? And yet ... yes, it is strange, but true, that, viewed as a work of art, the shape of his life would not have been so perfect had he been left to grow old. Death often is the point of life's joke'. (181-2)

Seen through Rex's eyes, Albinus's death is the point of the joke set up by the author of Albinus's life. In that regard, Rex is a key element of the joke; he is the 'tin of preserved peaches' that cuts Albinus's skin.[19]

Albinus's death, read as a consequence of his own blindness to the external world and insensitivity to the interiority of those around him, and propelled by Rex's sense of humour, exemplifies the complex trajectory of humour that encompasses three types of movements. His death is the logical conclusion to the downward movement of 'life [...] slid[ing] helplessly into caricature' (143), helped by the humorist's own personal touch. It is just as much the logical conclusion of the inversion of the wheel of fortune within the framework of a game played by a king and a fool. Finally, it exemplifies the paradoxical movement of the 'super-humour' described by Rex, that takes the form of a syllogism: 'Thesis: Uncle made himself up as a burglar (a laugh for the children); antithesis: it *was* a burglar (a laugh for the reader); synthesis: it still was Uncle (fooling the reader)' (143; original emphasis). The oppositional movement between the thesis and the antithesis of the humoristic syllogism is not solved by a synthesis that eliminates the opposition. The synthesis rather confirms the opposition and the co-existence of two seemingly incompatible aspects, that is, two aspects that cannot be perceived from the same point of observation. As Stuart observes, the whole novel can be read as an illustration of the syllogism: 'This brief dialectic loosely parallels the structure of the "joke" that happens to Albinus, in which Rex adds his "little touch": Albinus dresses himself up as lover in a film; it *is* a lover in the film; it is, as the bullet enters the flesh, still Albinus' (101; original emphasis). Focusing on the ending in particular, we can say that Albinus dresses himself up as Margot's murderer; he is actually Margot's murderer (since his death brings the destruction of his fantasy of Margot, the only Margot accessible to him); he is still Albinus, and thus dies in his attempt to kill his lover.[20]

The death scene conjoins the three movements of humour: downward movement, inversion and dialectical oscillation synthesized in the dynamic stability of two incompatible states that recalls Pirandello's 'equilibrio mobile' ['mobile balance'] (Pirandello [1920] 1992: 144). All three converge in Albinus's imprisonment within his body, an imprisonment that progresses by degrees in the course of the novel, and that is both finalized and put to an end by the death of the character. Paradoxically, Albinus's death means both the possibility and the impossibility of humour. The possibility, because it completes and informs the movements of the humoristic trajectory. The joke is actualized only when the point is given, and the movement of the joke is fully understood only when one knows the ending. But death is also the impossibility of the perpetuation of humour, since Albinus's death breaks all three movements for good. Like Moscarda's shelter, Albinus's dead body completes the humoristic trajectory, while signalling the end of humour. The enclosure and the end of humour are the conditions of its possibility.

Guareschi's inner prisoner: Companion selves and synecdochical selves

In Guareschi's fiction, the condition of bodily imprisonment as the impetus for the development of humour is illustrated by resorting to a form of duality that complements the two configurations analysed so far.[21] The humoristic process is built through a dialogue between two autobiographical characters: Guareschi's *persona*, who is generally given the narrative voice, and 'Giovannino' (or 'Giovannino fatto d'aria'), who dialogues with him. In his war writings, they are presented respectively as his bodily and his immaterial self, or the body and the soul, but their clear-cut separation is challenged by later writings. From 1945 to his death in 1968, Guareschi also resorted to the image of the moustache as a material representation of 'Giovannino fatto d'aria'. The separation between the body and the soul no longer stands, and the representation of the body of Guareschi's *persona* becomes a site of cohabitation of the two identities, within which humour becomes possible.

The existence of two autobiographical characters stems from Guareschi's internment in war camps, narrativized in *Diario clandestino*. The experience acted as a turning point in his life and in the development of his work as an author and a caricaturist. Perry shows how it led to Guareschi's discovery of humour, in contrast to his former use of the comic (see Perry 2001 and 2007). Imprisonment, he argues, made humour possible because it 'figuratively split him in two' (2007: 47). Perry also notes how the two selves become permanent features of the author's work, that is permeated by a 'leitmotif of doubling' (Perry 2007: x). As he remarks, the short piece 'Finalmente libero', from *Diario clandestino*, best represents the author's new awareness of his divided self (Perry 2007: 47). 'Finalmente libero' inverts the notion of the imprisoned self: it is not the bodily self imprisoned in the camps, but his inner, immaterial one that should be considered a 'prisoner'. The experience of imprisonment actually liberates this character, formerly trapped in his body, his society and his way of conceiving life: 'C'era qualcuno che era prigioniero di me stesso. Stava chiuso entro di me come in uno scafandro, e io lo opprimevo con la mia carne e con le mie consuetudini. Egli si affacciava ai miei occhi per vedere, e i suoi occhi erano acuti, ma il cristallo dei miei era appannato dai grassi vapori del vivere convenzionale.' (Guareschi [1949] 2009: 142) ['Somebody was a prisoner within me. He was shut up as if in a diving-bell, and my fleshly garments and habits oppressed him. He looked out of my eyes, and his sight was keen, but my eyes were clouded over with the thick steam of conventional living' ([1949] 1958: 120)]. In a chiasmic fashion typical of Guareschi's style, the short piece inverts the terms of imprisonment, locating freedom in the self imprisoned in the camps, and imprisonment in the 'fleshly shell' that Guareschi is afraid to find once he comes home: 'Ritroverò l'altro me stesso? Mi aspetta forse fuori del reticolato per riprendermi ancora? Ritornerò laggiù oppresso sempre dal mio involucro di carne e di abitudini?/Buon Dio, se dev'essere così, prolunga all'infinito la mia prigionia. Non togliermi la mia libertà.' (Guareschi [1949] 2009: 143) ['Shall I encounter my other self again? Will he be waiting, outside the enclosure, to re-possess me? Shall I go home weighed down by my old, fleshly shell?/If so, dear God, let my imprisonment never come to an end. Don't take my freedom away' ([1949] 1958: 121)]. The splitting of the self also makes humour possible, since the 'inner prisoner' becomes a tool to look at himself from a distanced point of view. The Guareschian dialogue thus illustrates the Freudian idea that humour necessitates a dialogue within the self. At the same time, it puts to the test the power dynamics implied by the Freudian notion, as well as its past-oriented temporal framework.

In the pieces considered in this section, Guareschi's *persona* is confronted with the difficulty to translate his 'freedom of imprisonment' (Perry 2012: 67) to Italian society after his return from the camps, something the author had anticipated in some stories of *Diario clandestino*. Guareschi also spent four hundred and nine days in Parma's San Francesco del Prato prison in 1954–1955, following a questionable trial for defamation against former Prime Minister Alcide De Gasperi (see Perry 2005 and 2016; Franzinelli 2014). The writings considered here are therefore written after two crucial episodes of imprisonment. The postwar pieces confirm the Guareschian conceptualization of imprisonment along a continuum, spanning from the internment camps to society, to the body. While the modality of imprisonment varies, its relationship with humour remains constant. The conception of the body as a prison creates the need for a dialogue between two selves that results in the creation of humour. I'll consider two main types of configurations of this dialogue. In the first case, the selves evolve in parallel, as two distinct characters who can dialogue with one another, as in the piece 'Colloquio nel bagno' (1955).[22] In the other case, the relationship is one of imbrication between an inner and a bodily self. In 'Era giovane, bellissimo...' (1967), the relationship manifests itself through the synecdoche of the moustache, which illustrates the symbolic intrusion of wartime 'Giovannino' in postwar bourgeois Guareschi and serves as a reminder of his experience of the camps and of his discovery of humour.

Selves in dialogue – 'Colloquio nel bagno'

'Finalmente libero' introduced an unnamed entity that becomes one of the selves central to Guareschi's writing. It generally takes the name of 'Giovannino fatto d'aria', as in the piece 'Colloquio nel bagno'. Built as a dialogue between Guareschi's *persona* (who is also the narrator) and 'il Giovannino fatto d'aria',[23] 'Colloquio nel bagno' was published in the journal *Candido*[24] in 1955, after Guareschi was released from the San Francesco del Prato prison in Parma but at the beginning of his conditional release. Parts of it were published in 1993 in *Chi sogna nuovi gerani? Autobiografia* (497–9), an 'autobiography' constituted of writings of the author compiled and completed by Alberto and Carlotta Guareschi, and again in a more complete form in 1989 in *Ritorno alla base* (206–13).[25] In *Chi sogna nuovi gerani?*, the 'colloquio' is followed by a series of 'Lettere dal carcere' ['Letters from prison'] that also appeared in *Candido*. Since the 'letters' were not written while Guareschi was in San Francesco, the ironic title of the series highlights how the author felt about his conditional release. Overturning again the conceptions of the prison and of freedom, he explains: 'Non mi è facile ritornare alla libertà, sia pur vigilata. [...] Non ho sentito il carcere quand'ero a San Francesco: lo sento adesso che sono a casa' (Guareschi [1993] 2009: 497) ['It is not easy for me to go back to freedom, even if monitored. [...] I have not felt the prison when I was in San Francesco: I feel it now that I am home'].

As its title indicates, 'Colloquio nel bagno' ['Interview in the bathroom'] takes place in the closed space of the bathroom, in the Guareschis' house. The opening lines of the piece immediately picture the bathroom as the only space where the dialogue between the two parts of Guareschi can take place, the only space of freedom in spatial containment:

Ogni tanto io mi ritrovo con l'altro me stesso e, stavolta, il Giovannino fatto d'aria era ad aspettarmi alle Roncole,[26] dentro lo stanzino del bagno.
–Con questa confusione di fotografi e di giornalisti – mi spiegò – era l'unico posto nel quale potevo sperare di rimanere solo con te.
Chiusi a chiave l'uscio perché niente può fermare la marcia di un fotografo, poi parlammo. (Guareschi [1989] 2011: 206)

[Every now and then I find myself with the other part of myself and, this time, the Giovannino made of air was waiting for me at Roncole, inside the small toilet room.
–With this confusion of photographers and journalists – he explained – it was the only place in which I could hope to stay alone with you.
I locked the door since nothing can stop the march of a photographer, then we talked.]

The bathroom is immediately set in opposition with the bustle of Guareschi's public – and publicized – life, represented by the figures of the photographers and the journalists that await his comments on his release from prison. The bathroom is a mirror image of the prison: it is the only space where Guareschi can choose to be alone, and the only space for which he can control the access. It is thus where the dialogue with himself can occur, and where a humoristic relationship between parts of himself can be built. The last line of the incipit acts as a signal of the spatial and conceptual shift between the social Guareschi and the private one,[27] marking the beginning of the extended dialogue with the self. Guareschi indeed indicates that he has not only entered the new spatial setting, but also taken control of it, locking the door from the inside, and upturning the dynamic of being locked in, which was his daily life for more than a year. The last line also signals the beginning of humour, made at the expense of the mediatic practices Guareschi criticizes. He is indeed hiding from the unstoppable photographers ('niente può fermare la marcia di un fotografo' ['nothing can stop the march of a photographer']) who are depicted as driven by their hunger for scoops. Yet Guareschi himself was one of the most read media voices of postwar Italy. It is even because of this importance that the publication of the De Gasperi letters had such consequences. After having been extremely influential in the 1948 election of the Democrazia Cristiana (DC) led by De Gasperi, Guareschi was indeed sent to court for libel for having published letters he thought were written by De Gasperi, who was asking the Allies to bombard Rome. Thus, the remarks about the impact of the public gaze must be integrated within the framework not only of criticism, but also of self-criticism and self-observation.

The 'Colloquio' is set at the boundary between public and private, and between Guareschi's satirical practice and his self-criticizing humoristic practice.

The dialogue between Guareschi and Giovannino can be read as the narrativization of the process of coping with the year in prison, through the humoristic dialogue. With Giovannino's help, Guareschi reflects on his sojourn in the San Francesco prison, comparing it to his time in Second World War prisoner-of-war camps. During their conversation, the comparison between present and past leads to an erasure of the period of imprisonment in Italy, which paradoxically highlights it. In order to deal with the discordance between the past experience and the desire to erase it from memory or from narratives, the two characters also discuss the embodiment of the experiences of imprisonment. Guareschi's body, enclosed in the bathroom, becomes a site of integration of the two periods of incarceration, and the space of the bathroom, a setting in which the private Guareschi can materialize his feeling of imprisonment through a dialogue with his immaterial self, using as we will see his 'mal di stomaco' ['stomach pain'] as a material reminder concretizing his feelings.

As in the incipit, the rejoinders between Giovannino and Guareschi enable the author to comment on the same element according to two different perspectives, represented by the two voices. The initial and last pages of the text deal with the experience of the Italian prison; the middle section goes back to the times of the war camps to draw a parallel between the two. After recalling a song Guareschi sang in the camps, both characters comment on the time that has elapsed:

> Il Giovannino fatto d'aria sospirò:
> –Altri tempi! ...
> Sospirai anch'io:
> –Altri tedeschi! (Guareschi [1989] 2011: 209)

> [The Giovannino made of air sighed:
> –Different times!
> I also sighed:
> –Different Germans!]

The four lines are built symmetrically. The characters sigh and comment on the difference between past and present. Giovannino's perspective is nostalgic: born in the camps, the character who just recalled with enthusiasm ('il Giovannino fatto d'aria si era eccitato' (208) ['the Giovannino made of air got excited']) the song he used to sing clearly thinks about the camp temporality and community with longing. Guareschi's remark is more critical and ironic: the 'Germans' are now within the country, and even include his former allies. The clash between nostalgia and criticism creates the humoristic movement of the piece, which can be read from both perspectives simultaneously. The association of the two perceptions also leads to the equation of the Italian State and of Nazi Germany and, at a personal level, of the war imprisonment and the imprisonment for libel.

The comparison between the two periods also introduces a phenomenon frequent in Guareschi: the juxtaposition of two levels of temporality that leads to the erasure of the intervening period. Indeed, immediately after in the dialogue, Giovannino tries to access Guareschi's prison time suffering, but the latter elliptically diverts the question and eludes the period of the San Francesco prison:

> Il Giovannino d'aria mi guardò con apprensione:
> –Hai sofferto molto?
> –Non mi ricordo – risposi. – Dovrei sfogliare il mio quaderno di appunti.
> –C'è, almeno, nella tua vicenda carceraria, qualche episodio che t'è rimasto impresso?
> –Sì: un pomeriggio, improvvisamente, mi trovai chiuso nel carcere di San Francesco e mi sentii un po' perplesso: ma, poco dopo, mentre il detenuto-barbiere stava radendomi, arrivò il Giudice di Sorveglianza e mi disse: 'Appena finisce, prepari la sua roba per uscire…' Ed eccomi qui.
> Il Giovannino fatto d'aria riconobbe che la storia era curiosa, poi mi domandò se mi erano stati usati particolari riguardi. (Guareschi [1989] 2011: 209)
>
> [The airy Giovannino looked at me with apprehension:
> –Did you suffer a lot?
> –I don't remember – I replied. – I would have to leaf through my notebook.
> –Is there at least in your carceral affair any episode that stayed impressed in your memory?
> –Yes: one afternoon, all of a sudden, I found myself locked in the San Francesco prison and I felt somewhat puzzled: but, shortly after, while the barber-inmate was shaving me, the Supervisory Judge arrived and told me: 'As soon as you're done, prepare your stuff to leave…' And here I am.
> The Giovannino made of air admitted the story was odd and asked me if I had had right to any special provision.]

Giovannino insists on the time of the suffering both at the beginning and at the end of this section of the conversation, asking whether Guareschi has suffered and enquiring into the specifics of his conditions as inmate. On the other hand, Guareschi erases the period of his incarceration from his narrative, in a similar way as he did in 'Lettere al postero' when he told his story to the child addressee (see Chapter 2). Although Guareschi ends up recalling certain aspects of his life in prison, the narrative separation between his voice and Giovannino's allows him to be pictured as reluctantly communicating his experience to his readers.

The enclosed bathroom thus sets the stage for a reconfiguration of the temporalities of imprisonment. Like the war camp in *Diario clandestino*, the space of the bathroom – and the discursive space of the dialogue with Giovannino – condenses the narrator's experience and leads to the reintegration of the narrator's past in his bodily self. Guareschi's inner prisoner, first described in 'Finalmente libero', is still a part of him that needs to be conveyed and expressed by the character. Unlike the 'Giovannino fatto d'aria', Guareschi has a body and the text reasserts his embodiment. Both Giovannino and Guareschi may 'sigh', but only Guareschi's sigh is marked by lived experiences of imprisonment that left physical traces. Indeed, the text keeps reasserting the differences in the embodiment of imprisonment.

> Il Giovannino d'aria mi osservò attentamente:
> –In compenso sei più grasso di allora.
> –Non 'più grasso': più pesante – precisai. (Guareschi [1989] 2011: 207)
>
> [The Giovannino made of air looked at me attentively:
> –On the other hand, you are fatter than before.
> –Not 'fatter': heavier – I specified.]

While Giovannino highlights Guareschi's bodily transformation, Guareschi immediately transmutes it from the physical ('grasso') to the immaterial ('pesante'), thus granting a symbolic sense to the physical attribute.

The transition from physical to symbolic is at play in the most important series of images of the embodiment of the imprisonment, built around Guareschi's 'mal di stomaco' ['stomach pain'].[28] As for Moscarda (see Chapter 3), Guareschi's capacity to feel pain is associated with his sense of self. In rejoinders about the use of bicarbonate to ease stomach pain, Giovannino leads Guareschi to explain why his pain is so important to his self-conception and to his conception of freedom:

> Aprii lo zaino[29] e presi a frugarvi dentro per trovare il barattolo del bicarbonato.
> –Quanti chili ne hai usato? – s'informò il Giovannino fatto d'aria.
> –Poca roba e soltanto in principio – risposi mostrandogli il barattolo quasi pieno. – Ma, adesso, devo ritrovare il mio mal di stomaco. Mi manca. [...] [P]er quattrocentonove giorni, i miei pensieri hanno appartenuto all'amministrazione statale, e, tre volte ogni notte, le guardie venivano in cella a controllare i sogni

che io sognavo per conto dello Stato. Adesso, per trovare pensieri miei, ho bisogno di ritrovare il mio mal di stomaco. (Guareschi [1989] 2011: 207–8)

[I opened the backpack and started to rummage in it to find the bicarbonate jar.
–How many kilos have you used? – enquired the Giovannino made of air.
–Not much and only at the beginning – I replied, showing him the jar almost full.
– But now, I have to go back to my stomach pain. I miss it. […] [F]or four hundred nine days, my thoughts belonged to the state administration and, three times a night, the guards came in the cell to inspect the dreams I dreamed on behalf of the State. Now, to regain my thoughts, I need to get my stomach pain back.]

A few weeks later, in *Candido*'s new section 'Lettere dal carcere', Guareschi tells his fictional wife Margherita that he has finally found his 'mal di stomaco':

Ho ritrovato il mio mal di stomaco. In questi lunghi mesi di riposo si è irrobustito e mi sveglia tre volte ogni notte. Ha preso il posto delle tre ronde notturne di San Francesco.
   E, ogni volta, mi alzo e porto a spasso il mio mal di stomaco per la casa deserta e silenziosa fino a quando non si riaddormenta. Mi pare di avere un bambino da cullare e mi sento meno solo e meno prigioniero. ([1993] 2009: 504)[30]

[I got my stomach pain back. In those long months of rest, it got stronger and it wakes me up three times a night. It took the place of San Francesco's three night patrols.
   And, every time, I get up and I walk my stomach pain in the deserted and silent house until it goes back to sleep. I feel like I have a baby to cradle and I feel less alone and less of a prisoner.]

The reintegration of personal, physical pain into Guareschi's body becomes a symbol of the capacity to conceptualize oneself as a free individual. Even if Guareschi is not accompanied by Giovannino in this particular letter, the presence of the split self is instrumental in his self-construction. The stomach pain is a symbol of the past and of Giovannino, this other part of Guareschi. It enables him to enter in dialogue, and to feel 'meno solo' ['less alone']. His stomach pain expresses itself as a separate entity inside of him and trapped by his body. Paradoxically, this entrapment of an inner entity prompts Guareschi to move towards a stronger feeling of freedom (or a lesser feeling of entrapment), not unlike in 'Finalmente libero'.

   'Colloquio nel bagno' thus concretizes the humoristic split selves, thematizing the psychic process of humour through literary creation. In a similar way as 'Finalmente libero', the portrayal of two parts of one's self in distinct literary characters creates jest out of a distressing situation. In Freud's explanation, the communication between the two figures is not made on an equal footing. Freud makes clear that the part of the self that soothes the other part has a position of superiority that grants it authority and thus the capacity to reinforce the distance between itself and the inferior part. Indeed, the two instances are compared to a father and a son, where the father smiles at the triviality of the suffering of his child (Freud [1927] 1961: 163). Guareschi appears to be such a figure of authority. As both character and narrator of the story, he has the control over the narrative. Being the only embodied character, he also has control over the actions, and especially over deciding to enter and exit the space of the bathroom.

However, the positioning of the two characters is not as simple as that. As in other stories, Giovannino can be perceived as the highest moral figure, who is to be consulted in the bathroom (as one would look in a mirror to talk to oneself and make sense of a situation). He also has his own agency, deciding when to appear in Guareschi's life. If a correspondence with the Freudian framework should be drawn, we would have to relate Guareschi to the ego and Giovannino to the super-ego, and their conflict to the one between the external and internal worlds:

> Whereas the ego is essentially the representative of the external world, of reality, the super-ego stands in contrast to it as the representative of the internal world, the id. Conflicts between the ego and the ideal will, as we are now prepared to find, ultimately reflect the contrast between what is real and what is psychical, between the external world and the internal world. (Freud 1923: 26)

Even more importantly, the two characters are depicted as complementary and at the same level, able to build a true dialogue together. Of course, Giovannino is both a past self and an internal presence within Guareschi, that somehow speaks through Guareschi's public voice. Still, the author makes a point of representing his social *persona* and Giovannino as two distinct selves. The internal relationship is hinted at, but the external representation of both selves dominates in this story.

Synecdochical selves – Giovannino and his moustache

The dynamics between Guareschi and his stomach pain are exemplary of a subtler form of co-habitation of selves that materializes the immaterial but that does not embody the two selves in two distinct characters. Another image that is often used to give shape to the other self is the moustache. A passage from a late text gives an idea of this pervasive use.

In *Vita con Gio'*, an anthology collecting stories published in the magazine *Oggi* from 1964 to 1968, Guareschi uses the character of Gio', to contrast his point of view with the one of the new generation. Gio' (short for Gioconda) is the Guareschis' hired help or 'giovane collaboratrice familiare' ['young family collaborator']. In the story 'Era giovane, bellissimo... ' ('He was young, beautiful...'), which is illustrated in the anthology by a self-portrait of an angry-looking Guareschi displaying an enormous, ruffled moustache, the characters of Guareschi and his fictional wife Margherita recount Guareschi's prewar youth, when he used to chase young women, something that Gio' has a hard time believing:

> Gio' scoppiò in una risata:
> 'Lui[31] correva dietro alle ragazze?' domandò ululando.
> 'Sì' spiegai: 'ma non era una gran fatica perché io marciavo sempre in bicicletta.'
> 'Con quei baffi lì' gridò la ragazza.
> 'No' intervenne Margherita. 'Allora non li aveva. Se li è fatti crescere in campo di concentramento per avere qualcosa cui aggrapparsi quando la fame gli toglieva la forza dalle gambe.'
> 'Io non me lo so immaginare senza baffi!' disse Gio'. ([1995] 2011: 431–2)[32]
>
> [Gio' burst into laughter:
> 'You ran after the girls?' she asked, howling.
> 'Yes', I explained, 'but it wasn't too much of an effort since I always got around by bicycle.'
> 'With *that* moustache', shrieked the girl.
> 'No', Margherita intervened. 'He didn't have it then. He grew it in concentration camps to have something to grab onto when hunger took the strength out of his legs.'
> 'I can't imagine him without a moustache!' said Gio'. (emphasis added)]

The dialogue between Guareschi, Margherita and Gio' gives us an entry point into the use of the trope of the moustache. The first thing to note is that the moustache immediately opens up a temporal breach. In terms of Guareschi's personal past, it indicates how war imprisonment was a turning point that left a permanent trace in the protagonist's life – a trace that is made visible by the moustache. Through it, Guareschi's personal life can thus enter the social sphere.

Thanks to this bodily trace, Gio', for whom the moustache is associated with a bourgeois, unattractive lifestyle, highlights the clash of generations that is at the core of the *Oggi* pieces. Gio's remark can be read as a statement on Italy's history, or rather on the postwar perception of this recent history. To Gio', her boss cannot be anything but a moustachioed middle-aged bourgeois who has had no past as a fetching young man, and even less as a prisoner of war. 'Io non me lo so immaginare senza baffi!' illustrates the new generation's incapacity to imagine Italy 'without a moustache', that is prewar and wartime Italy, ungraspable epochs to the 'collaboratrice familiare'.[33]

A feature of the passage is also Margherita's role. Indeed, the passage differs from many of the author's reflections on his past in that it is not a direct self-reflection between Guareschi's *persona* of the present and his *persona* of the past. The remark on the moustache is mediated by Margherita, who has known both 'Giovannino senza baffi' – an expression that has become a common way to indicate the prewar period of Guareschi's life and works – and 'Giovannino con baffi' after the return from the camps in 1945. As an external observer, she is able to have a clear picture of the transformation. Unlike Guareschi, however, Margherita has not been there to witness the moment of the growth itself, and her construction of her husband's transformation must be built without access to the process of transformation. This absence from Guareschi's story in those two years thus stresses the gender division of the experience of the war, that Margherita spent in Italy, waiting for the uncertain return of her husband and giving birth in the meantime to their second child. This experience is at times acknowledged by Guareschi:

> Una settimana dopo, il 9 settembre del 1943, partivo in vagone-bestiame alla volta di un Lager in Polonia. Tornai a casa esattamente due anni dopo, nel settembre 1945, agile come una gazzella e con due meravigliosi baffi: ero quarantasei chili, però Margherita, che era ancora più magra di me, si limitò a rallegrarsi per il mio bell'aspetto. ([1995] 2011: 118)[34]
>
> [A week later, on September 9, 1943, I left on a livestock wagon in the direction of a Lager in Poland. I came back home exactly two years later, in September 1945, agile like a gazelle and with a magnificent moustache: I weighed forty-six kilograms, but Margherita, who was even skinnier than I was, limited herself to cheering up at my nice look.]

The two characters share the bodily imprint of the hardships of the war. While the imprint on Margherita's body remains enclosed within the domestic sphere, the imprint on Guareschi's becomes a social and political symbol forever recalling his choice of 'voluntary imprisonment'. In the context of the lack of recognition given to the IMI's role as another form of resistance, reclaiming the imprint left by one's decision becomes another political choice. The 'magnificent moustache' is even depicted as a war medal, earned through military valour and to be worn proudly – it becomes a visual mark of a recognition that the Italian state has refused to the IMI:

> Costretto per due mesi nel Lager a non potermi radere e guardandomi alla fine in uno specchio, scopro di possedere una pessima barba da venditore ambulante e due ottimi baffi da 'Romanzo di un giovane povero'.[35] Detestando il vagabondaggio e adorando tutto ciò che è romantico, elimino – appena possibile – la barba e mi tengo i baffi curandoli con amore perché, mentre senza baffi mi detestavo, con i baffi mi sono simpatico… Me li sono guadagnati onorevolmente e ho il diritto di portarli a naso alto.[36]

> [Forced not to shave for two months in the Lager and looking at myself in a mirror at the end, I discovered I possessed an awful peddler's beard and an excellent moustache worthy of the *Roman d'un jeune homme pauvre*. Detesting vagrancy and adoring everything that is romantic, I removed – as soon as it was possible – the beard, and I kept the moustache, nursing it with love because, while without a moustache I detested myself, with a moustache I like myself… I earned it honourably and I have the right to wear it with my nose held high.]

Speaking through Guareschi's body is this other Giovannino forever represented by the trace and only waiting to emerge again. Going back to Margherita's comment ('Se li è fatti crescere in campo di concentramento per avere qualcosa cui aggrapparsi quando la fame gli toglieva la forza dalle gambe.' ['He grew it in concentration camps to have something to grab onto when hunger took the strength out of his legs.']), we can see how the moustache becomes a leitmotiv illustrating inner strength.[37] The paradoxical image created by Margherita – of a man relying on a part of his body at the moment when his body itself is failing – is made possible by the split enacted within the self through the humoristic process. Margherita's sentence is a semantic syllepsis, that is both realistic (a man is grabbing his moustache in despair) and surrealistic (a man is suspending himself on his moustache when his legs grow too weak). It juxtaposes two incompatible conceptions of the body: one that is unifying, and one where the moustache and the man pertain to two different yet inseparable realms.

The humoristic image therefore underlines the liminal status of the moustache, pictured as almost outside one's body while central to it. An external tool to sustain oneself, the moustache is also an expression of interiority, the externalization of an internal self. From the moment of the camps onwards, the moustache acts as a ventriloquist, expressing itself from inside a Guareschi-puppet. Recalling 'Finalmente libero', the moustache concretizes the inner self trapped within the bourgeois crust. Going back to the role of political imprisonment in Guareschi's development of humour, I read the moustache as the trace that remains from the process of humour that has split the self in two. If, as Freud posits, humour arises when the super-ego addresses itself to the ego to soothe it, we can read Guareschi's use of this trope both as a reminder of this past process and as a tool to externalize again the inner prisoner. In the fiction, there is thus an extension of the humoristic process in time; it is not considered only as an instantaneous event, but it can reverberate through time. In the threefold conversation between Guareschi, Gio' and Margherita, humour displaces the inner transformation on the social and political levels, while creating a comic clash between the perspective of the young and of the mature.

In the texts analysed, Giovannino and the moustache can be read as fictionalized super-egos. The relationship between Guareschi and Giovannino (or the moustache synecdoche) enacts the process of humour, where the super-ego soothes the ego to help it live in the real world without being broken by painful affects. Some differences between the Freudian framework and the Guareschian use of the double image however arise.

First, as I have underlined in the initial analysis, the relationship between the split selves is one of complicity rather than domination. In *The Ego and the Id*, the super-ego is described as a 'tyrant', giving 'dictatorial' imperatives, a severe and aggressive master to the ego (Freud 1923: 43, 45, 46). This relationship of power gives rise to the ego's sense of guilt (41). It is true that the super-ego has a more comforting role in 'Der Humor', something that indeed puzzles Freud: 'If it is really the super-ego which, in humour, speaks such kindly words of comfort to the intimidated ego, this will teach us that we have still a great deal to learn about the nature of the super-ego' (166). The relationship between the Guareschian selves retains a form of hierarchy in that the figure of Giovannino and the image of the moustache are given moral supremacy. This supremacy, however, does not lead to the diminishment of the other self. The *persona* Guareschi is not a representation of an 'intimidated ego'. The Guareschian dynamic thus removes the guilt or intimidation present in the Freudian system. The role of Guareschi's

Catholic faith in his literary creation can explain the positioning of the super-ego figure as a form of internal guide.[38] Freud also points to the connection between the super-ego and religion (Freud 1923: 27), but once again, the development of religion is put into relation with the role of authority figures and not that of a moral guide as is the case for Guareschi. By giving the role of collaborator to the thematized 'super-ego', Guareschi gives a positive value to this psychic instance, transforming the negative image of the 'dictator', 'master' or controlling ventriloquist into one of a non-paternalistic, internal beacon that works with the bodily self to survive hardships through humour.

The different quality of the relationship in Guareschi is intimately related to the second major difference with the Freudian theory: the shift in temporal framework. For Freud, the super-ego is a memorial trace of the past, an ideal image of the ego (the 'ego ideal' or 'ideal ego' is the other name of the super-ego) formed before the constitution of the ego as a definite entity (Freud 1923: 38). In temporal terms, the humoristic process is thus the intrusion of the past, ideal self in the present life of the ego. The weight of the past explains the weight of the authority of the super-ego, always associated with past figures of authorities in the Freudian framework. For Guareschi, Giovannino and the moustache are also traces of the past, memorials, as well as guides. However, the weight of the past does not make of Giovannino a master figure. Contrarily to Freud's, the temporal framework of Guareschian humour gives a prominent place to another component: the future. The 'new generation', incarnated in the character of Gio' of 'Era giovane, bellissimo...', propels the figure of the past into the future. As seen previously, one of Guareschi's definitions of a humorist is indeed: 'chi sa retrodatare le sue azioni e le sue sensazioni'; 'one who can backdate their actions and their sensations' (Guareschi [1989] 2011: 64), that is, one who is able to relativize one's present self by imagining a future self looking at it. The impact of the split part of the self that represents the past in Guareschi is thus given a new dimension thanks to this intrusion of the future. Seen under this new light, Guareschi's humour transforms the father—son dyad of Freud's theory into a new, triadic relationship. The figure of the son (ego) has to be considered, in turn, as a father figure. The new relation is one of father—son(father)—son. Yet the extension of the past into the future is not a smooth process that erases the particularities of the past or of the present. On the contrary, Guareschi's work stresses the importance of the materiality of the body of the present self, which constitutes the link between the past and the future. Guareschi's past self and Giovannino's moustache that shines through him refuse to be fully integrated and overtaken. The materialization of the past in the moustache shows the resistance against a notion of the passing of time as a smooth linear progression. The process of humour and the coexistence of divided selves that it necessitates thus make possible a reconfiguration of the temporal framework that leads to the juxtaposition of temporal periods within the humorist's body and work.

The temporality of humour in imprisonment

Conceiving the body as a site of confinement, this chapter has looked at three pairs of characters whose relationships create conditions of imprisonment for at least one of them. In Gary's *La danse de Gengis Cohn*, the immaterial Jewish *dybbuk* Cohn is initially trapped in the body of former Nazi officer Otto Schatz. The novel insists on Cohn's condition of prisoner by spatializing Schatz's subconscious, described via an isotopy of confinement as a new ghetto for the Jewish character. As the novel unfolds, however, the shared use of humour by Cohn, Schatz and their creator leads to a complete reversal of the situation, where Schatz can be conceived as a prisoner of Cohn, and both as prisoners of their creator. The humoristic discourse plays with the endless reversibility between the characters' positions and creates an oscillation between Cohn's desire to free himself from Schatz (which would entail his second death), and his immortality as a character.

Unlike Gary's characters, Axel Rex and Albert Albinus, protagonists of Nabokov's *Laughter in the Dark*, do not share the same frame of reference, and therefore cannot partake in a conscious collective creation of humour. Albinus's and Rex's visions do not dialogue with one another within the diegesis, yet they become complementary characters for the reader. Rex's main power is to make us see, to act as a counterpoint to Albinus's blindness. Rex's 'seeing, remembering, gathering, and unifying self-activity' allows to produce Albinus's 'finished personality' that 'could not exist, if the other did not create it' (Bakhtin 1990: 35–6). His distanced position, akin to the Lewisian laughing observer's, enables us to see beyond Albinus's vision of his own world. Conversely, Albinus's entrapment within his flawed perspective and within his body makes Rex's role possible. The condition of imprisonment becomes a starting point of humour, that in turn cements this imprisonment. The combination of Albinus's blindness (as a symbol of imprisonment within one's incomplete perspective) and of Rex's external power of observation leads to the rise of cruel humour, setting in motion its downward, inverting and dialectical trajectory towards definitive bodily entrapment. In reducing Albinus to the materiality of his dead body, *Laughter in the Dark* strips the character of his consciousness and of his spiritual dimension, and thus signals the end of art, and of humour.

The articulation between pairs of characters gets further complicated in Guareschi's two sets of imprisonment writings (about Second World War camps and his imprisonment for libel in the 1950s), and particularly in his postwar pieces which challenge the clear-cut separation between bodily and immaterial selves. The body-as-prison creates the need for a humoristic dialogue made possible by the fictional split between 'Giovannino' and 'Guareschi'. In 'Colloquio nel bagno' (1955), the washroom frames the dialogue between Guareschi, freshly out of his cell in the San Francesco del Prato prison, and Giovannino, first encountered in the Nazi camps. As a trace of his past, Giovannino engages Guareschi to compare both experiences of imprisonment. This form of dialogue is reinforced by subtler occurrences in later stories. In 'Era giovane, bellissimo…' (1967), the moustache acts as a synecdoche through which wartime Giovannino intrudes in postwar bourgeois Guareschi. As a reminder of the experience of war imprisonment, the moustache is a trace of the split self which makes humour not only possible but necessary. Through the recourse to images conjoining different conceptions of the body, such as the syllepsis, the body becomes a site of cohabitation between the material and the immaterial, between multiple identities and temporalities.

The analysis of the postwar image of the prisoner in Guareschi's works brings to the fore some considerations about the temporal framework of humour in the context of imprisonment. For Guareschi and Giovannino, the body, understood as a space imprisoning one's past selves, condenses the temporality of one's life into a single location, and leads to the juxtaposition of temporal planes in the spatial setting of the body. The condensation is an active process. It implies a temporal extension that integrates the present into a larger frame. The point of origin and the direction of the extension differ according to the frameworks. For Freud, the temporal orientation of the humoristic process is directed towards the past. This aligns with the idea behind superiority theories of humour, which emphasize the contrast either between oneself and the other in the present, or between one's present self and one's past self. Other frameworks rely on hypothetical images of one's future self in order to redress the image one forms of the present. Guareschi's humorist 'backdates' actions. They need to posit a future self in order to readjust their perception in the immediacy of the present. In that regard, the orientation of the movement is the same as for Freud, but the point of departure differs. At the same time, the Guareschian framework implies a movement that originates in the present and that extends towards the future. Humour becomes a tool of transmission of memory, leaving traces that emphasize the continuity between the present and the future self. Humour resemantizes the present and opens the door to future resemantizations of its traces by the reader. In that sense, the Guareschian definition of humour is 'future-oriented' and brings to mind the temporality of the carnival: 'Laughter opened men's eyes on that which is new, on the future' (Bakhtin 1984b: 94). This temporal orientation also incorporates the individual in the group's (or the other's) temporality, extending one's present location and temporality to a larger spatial and temporal frame. Albinus's story is part of a cycle that he himself cannot perceive in its entirety. That is also why he cannot perceive the humoristic arc of his trajectory, that becomes such only through its completion with Albinus's death. The externality of Rex, the laughing observer, extends the temporality of Albinus's humoristic imprisonment. That is also why Cohn, who is 'past' death, can perceive the humoristic aspect of his existence. As he explains: 'Je me marre. Au fond, si la mort n'existait pas, la vie perdrait son caractère comique' (164) ['I giggle. After all, if death didn't exist, life would lose its comic nature'].

For the characters in this chapter, the negotiation of bodily imprisonment through humour thus implies the reconsideration of one's temporal limits. Gengis Cohn's imprisonment within Schatz's body questions the finalization of the character in death, as Cohn's life is extended after his death in Nazi imprisonment. Death is thus the starting point of humour in *La danse de Gengis Cohn*. It is its end point in *Laughter in the Dark*, where it completes the trajectory of the 'joke' perceived by Rex and the reader: 'Death often is the point of life's joke' (Nabokov [1938] 1960: 182). Albinus's death leads to the finalization of his trajectory, making humour possible. Gengis Cohn, for his part, dreads finalization, and combats his creator, working against the finalization of the narrative and of the character within the narrative. Its reappearance in other novels, illustrating Gary's plea for the return of the picaresque character, indissociable from his laughter (see Gary [1965] 2003: 358),[39] extends the narrative's boundaries to the work to come. Similarly, Guareschi's episodic recourse to the immaterial Giovannino, in the form either of a separate character or of a materialized moustache, extends the life of the character Guareschi beyond its future death. The serial nature of Guareschi's *oeuvre* contributes to the understanding of the situation of imprisonment as part of a continuum. The movement of the humoristic narrative includes spatial imprisonment within the frame of one's constitutive imprisonment inside one's society, and one's body. The spatial and temporal boundaries of the prison are given new dimensions by the narratives, extending beyond four walls (in the social realm, beyond the present tense), and condensing the experience on an even smaller scale (in the instantaneity of one's bodily life).

Conclusion: A Geometry of Humour

The continuum of imprisonment

This book's enquiry into the deep-rooted connection between humour and imprisonment has been structured according to a 'continuum of imprisonment', that is the idea that there is a conceptual similarity between figures of containment that are shaped in various ways in humoristic literature. I have organized the presentation of the analyses to establish a progression from concrete situations of imprisonment (in prison cells and war camps) to metaphorical figures of containment (the mask and the body). Yet I have also ended by going back to the role confinement plays in the formation of the first character discussed in the book, Giovannino Guareschi's autobiographical *persona*, conceived as a figure balancing multiple split selves (most importantly the bourgeois Guareschi and the interior Giovannino). By moving from and then back to Guareschi, this book shows how the continuum can be read as both progressive and circular. In Guareschi's work, for example, the experience of war imprisonment and the discovery of humour as a way of life and as a new literary style shed light on forms of constitutive entrapment within roles and within the body already present before the experience of imprisonment. Indeed, humour in the specific sense defined in this book can be conceived both as a form of narrative and a way to identify and negotiate individual, social and bodily confinement.

The figures of confinement explored in this book connect with each other to the extent that they blur their own boundaries. Stressing the fluidity of this notion by comparing actual and metaphorical situations of imprisonment in works born in different political contexts entailed certain risks. Gengis Cohn's death during the Shoah is not equivalent to Snooty Baronet's frustrated entrapment in his role of the Douanier. Yet the continuum does not create equivalences; it highlights a connection emerging from the theories and the narratives themselves and a set of conceptual schemes born in twentieth-century literature that make the existence of humour possible.

In Chapter 1, I show how the notion of imprisonment is not only at the core of theories of humour in the restrictive sense, but also at play in the conceptualization of connected notions, such as the comic. Henri Bergson conceives laughter as a collective signal which should correct comic characters trapped in their own 'unnatural' rigidity. The comic gives us the flip side of humour's connection to imprisonment, in that it looks at the character trapped in rigid forms from a collective, external point of view. Theories of humour proper, on the other hand, look at the phenomenon from the point of view of the humorist or the humoristic character. Sigmund Freud, for example, distinguishes humour from jokes and the comic and shows humour as an impulse to free oneself from the expression of overwhelming negative feelings. Born out of a dialogue between parts of a split self, humour is a highly unstable phenomenon. Luigi Pirandello further explores humour's contradictory nature and its literary expressions. Humoristic narratives and the humoristic character appear as relatively 'formless forms' precisely because they reveal interior movements of oscillations between contradictory states and do not try to annul the contradictions by the creation of syntheses.

Compared to comic characters who are unconscious of their rigid entrapment, then, humoristic characters set an oscillatory movement in motion by self-consciously looking at their own condition as one of imprisonment intrinsic to their human nature. This is what Wyndham Lewis sheds light on with his twist on the Bergsonian formula. While for Bergson comic laughter is provoked by a person behaving as thing, for Lewis, the comic is born out of 'the sensations resulting from the observation of a *thing* behaving like a person' (Lewis 1927: 246; original emphasis). The mere fact of being human (a thing behaving like a person) is a source of laughter for the individual able to reflect upon it. It makes possible the development of the 'metaphysical satire' conceived as a satire for all mankind (Lewis 1934). Once again, humour brings to the fore an already present condition of imprisonment that in turn enables the creation of humour. Indeed, the humoristic impulse is born out of the recognition of one's constitutive imprisonment. In Mikhail Bakhtin's framework, carnivalesque laughter would provide a powerful but extremely circumscribed liberation that actually reveals more on the moments on non-liberation, that is, on what laughter 'frees from': social hierarchies, fear and the individual body. Literary humour as an impulse is made possible by the always sustained tension between oppressive structures and attempted liberation. In humoristic narratives, the tension is spatialized in key sites of confinement that form localized images while also connecting with each other, most notably sites of political imprisonment (the prison cell, war camps), of social entrapment (social roles framed by the image of the mask) and of bodily confinement (individual bodily limits and multiple selves that connect and contain each other).

The conceptual continuum between those three key sites emerges along with a specific way of conceiving the temporality of imprisonment. In Chapter 2, I showed that for Guareschi's autobiographical character (*Diario clandestino 1943-1945*), Duparc and Morel (*Les racines du ciel*), and Cincinnatus C. (*Invitation to a Beheading*), the moment of imprisonment marks a clear temporal break in the continuity of their lives. However, paradoxically, this temporal and spatial rupture provokes a conceptual shift that leads them to reframe the understanding of their whole lives as the lives of prisoners. The concreteness of the episode of imprisonment gives shape to a state of entrapment always already present, but not yet named. In that context, humour becomes a conceptual and aesthetic tool enabling the humorist to perceive the imprisonment continuum with the distance that is essential for the shift to occur and for the condition to be named. The transformation of the prisoner's dream into a humoristic story by seeing today with the eyes of tomorrow (Guareschi), the creation of a myth that enables one to laugh at the Nazi's attempt to confine one (Gary) and the epiphanic moments of humoristic laughter that negate the power of the gaolers' comedy (Nabokov) signal the transformation of the characters' perspective through the lens of humour. In each case, the humoristic transformation stresses the continuity between imprisonment and what precedes or follows it. Guareschi's *Diario clandestino* emphasizes the similarities between the rules of the war camps and the rules of his pre-war (and postwar) bourgeois lifestyle. In *Les racines du ciel*, the blurring of voices and temporalities establishes a direct continuity between Duparc's wartime resistant humour and Morel's postwar mythic *persona*. By his endeavour to save African elephants, Morel literalizes the ideal image of free elephants that Duparc had summoned within his solitary confinement. Finally, Cincinnatus's nineteen days in prison (*Invitation to a Beheading*) lead him to the conclusion that his life before then has only been a more veiled form of prison.

While spatially circumscribed images of imprisonment spur the creation of humour in the first narratives analysed, they are also the end point of other narratives, such as Pirandello's *Uno, nessuno e centomila*. In that case, the shelter in which the protagonist Moscarda takes refuge at the end of his journey concretizes and spatializes a feeling of social imprisonment that has been gradually revealed by humour throughout the novel. This ongoing unveiling is made possible by Moscarda's reflection on the multiple social masks he has been framed in, and most crucially (especially towards the end of the novel), the mask of the fool. My analyses of Chapter 3 show how the fool, the rogue and the clown, three key novelistic masks, reveal the 'inadequacy of all available life-slots to fit an authentic human being' (Bakhtin 1981: 163). The mask becomes a tool for understanding the characters' entrapment, and a weapon to fight against it. In Lewis's *Snooty Baronet*, the roguish literary mask of the eponymous character is set up in reaction to other discursive masks imposed onto him by other characters. The rogue figure comes into being through its playful and violent use of language, full of logical malpractices (Nash 1985: 112) and conceptually based on flawed syllogisms. Snooty's self-creation shows how the literary text itself can be conceived as yet another site of imprisonment. As one of Romain Gary's *Clowns lyriques*, La Marne conceives himself as a caricatured, exacerbated surface that gives him the right 'to hyperbolize life; the right to parody others while talking, the right to not be taken literally, not "to be [him]self"' (Bakhtin 1981: 163) while trapping him in his very surface. Using the mask of the clown, he reveals social tensions being pairs of characters who feed each other and form micro social settings that make their very existence as literary characters possible.

In certain cases, humour sets up relationships between pairs of characters whose boundaries are porous. The borderline cases studied in Chapter 4 contribute to reframing the conception of literary imprisonment. In Gary's *La danse de Gengis Cohn*, Gengis Cohn is as much of a prisoner in Otto Schatz's subconscious as he was in a Nazi concentration camp, and as he ends up being in a Jewish author's novel. By spatializing Schatz's subconscious as a ghetto enclosing Cohn and by alternating between the voices of Cohn, Schatz and their creator, the novel builds a humoristic discourse that leads to the reversibility of the characters' positions and to the oscillation between Cohn's desire to die so as to escape his host's body, and his immortality. The humoristic impulse both stems from conditions of confinement and creates them. This is strikingly the case in Nabokov's *Laughter in the Dark*, where humour constitutes a cause of imprisonment for some, and a source of enlightenment for others. Albert Albinus is trapped within his romantic relationship by his own blindness, just as much as he is by the prison of Axel Rex's humour. Yet Rex would not be able to generate humour without Albinus's existence; humour is a dynamic that calls for an 'other'. Its duality is incarnated by figures that oppose, reverse or conjoin opposition and reversals in chiasmic unions or paradoxical syntheses. In Guareschi's two sets of imprisonment writings (in Nazi war camps and in the San Francesco prison in the 1950s), the 'other' is to be found in his very body, conceived as a site of imprisonment. The humoristic process unites material and immaterial realms, past, present and future temporalities, and multiple identities by using figures such as a syllepsis, which paradoxically conjoins realistic and surrealistic conceptions of the body. The cohabitation of identities is also incarnated in bodily parts such as the moustache, which becomes the trace of the process of humour that had split the self in the first place. Guareschi's fictional *persona*, like Cohn, uses humour to negotiate the impossibility to free the part of himself that is trapped, since it is constitutive of his human essence.

The movement from an imprisoned body to the prison-body makes us see not so much the differences between types of imprisonment, as their commonality. Going back to Berchtold's analysis of seventeenth- and eighteenth-century picaresque novels, we can see that twentieth-century narratives of imprisonment also stress the '*absence de rupture* plus surprenante, qui souligne une *homogénéité* entre le monde carcéral et le monde extérieur égalisés dans une relation d'identité spéculaire' (2000: 750; original emphasis) ['a more surprising *absence of rupture* that underlines an *homogeneity* between the prison world and the outside world, levelled out in a relation of specular identity'].

Comic circles and humoristic spirals

The emphasis on the continuity of imprisonment could entail that the dominant mode of apprehension of the relationship between humour and imprisonment is close to Lewis's metaphysical satire (Lewis 1934): literary humour would only stress the constitutive imprisonment of humankind, without providing liberation. Yet, even in Lewis's fiction, the continuum of imprisonment is always set in opposition with impulses towards liberation that at times seem to succeed and that appear to break the continuum. The most powerful impulse is certainly Cincinnatus's (Chapter 2). The novel has set up a spatial opposition between the world of the prisoner and the world of his gaolers. The opposition is signalled by two types of laughter: the gaolers' comic laughter, uttered by figures of doubles who strengthen the repetition of the same and create a comic circle, and Cincinnatus's humoristic laughter, which comes out of his capacity to perceive a disconnect within his own experience of life. In his case, epiphanic moments of humour hint at another space that exists outside of his prison, and the last lines of the novel simply show Cincinnatus's acknowledgement of the reality of that space. Cincinnatus's escape resonates with Sartre's idea that literary prisoners have to *invent* their own way out, that they do not find a hole from which to escape but they create it (see Brombert 1978: 198). By destroying the world of his gaolers and heading towards the 'other space', Cincinnatus also signals the end of humour. Unbounded, without any prison walls against which his humoristic laughter would resonate, we can assume he will not need humour anymore (or the novel, for that matter). He has broken away from the narrative circle.

Cincinnatus's extreme case also dramatizes an idea that is present in more or less veiled ways in most narratives: that death would constitute the only complete escape from the prison of the body, of society, of form and even of humour. This is particularly true in Nabokov's fiction, but also in Gary's, especially for Gengis Cohn. However, the clash between Cohn's desire to die in order to escape from the prison of Schatz's body and his will to live lead not to the death of the character, but to his perpetual renewal in new narratives. Humoristic fiction wishes to renew its form by providing new fictions of regeneration and perpetuation to fight against the trap of form. The humoristic novel of entrapment longs for a 'non-conclusion' for its protagonist, as is best exemplified in *Uno, nessuno e centomila*. One way not to conclude (to close up the character and the novel) is to operate a displacement between narrative realms. Moscarda and Snooty Baronet both operate displacements between one form of imprisonment they deem unbearable and another, chosen one. Moscarda opts for a life in the spatial enclosure of the shelter, to escape society. Snooty shifts from the discursive masks others have created for him to his own narrative. In this light, Moscarda's choice of a life in the shelter can be read both as the choice of social death and as the 'invention' of another space that displaces him from a realm to another, therefore allowing him to be perpetuated rather than concluded.

Perpetuation by means of displacements is to be found in all aspects of the narratives. Humour operates displacements at the linguistic, psychical, formal and conceptual levels. As Jardon puts it, humour activates a linguistic movement from A to A^{+x} (45). When Guareschi's 'schiocco formidabile' (Guareschi [1949] 2009: 11) ['resounding click' (Guareschi [1949] 1958: 22)] is resemantized at the end of 'Lettere al postero', passing from the A of clapping one's boots in a military setting in Italy to the A^{+x} of the clapping of wooden shoes in war camps, it triggers a linguistic displacement that reveals the contribution of humour. The return to the 'schiocco formidabile' does not close the circle by going back to the same. By bringing to the fore a 'surplus' meaning now contained in the word, Guareschian repetitions expand the circular movement into a spiral linguistic impulse that brings the word to another realm.

Similarly, for Freud, humour constitutes a psychical displacement, or, in Morin's words, a movement from dysphoria to euphoria (Freud [1905] 1960: 228–36; Morin 2006: 9). Humour's 'grandeur' and 'dignity' (Freud [1927] 1961: 162–3) enable the protagonist to operate a movement towards a new psychical space to negotiate imprisonment. The relief created by this psychical displacement thus leads to the formation of a spiral impulse. Except in the case of Cincinnatus, however, the narratives analysed present spiral impulses that do not lead to the formation of a complete spiral movement. The overarching structures of the narrative generally incorporate the spiral impulse into a sequence of movements that circle back on themselves, from euphoria back to dysphoria, and back to euphoria again. The moment of euphoria – the relief – is an instant in the larger frame of the novel or, in the case of Guareschi, an episode in a prolific series of periodical short pieces. The Freudian branch of humour theories that sheds light on the moment of relief is therefore integrated within the frame of the narrative theories of humour's oscillation.

Containing humour

Thus, relief and spiral impulses can be read as moments along the temporal continuum of the narratives, which are integrated within the larger temporality of the oscillation. However, if we posit the oscillatory movement as the essential condition for the development of humour, episodic relief and liberatory impulses appear as consequences of the oscillation rather than the opposite. They arise when the pressure created by the containment of the oscillation within the 'square of the prison' (Berchtold 2000) becomes so great as to create a longing for escape in the character. Guareschi's narratives, read out loud to his fellow prisoners, constitute such moments, just as Cohn's temporal escape from Schatz, which is made possible through the laughter induced by the Ennoctal. In both cases, though, the moment of escape is reframed within the larger oscillation of the *diario* or the novel. We can also read the moments of escape as vertical expulsions of the pressure contained in the cells, that, again, lead to another oscillation, this time between the vertical axis of escape and the horizontal axis of entrapment.

The containment within the cell does not only lead to breaches of vertical expulsion; it makes possible the very oscillation of humour. The shape of humour can be read as a fight between humour's longing for the un-formed and the narrative genre's attempt to give a defined shape to the amorphous, or a fight between the closeness of imprisonment and the openness of humour. To Pirandello, the humoristic work of art is by definition formless: 'L'umorismo ha bisogno del più vivace, libero, spontaneo e immediato movimento della lingua, movimento che si può avere sol quando la forma a volta a volta si crea' (Pirandello [1920] 1992: 43) ['Humor needs a highly spirited, free, spontaneous, and direct movement of language – a movement that can be achieved only when form creates itself anew each time' (Pirandello [1920] 1974: 35)]. However, the 'formlessness' of the humoristic work is an objective rather than a given. The humoristic narrative fights to be formless, trying to pull the work out of its defined boundaries. And this is where the 'square' of the prison comes in. The prison gives a clear set of boundaries to the amorphous, incessant fluctuation of humour. It makes the oscillation possible, giving the centripetal force of humour limits against which it can bounce, even intensifying the movement. It is as if the association between contraries were created by the rebound of the narrative movement from one wall of the narrative cell to another.

Humour and the image of the prison also share a crucial characteristic: their faculty to condense. Humour can conjoin two or more linguistic, temporal, psychological or social planes within one space – the space of the text – mirroring the prison cell's capacity to condense the experience of an individual in a small, finite spatial perimeter. More than a capacity, the juxtaposition of two or more planes arises as a structural prerequisite of humour. By compressing the personality of a protagonist in a two-dimensional image and confining the character to one particular social positioning, the mask can become a root for the development of humoristic condensation. Similarly, the body conceived as a figure condensing one's temporal experience within a bounded space enables characters to conceptualize their life's continuum as a condensed temporality that can create a conceptual distance between parts of the self, and thus foster the internal humoristic dialogue.

The frame of the prison – and by extension of the mask and the body – through its spatial fixity makes possible the cohabitation of simultaneous temporalities and the formation of the oscillatory movement of humour. The condensation of the temporal spectrum in spaces of imprisonment can be read as a way of responding to a shift in the conception of time introduced by modernity. The rise of the novel itself has been connected to the 'quite sudden and enormous lengthening of the scale of history' (Kermode 1967: 166–7) and the conceptual and literary consequences of this new comprehension of the unfolding of time are still felt in twentieth-century novels. By resorting to the frame of the prison, the humoristic narrative, a quintessentially formless genre, gives literary shape to the problem of the expansion of time. Condensing time, the prison contains the expanding time and the expanding form of the novel. It becomes a conceptual and stylistic tool to frame the humoristic narrative, with its fight against endings and against the creation of a coherent protagonist or a coherent plot. The dynamic oscillation between the frame of the prison and the humoristic expansion thus reasserts the humoristic work's desire not to conclude and not to propose syntheses. In the economy of the narratives, the concept of the prison does not conclude the humoristic oscillation; it contains it.

Moving frames

Literary humour deals with the formless. It needs formlessness to be, yet it needs formlessness to be contained. Hence its recourse to figures of containment. The narratives analysed in this book establish a dialogue between the humoristic characters' entrapment and their fluidity. As incoherent characters, they cannot settle on a form. Their flowing nature born out of the consciousness of their own contradictions calls for frames that the oscillation can bounce on, such as the cell, the mask, the body. The force produced by the powerful movement does not result in a liberating escape, but in a spiral impulse that often provokes a displacement from a frame to another. Moving between those frames, humoristic characters translate along the imprisonment continuum, creating their existence in the continuity of their renewed forms.

Acquiring their identities through their displacement, those shape-shifters are like Rowling's Boggart, the non-being that assumes the shape of the onlooker's worst fear. Trapped in wardrobes or curled in cupboards, 'the Boggart sitting in the darkness within has not yet assumed a form. He does not yet know what will frighten the person on the other side of the door. Nobody knows what a Boggart looks like when he is alone' (Rowling 1999: 101). Like the humoristic character, the Boggart *becomes* only when confronted to an external perspective that can define it, albeit temporarily. It becomes itself, 'someone who is no longer the person, no longer the *I*, but the *other*' only as a reflection 'in the empirical other through whom one must pass in order to reach *I-for-myself*' (Bakhtin 1986: 137; original emphasis). Literary humour's inner workings shed light on the ways in which identities are constructed, in tension between the expression of our singularities and a desire for protean fluidity and possibilities of existential and experiential transformations. The humoristic conception of identity as a precarious balance between a frame and the endless movement it contains points to a vision of identity that moves away from the dichotomy between coercive and liberating ways of being.

Notes

Introduction

1 For a detailed discussion of the terminology of humour in French and English specifically, see Noonan (2011).
2 Morreall's classification can be a useful guideline for an overview of theories of humour, but each theory I discuss can hardly fit perfectly in any of the categories. As Bown (2018) points out in his critique of the 'type' theories, 'it seems impossible to maintain a system of dividing laughter into types: each laugh seems to have features of more than one "type" operating at once' (27).
3 For a critical overview of the theoretical connections between laughter and liberation, see Bown 2018: 23–50.
4 Holland (1982) is an exception; he dedicates a paragraph to Pirandello's theory in his section on formal incongruity (25).
5 Brombert also published an English version of the same study (1978). There are slight differences between the two versions. I refer to the French one.
6 Note on quotes and translations:
I quote the works in Italian and French in the original language and I cite the available translations when possible. Some works have a complicated translation history, particularly those of Romain Gary. When necessary, I provide my own translation or I supplement existing translations with additional material.

Nabokov's *Invitation to a Beheading* and *Laughter in the Dark* were originally written in Russian, but Nabokov himself has collaborated with his son on the translation of *Invitation to a Beheading* and re-translated *Laughter in the Dark* after a first translation that he disliked. Both can be considered works of Nabokov or approved by Nabokov as accurate translations.

Chapter 1

1 *Le rire* was published as three articles in *La revue de Paris* in 1899, and as a book in 1900.
2 All English quotes are from Brereton and Rothwell's translation.

3. What Bergson calls 'repetition' when dealing with the comic of situations is called 'transposition' in the context of the comic in words. 'Repetition' is understood as the repetition of a situation in new circumstances, and 'transposition' as the use of an expression in a new tone. The latter is therefore a form of repetition, but generally with one of the two forms actually expressed (Bergson [1900] 1975: 93, [1900] 1911: 121–2).
4. Although Bergson insists throughout his book on the corrective role of laughter, when dealing with the comic of situations, and particularly with the vaudeville, he states that the laughter arising from it does *not* seek to correct but is simply a way to obtain pleasure (Bergson [1900] 1975: 78, [1900] 1911: 102).
5. 'Cesser de changer serait cesser de vivre. […] la loi fondamentale de la vie, qui est de ne se répéter jamais !' (Bergson [1900] 1975: 24).
6. On the connection between humour and self-consciousness, see Escarpit (1972), who defines the sense of humour as 'la conscience de son propre personnage' (27) ['the consciousness of one's own character'].
7. Freud considers some literary works in his section on humour of the 1905 book, yet he reads them as though they mimic the structure of the joke (the story raises an expectation of pity and a punch line nullifies this need for pity, thus saving the expenditure in feeling) (1905: 230–1), and he does not consider the aftermath of the punchline. In a footnote, he mentions the place of humour in the creation of literary characters but does not elaborate (1905: 232).
8. I use Strachey's translation of *Jokes and Their Relation to the Unconscious* and of 'Der Humor'.
9. Noguez (1996) critiques Freud's idea of the elimination of affects through humour by emphasizing the communicational aspect of humour: 'Même dans le cas où, comme dit éloquemment Freud, "le processus humoristique tout entier a pour *théâtre* sa propre personne", l'humoriste est pour ainsi dire double et se joue une comédie. L'humour est peut-être narcissique, il n'est pas solipsiste. Pour en faire, il faut être deux' (15; original emphasis) ['Even in the case in which, as Freud eloquently puts it, "the entire humoristic process is *staged* within one's own self", the humorist is in fact double and acts for themselves. Humour might be narcissistic, it is not solipsistic. To create some, you must be two']. According to this communicational process, the affects leading to the creation of humour would not disappear but reappear, stripped down but even stronger, in the humoristic creation. Noguez concludes that humour 'est moins *catharsis* que transsubstantiation' (15; original emphasis) ['is less *catharsis* than transubstantiation']. I agree with Noguez's reading; humour, especially narrative humour, does not eliminate the affects.
10. English quotes are from Illiano and Testa's translation of the 1920 edition.

11 Della Terza translates *umorismo* into 'humorism', clearly distinguishing Pirandello's concept from the broader notion of humour. The term has not been kept by Illiano and Testa in their 1974 translation, *On Humor*.
12 In his 1903 *Aesthetik*, Lipps also defines the comical as a 'conceptual' or 'psychic' oscillation (396–7). Although he first presents it as an alternation between a motive of joy (*Lustmoment*) and a motive of displeasure (*Unlustmoment*) (394–5), he concludes by framing it as a succession between bewilderment and enlightenment (396–7), stressing the conceptual aspect. Lipps's oscillation is also not a dialectics; it repeats itself over and over again. However, for him, the movement then simply fades out and mysteriously 'dissolve[s] in itself' (397). Lipps has influenced both Freud and Pirandello, who refers to *Komik und Humor* (1898) in *L'umorismo*. Pirandello's main point of contention with Lipps is the ethical dimension the latter gives to humour.

More recently, Zupančič (2008) has theorized the 'comic sequence' as a continuous movement of oscillation that originates from the split of a unity (145). She explains that the split takes place thanks to comic techniques such as the 'introduction of a surplus-object', redoublings or repetition (145), and insists on the duration of the comic sequence (opposed to the joke's instantaneity). Zupančič's idea that 'one of the crucial conditions of comedy' is 'continuity that constructs with discontinuity' (147) is very pirandellian.
13 Lewis is said to have been the main (or even sole) writer of the manifesto (Somigli 1995: 21).
14 I retained as much as possible the original typographical presentation of the Manifesto.
15 The term 'laughter' most pervades Lewis's work, while the use of 'humour' and 'satire' is more restricted in time. The term 'comic' is particularly present in *The Wild Body*. One of the most important sections of the book, the second part of 'The Meaning of the Wild Body', is entitled 'The Root of the Comic', and explains central features of Lewis's theory of laughter. In this section, 'humour', 'comic' and 'ridiculous' are used almost interchangeably, although 'comic' is the most frequent. As for 'satire', it is only used on one occasion in the collection (235).
16 Unlike the Wild Body, the expression 'laughing observer' is not capitalized by Lewis.
17 Bakhtin discusses the possibility that the individual be the vehicle for a form of carnival in the second edition of *Problems of Dostoevsky's Poetics*, where he develops the notion of 'reduced laughter'. Whereas in *Rabelais* Bakhtin is prone to denigrate forms of laughter that are not as 'strong' as carnival laughter, in *Dostoevsky*, he studies the presence of 'reduced laughter' as a phenomenon significant in itself (Morson and Emerson 1990: 464). This concept could share important aspects with humour, but I want to remain cautious about it. As Morson and Emerson warn: 'one cannot help feeling at times that, however illuminating the concept of "reduced laughter" may

Chapter 2

1. I quote the only existing English translation of the book, Frenaye's *My Secret Diary* (1958). I use the original title when referring to Guareschi's book, and the English title only when referring to the translation. The translation does not include the original appendix on the months following the Liberation. Instead, it contains an epilogue entitled 'Fourteen Years Later', which is a shortened translation of the section 'Ritorno alla base' of the eponymous book. When useful, I highlight the discrepancies between the original and the translation. This is particularly important for the title. The 'my' of *My Secret Diary* erases the collective aspect that Guareschi insists on, while 'secret' eliminates the relation to wartime conveyed by 'clandestino'. The movement from specificity to generality is reinforced by the disappearance of the dates (1943–1945) that were part of the Italian title, although the context is still evoked by Guareschi's self-portrait as a soldier, which has been kept on the cover of the English edition. The simplicity and voluntary repetitiveness of Guareschi's style are often lost in Frenaye's translation, which often replaces the second utterance of a word or a phrase by synonyms. This is unfortunate, since Guareschi's style and humour depend on devices such as literal repetitions which take on new meanings in different contexts.
2. 'Most of it' is an addition by Frenaye.
3. Jonathanisms are named after 'Brother Jonathan', the 'tall-ordering personifier of American folk humour' (Nash 1985: 46). They can be read as a form of incongruity-resolution (IR) humour, in which the resolution is either partial or null. On IR forms of humour, see Ritchie (2009).
4. Frenaye's translation of the last sentence does not retain the idea of the voluntary aspect of imprisonment. I would translate it as: 'They are the disappointed ones: maybe the most honest of all of us volunteers of the camps'.
5. The translation omits the insertion 'come dicevo al principio della mia storia' ['as I said at the beginning of my story'] in which the narrator highlights that he is repeating the beginning of his story. It also adds the precision 'of war', while Guareschi had stopped with 'prisoner'.
6. In Italian, 'urla scomposte' is a lot stronger. It would be closer to 'wild screams'.
7. The Goncourt cannot be awarded twice to the same author. Gary is the only exception, since his novel *La vie devant soi*, published under the pseudonym Émile Ajar, received the award in 1975.

8   First published in 1956, *Les racines du ciel* was revised and republished by Gary in 1980. The structure of the two versions is similar, except that Chapter 28 of the 1956 version is divided into two chapters in the 1980 version. I am working here with the 1980 version. The only English translation, Jonathan Griffin's *The Roots of Heaven*, dates from 1958. It omits certain sentences or passages that appear both in the 1956 and in the 1980 French versions. Robert's role is diminished in the translation, and Morel seems to come up with the idea of imagining elephants. I am quoting this translation when possible, and I translate when the passage in French is not present in the 1958 English translation.

9   The 'unburstability' of the Garyan character can recall the Beckettian character, as analysed for example by Dolar (2005: 159) and Zupančič (2008: 53).

10 This distinction recalls what Toker has called Nabokov's 'consciousness of two worlds', one of quotidian reality, and an 'otherworld'. See Toker 1995 as well as Alexandrov 1991. Glynn criticizes the association many Nabokovians make between Cincinnatus and a mystic or transcendental world, and associates, on the contrary, Cincinnatus with the capacity to perceive the material world. My vision is closer to Glynn's, and I do not associate the 'world of others' with the quotidian and 'Cincinnatus's world' with the otherworldly.

11 Toker credits Hyde for having been the first to connect Nabokov with the Bergsonian notion of laughter (Toker 1995: 373n). On the comparison between Nabokov's fiction and Bergson's laughter, see Hyde (1977: 26–31, 36–7n, 44, 156, 159–60, 169n); Toker (1989: 8, 1995: 371–2); Couturier (1993: 253–304); Toker (2005: 233, 245n) and Glynn (2007: 76–7). See also my analysis of *Laughter in the Dark* in Chapter 4.

12 Unlike in the Bergsonian framework, then, it is the comic character (M'sieur Pierre) who tries to bring the non-comic character back in the social circle. However, we should distinguish between the diegetic and the extradiegetic levels. Inside the diegesis, Cincinnatus is a comic character, the object of M'sieur Pierre's laughter. Looking at their dynamic from outside, though, M'sieur Pierre is a comic character, and Cincinnatus, a humoristic one.

13 Hyde associates Cincinnatus's new time, that I have identified as the 'time of the hiatus', with Bergson's 'durée': 'It is evident that Cincinnatus's liberation cannot take the linear and material form in which he conceives it: it can only be a liberation from time into what Bergson called "durée" and Nabokov himself elsewhere talks of as "spacetime" (in order to emphasize its characteristic relativity)' (133–4).

14 On several occasions, the narrator notes that the characters of the 'world of others' never quite correctly place the centre of things. This is the case with the light placed on the ceiling of the cell (119, 125) and more importantly with the scaffold on execution day (218).

Chapter 3

1. Macchia relates Moscarda to another type of figure identified by Bakhtin in 'The Functions of the Rogue, Clown and Fool in the Novel': the *crank*, the eccentric man ('lo strambo' for Macchia). See Bakhtin (1981: 164) and Macchia (1981: 77).
2. The Italian term is 'ospizio di mendicità' (Pirandello [1926] 1973: 899). Weaver translates it as 'home for the destitute' (158). I prefer to use the more neutral 'homeless shelter' or simply 'shelter' to render the Italian 'ospizio', which indicates a space set apart from a home.
3. All translations of *Uno, nessuno e centomila* are Weaver's.
4. Macchia discusses the symbolic place of the nose in humoristic writings from Erasmus to Bruscambille, Gogol and Rostand, and compares Pirandello's use of the nose to Sterne's in *The Life and Opinions of Tristram Shandy, Gentleman* (Macchia 1981: 77). In his notes to the Giunti edition of *Uno, nessuno e centomila*, Cudini highlights the crucial role of the nose as an element that makes the story progress throughout the novel (22, note 30).

    On the importance of the nose in humoristic literature, see also Bertoni (2007) and Bakhtin (1984b: 315–18).
5. Lafourcade comments on Lewis's 'paradoxical handling of time centrally concerned with the rather Augustinian impossibility of the present moment, or vortex' (1984: 261).
6. Not capitalized by Lewis.
7. On the importance of the male dyad in the economy of Lewisian narratives, see also Hickman (2005), who reads the construction of male interactions as a reaction to the Wildean effeminate aesthete that the Vorticists are both attracted to and anxious about (72).
8. Kell-Imrie's solution is close to other Pirandellian protagonists who decide to set aside other masks by choosing their own. Such is the case of the heroes of *Enrico IV* and of *Il fu Mattia Pascal*. Both realize, however, that their new mask cannot set them free but constitutes a new prison.
9. On the connection between Bakhtin and Gary, see also Östman (1994), Lecarme-Tabone (2005), Gelas (2009) and Roumette (2011). Gelas discusses the figure of the clown in *Les enchanteurs* and *Les clowns lyriques* but strangely pays little attention to La Marne.
10. Hélène Baty-Delalande (2014) notes the recurrence of the notion and of the phrase 'lyrical clowns' in Gary's novels *Lady L., Les couleurs du jour, Pour Sganarelle, Charge d'âme* (80).
11. Gary's novel *Les couleurs du jour*, published in French in 1952, was considered a failure, both in terms of sales and by the critics. An English version, *The Colours of*

the Day, translated by Stephen Becker, came out in 1953. The 'Author's Note' of this version states: 'the opportunity has been taken by the author to add certain passages to the translation of the original French text and to make some rearrangements and changes which will be incorporated into future French editions' (Gary [1953] 1976: 6). Seventeen years later, Gary, as he often did, revisited the novel and re-submitted it to his editor, Gallimard, who republished it (unknowingly?) under the title *Les clowns lyriques*. This version has never been translated into English. Since the particular passage of *Les clowns lyriques* I analyse is similar to the corresponding passage of the 1952 and 1953 versions, I quote the English *The Colours of the Day* whenever it is similar to the version of *Les clowns lyriques* and provide my own translation in other cases. In terms of the structure of the novel, I analyse the episode of La Marne's monologue within the economy of the later version, *Les clowns lyriques*.

12 On the alternation between the lyrical and the parodic in Gary's works, see Baudelle (2005: 293) and Huston (1995: 55). Huston noted the alternation throughout Gary's *oeuvre* between novels written in a dominantly lyrical and idealistic tone, and novels with a dominantly sarcastic and denunciatory tone. In *Les clowns lyriques*, oscillation is present within the narration, with lyrical sections alternating with parodic ones.

13 On the importance of the 'carnivalisation de soi' ['carnivalization of the self'] in Gary, set in opposition to the cult of the 'I' in contemporary French fiction, see Baudelle (2005: 297). This carnivalization is definitely present in Gary, but always countered by an equally powerful assertion of an ideal. In *Les clowns*, La Marne is the emblematic carnivalesque character, but he counterbalances the equally strong idealistic Jacques, who is not pictured negatively by the narration.

14 While the narrator mentions La Marne's Polish origins (Gary 1979: 29), his birth name is never revealed. The opening line of the chapter already problematizes his identity: 'La Marne – de son vrai nom, qui sait – [...]' (29) ['La Marne – who knew what his real name was – [...]']. It is later made clear that the character chose both his names of 'La Marne' and 'Bebdern'. Since we are told that he has spent five years in the Foreign Legion (1979: 33, [1953] 1976: 19), the choice of a name might play with the Legion's placement under 'identité déclarée', which enables a new member to assume a new identity.

15 Although Willie shares many traits of the clown figure, he is further from the carnivalesque clown than La Marne/Bebdern, and his movement at the 'surface' is connoted differently. While La Marne/Bebdern's surface is a positive counterpoint to idealism, Willie's life at the 'surface' is closer to escapism. Willie is more pathetic than parodic, and the reader has more access to his interiority and personal drama. His choice of suicide is also opposed to La Marne's death as a support *and* a counterpoint to Jacques's heroism.

16 *The Colours of the Day* does not mention Bebdern here.

17 The title of the early short story 'Stefano Giogli, uno e due' (1905), which influenced the writing of *Uno, nessuno e centomila*, places more emphasis on the notion of the double. The two selves become an infinite multiplication in the later novel. Stefano Giogli can be read as a proto-Moscarda (Macchia 1981: 38).

Chapter 4

1 *Frère Océan* is composed of the essay *Pour Sganarelle* and the novels *La danse de Gengis Cohn* and *La tête coupable* ([1968] 1994). The essay develops the concept – then articulated in the novels – of the 'frère Océan', an ideal cultural fraternity connecting human beings.
2 This is Gary's term. It first appears as the title of the first of three parts, 'Le *dibbuk*' ['The Dybbuk']. Although Gary does not make explicit references, *La danse de Gengis Cohn* can be connected to other works created around the figure of the *dybbuk*, such as S. Ansky's ([1917] 2002) play *The Dybbuk*.
3 The French and English versions of the novel differ substantially. The English version, published a year after the French one and presented in the colophon as being 'translated from the French by Romain Gary with the assistance of Camilla Sykes', is not a direct translation. Both Bellos (2010) and Huston (2010) have commented on this 'translation' story. Bellos reveals that Gary started to write the work in English, before switching to French, finally revising and adapting the work for an American audience following the French publication and reception of the novel (335). According to Huston's comparative analysis of the last chapter of the novel, the English version explicitly details some concepts that remained implicit in the French version (38, 39, 42). It also contains cultural references adapted to a different public. The substantial structural differences between the two versions are apparent when considering 'L'un dans l'autre'. In the English version, the material from this chapter is included in Chapter XVII, entitled 'The Jewish Holes' which condenses both 'L'un dans l'autre' and the following chapter 'Les trous juifs'. The situation of imprisonment and ventriloquism and the role of laughter are much more elaborate in 'L'un dans l'autre' than they are in 'The Jewish Holes'. For this reason, I will quote the French version and provide my own translations, and I will use the French spelling *Gengis* Cohn.
4 I follow Gary's terminology. Whereas he uses the term 'insconscient' in his essay *Pour Sganarelle*, he opts for 'subconscient' in *La danse de Gengis Cohn* ('subconscious' in the 1968 English version).
5 I am not aware of Gary commenting on Freud's theory of humour in particular.
6 Cleanliness is a deeply ambivalent notion for Gary, a symbol of inhumanity (see for example Gary [1967] 1995: 79, 1966: 261 and Kauffmann 2009: 133–4) and a

defining feature of the human figure who can never be tarnished by atrocities (see Gary 1979: 147, 1966: 255).

7   The English version is substantially more elaborate and explicit on that aspect (Gary 1968: 4).
8   Judith Kauffmann also notes the close proximity between Cohn's humour and Freud's definition. However, her analyses focus solely on Cohn's use of humour as a protection against Schatz, whereas I read the two characters as inseparable beings who share the power of humour and participate in its creative process. See Kauffmann (2005 and 2009: 135).
9   On the reversibility of identities in Gary's *oeuvre* in general, see Schoolcraft (2002: 114).
10 *La danse* announces Cohn's reappearance in Tahiti on several occasions. See for example 192, 310, 341.
11 The novel was published in Russian in 1932 as *Kamera Obskura* and translated into English in 1936 under the title *Camera Obscura*. Nabokov disliked the translation and provided his own English version in 1938 as *Laughter in the Dark*. See Wyllie (2010: 70–1); Connolly (1992: 247) and Grayson (1977: 27–8). My analysis is based on the 1938 English novel.
12 As Stuart (1978) makes clear, the Nabokovian pair is not to be confused with any forms of doubles. According to him, true doubles are absent from Nabokov's novels (107). I would reconsider that statement in the case of Rodion and Rodrig in *Invitation to a Beheading* (see Chapter 2).
13 Couturier (1993) also finds similarities with Sternian (257), Gogolian (257, 274, 284, 292) and Dionysian laughter (290), thus stressing the complexity of Nabokovian laughter. He seems to weaken his own analysis when he later subsumes Nabokovian laughter under the Hobbesian definition (303).
14 To Connolly (1992), Rex's art is also parasitical (123). Yet there are major differences between the two types of parasitism. First, Rex is well aware of the parasitical nature of this work, whereas Albinus is not. Second, Albinus's parasitism always feeds on art. This is the case for Rex as a forger of works of art, but it is not in his practice of caricature. Rex's vision of caricature is actually derivative from life, and not art. Finally, Albinus does not possess Rex's technical mastery that enables him to create both copies and original works.
15 On the connection between Nabokov and Bergson's theory of the comic, see Chapter 2 on *Invitation to a Beheading*.
16 Stuart (1978) remarks the association between Axel and an axle (107). Rex is also Albinus and Margot's driver on the trip to France, literally turning the wheel that directs the movements of the other two (201). When Albinus decides to take the car himself – i.e. to take control of his own movement – he causes the near-fatal car

accident that leaves him blind. Rex is presented in mastery of the wheel, whereas Albinus cannot control its movement.
17 Poker is at the origin of Rex and Margot's relationship. Rex is introduced to Frau Levandovsky, Margot's pimp, by two travellers with whom he played poker.
18 On Albinus's moral and social blindness, see also Connolly (1992: 119–27) and Stuart (1978: 99–100).
19 The motif of death as a joke is recurrent in Nabokov. In *Invitation to a Beheading*, Cincinnatus's death is also depicted as a joke. Cincinnatus can overcome it by escaping the nature of the 'world of others' through his capacity to envision *something else* that exceeds the world of parody. In *Bend Sinister*, the superior narrative entity of the author's *persona* intervenes to stop Krug's death despite his having been shot twice, commenting that this intervention is 'a slippery sophism, a play upon words' (241). On the motif of death in Nabokov, see also Toker (2005: 238–41) and Wyllie (2010: 84).
20 See also Williams (1967) on Nabokov's use of dialectical structures.
21 A first version of this section has been published in *Post-Scriptum* (2016).
22 'Colloquio nel bagno' is written after another very significant piece featuring Guareschi's split self, 'Addio, Giovannino'. It appeared on the front page of the 8 June 1946 edition of *Candido*, a week after the Italian constitutional referendum that resulted in the victory of the republic over the monarchy, for which Guareschi had campaigned. The piece shows Guareschi and Giovannino walking side by side until they part, Guareschi staying in the newly founded Republic and Giovannino leaving it. The split between Guareschi and Giovannino becomes a metaphor for the division of the country in the aftermath of the referendum. In the piece, Guareschi addresses Giovannino but the latter does not speak. It is a monologue rather than a dialogue.
23 There is a third character in the piece, the 'angioletto', a guardian angel that first appeared in *Diario clandestino*. Guareschi, Giovannino and the angel constitute a trinity combined in Guareschi's body. However, only Guareschi and Giovannino have a narrative voice in the piece.
24 *Candido* is created in December 1945, with Guareschi as editor-in-chief. He remained in this position until 1957 and continued to collaborate until 1961. The newspaper closed almost immediately after Guareschi announced his resignation. See Conti (2008: 320–40 and 510–20).
25 I am quoting the version published in *Ritorno alla base*. All translations are mine.
26 Roncole Verdi is the locality where Guareschi lived from 1952.
27 The passage from the outside to inside of the bathroom brings to mind the passage from the streets of Nice to the hotel room in *Les clowns lyriques*.
28 Guareschi frequently discusses his 'mal di stomaco' in other writings. See for example Guareschi ([1993] 2009: 201) and the short stories 'Il fritto proibito' (116–26) and 'La faccia di Milano' (203–11) in *Corrierino delle famiglie* ([1954] 2009).

29 Guareschi's Second World War backpack is another object materializing the connection between different temporal planes.
30 The indication at the top of the letter reads: 'Dal carcere delle Roncole, 31 luglio 1955'. It appeared on *Candido* 32 (1955): 6–7.
31 Gio' ungrammatically uses 'Lui' instead of the formal, gender-neutral 'Lei' when addressing her male boss.
32 Originally published in *Oggi* 30 (1967): 65. All translations are mine.
33 Guareschi's use of a singular character to stand in for a whole generation is frequent and at times explicit. In the stories of *Ritorno alla base*, the narrator (again, Guareschi's *persona*) gives his son Albertino the nickname 'la nuova generazione' (see for example Guareschi [1989] 2011: 221, 225, 243, 244).
34 The quote is from the piece 'Va' fuori o stranier!' It was originally published in *Oggi* 28 (1965): 72.
35 Guareschi refers to Octave Feuillet's 1858 *Le roman d'un jeune homme pauvre* or, possibly, to one of its movie adaptations, more likely Guido Brignone's 1942 film.
36 Originally published in *Candido* 3 (1945): 4. Quoted in *Chi sogna nuovi gerani?* 231.
37 As Perry remarks in his analysis of the piece 'No, niente appello', 'Guareschi relies on his personal mystique of the prisoner-of-war camp as a font of strength' (2007: 45).
38 Others have extensively worked on the place of religion in Guareschian poetics (see particularly the works of Gnocchi (1995) and Perry (2007)).
39 In *Pour Sganarelle*, Gary insists on the picaresque novel's power to go beyond the boundaries of death (see 166, 272, 378). He asks, 'Pourquoi le roman choisit-il toujours la mort plutôt que la renaissance sans fin?' (378) ['Why does the novel always choose death over endless rebirth?']

References

Alexandrov, V. E. (1991), *Nabokov's Otherworld*, Princeton: Princeton University Press.

Alter, R. (1997), 'Invitation to a Beheading: Nabokov and the Art of Politics', in J. W. Connolly (ed.), *Invitation to a Beheading. A Critical Companion*, 48–65, Evanston: Northwestern University Press.

Amsellem, G. (2008), *Romain Gary et les métamorphoses de l'identité*, Paris: L'Harmattan.

Ansky, S. ([1917] 2002), *The Dybbuk and Other Writings*, ed. D. G. Roskies, trans. G. Werman, New Haven: Yale University Press.

Averintsev, S. (2001), 'Bakhtin, Laughter and Christian Culture', in S. M. Felch and P. J. Contino (eds), *Bakhtin and Religion. A Feeling for Faith*, 79–95, Evanston: Northwestern University Press.

Bakhtin, M. M. (1981), *The Dialogic Imagination: Four Essays*, ed. M. Holquist, trans. C. Emerson and M. Holquist, Austin: University of Texas Press.

Bakhtin, M. M. (1984a), *Problems of Dostoevsky's Poetics*, ed. and trans. C. Emerson, Introd. W. Booth, Minneapolis: University of Minnesota Press.

Bakhtin, M. M. (1984b), *Rabelais and His World*, trans. H. Iswolsky, Bloomington: Indiana University Press.

Bakhtin, M. M. (1986), 'From Notes Made in 1970–71', in C. Emerson and M. Holquist (eds), *Speech Genres and Other Late Essays*, trans. V. W. McGee, 132–58, Austin: University of Texas Press.

Bakhtin, M. M. (1990), 'Author and Hero in Aesthetic Activity', in M. Holquist and V. Liapunov (eds), *Art and Answerability. Early Philosophical Essays by M. M. Bakhtin*, trans. V. Liapunov, Supplement trans. K. Brostrom, 4–256, Austin: University of Texas Press.

Bakhtin, M. M. (2014), 'Bakhtin on Shakespeare: Excerpt from "Additions and Changes to *Rabelais*"' trans. and introd. by S. Sandler, *PMLA* 129 (3): 522–37.

Baty-Delalande, H. (2014), 'Tout contre les clowns lyriques: Gary et la hantise de l'engagement (sur Frère Océan)', *Littératures* 70: 79–90.

Baudelaire, C. ([1855] 1955), 'On the essence of laughter, and, in general, on the comic in the plastic arts', in *The Mirror of Art. Critical Studies*, 133–53, ed. and trans. with notes and illus. by J. Mayne, London: Phaidon.

Baudelaire, C. ([1855] 1962), 'De l'essence du rire et généralement du comique dans les arts plastiques', in *Curiosités esthétiques. L'art romantique et autres œuvres critiques*, 241–63, Paris: Garnier Frères.

Baudelle, Y. (2005), 'Un cosaque dans nos lettres', in J.-F. Hangouët and P. Audi (eds), *Les Cahiers de l'Herne. Romain Gary*, 289–302, Paris: Éditions de l'Herne.

Bayard, P. (1990), *Il était deux fois Romain Gary*, Paris: Presses universitaires de France.

References

Bellos, D. (2010), *Romain Gary. A Tall Story*, London: Harvill Secker.
Berchtold, J. (2000), *Les prisons du roman (XVIIe–XVIIIe siècle). Lectures plurielles et intertextuelles de* Guzman d'Alfarache *à* Jacques le fataliste, Genève: Droz.
Bergson, H. ([1900] 1911), *Laughter: An Essay on the Meaning of the Comic*, trans. C. Brereton and F. Rothwell, London: Macmillan.
Bergson, H. ([1900] 1975), *Le rire. Essai sur la signification du comique*, Paris: Presses universitaires de France.
Bergson, H. (1970), *Œuvres*, annotated by A. Robinet, introd. H. Gouhier, Paris: Presses universitaires de France.
Bertoni, F. (2007), 'Naso', in R. Ceserani, M. Domenichelli and P. Fasano (eds), *Dizionario dei temi letterari*, vol. 2, 1600–2, Torino: UTET.
Boyd, B. (1990), *Vladimir Nabokov: The Russian Years*, Princeton: Princeton University Press.
Bown, A. (2018), *In the Event of Laughter: Psychoanalysis, Literature and Comedy*, New York: Bloomsbury Academic.
Brombert, V. (1975), *La prison romantique. Essai sur l'imaginaire*, Paris: José Corti.
Brombert, V. (1978), *The Romantic Prison. The French Tradition*, Princeton: Princeton University Press.
Chapman, R. T. (1973), *Wyndham Lewis: Fictions and Satires*, London: Vision.
Connolly, J. W. (1992), *Nabokov's Early Fiction. Patterns of Self and Other*, Cambridge: Cambridge University Press.
Conti, G. (2008), *Giovannino Guareschi: Biografia di uno scrittore*, Milano: Rizzoli.
Cotta, S. (1977), *Quale Resistenza? Aspetti e problemi della guerra di liberazione in Italia*, Milano: Rusconi.
Couturier, M. (1993), 'Les complicités du rire', in *Nabokov ou la tyrannie de l'auteur*, 253–304, Paris: Seuil (Poétique).
Critchley, S. (2002), *On Humour*, London: Routledge.
Cudini, P. (1994), introduction and notes, in L. Pirandello, *Uno, nessuno e centomila*, Firenze: Giunti.
Della Terza, D. (1972), 'On Pirandello's Humorism', in Harry Levin (ed.), *Veins of Humor*, 17–33, Cambridge: Harvard University Press.
Dolar, M. (2005), 'Comedy and Its Double', in R. Pfaller (ed.), *Schluss mit der Komödie!/ Stop That Comedy!*, 181–210, Vienna: Sonderzahl.
Douglass, P. (2013), 'Bergson on *Élan Vital*', in P. Ardoin, S. E. Gontarski and L. Mattison (eds), *Understanding Bergson. Understanding Modernism*, 303–4, New York: Bloomsbury.
Emerson, C. (1997), *The First Hundred Years of Mikhail Bakhtin*, Princeton: Princeton University Press.
Escarpit, R. (1972), *L'humour*, Paris: Presses universitaires de France (Que sais-je?).
Ferroni, G. (1974), *Il comico nelle teorie contemporanee*, Roma: Bulzoni.
Foucault, M. (1986), 'Of Other Spaces', trans. J. Miskowiec, *Diacritics*, 16 (1): 22–7.

Foucault, M. (1994), 'Des espaces autres', in *Dits et écrits 1954–1988*, tome IV 1980–1988, 752–62, Paris: Gallimard.

Franzinelli, M. (2014), *Bombardate Roma! Guareschi contro De Gasperi: Uno scandalo della storia repubblicana*, Milano: Mondadori.

Freud, S. ([1905] 1960), *Jokes and Their Relation to the Unconscious*, ed. and trans. J. Strachey in collaboration with A. Freud, *The Standard Edition of the Complete Psychological Works of Sigmund Freud*, vol. VIII, London: The Hogarth Press and the Institute of Psycho-analysis.

Freud, S. ([1923] 1962), *The Ego and the Id*, ed. J. Strachey, trans. J. Riviere, London: The Hogarth Press and the Institute of Psycho-analysis.

Freud, S. ([1927] 1961), 'Humour', ed. and trans. J. Strachey in collaboration with A. Freud, *The Standard Edition of the Complete Psychological Works of Sigmund Freud*, vol. XXI (1927–1931), 159–66, London: The Hogarth Press and the Institute of Psycho-analysis.

Gary, R. (1952), *Les couleurs du jour*, Paris: Gallimard (NRF).

Gary, R. ([1953] 1976), *The Colours of the Day*, trans. S. Becker, London: White Lion.

Gary, R. ([1958] 1964), *The Roots of Heaven*, trans. J. Griffin, New York: Time.

Gary, R. ([1965] 2003), *Pour Sganarelle: Recherche d'un personnage et d'un roman*, Paris: Gallimard (Folio).

Gary, R. (1966), *Les mangeurs d'étoiles*, Paris: Gallimard (NRF).

Gary, R. ([1967] 1995), *La danse de Gengis Cohn*, Paris: Gallimard (Folio).

Gary, R. (1968), *The Dance of Genghis Cohn*, trans. R. Gary with the assistance of C. Sykes, New York: Annal.

Gary, R. (1979), *Les clowns lyriques*, Paris: Gallimard (NRF).

Gary, R. ([1968] 1994), *La tête coupable*, Paris: Gallimard (Folio).

Gary, R. ([1980] 2010), *Les racines du ciel*, Paris: Gallimard (Folio).

Gary, R. (2005), 'Être deux c'est pour moi la seule unité concevable. Entretien avec Pierre Sipriot', in J.-F. Hangouët and P. Audi (eds), *Les Cahiers de l'Herne. Romain Gary*, 272–4, Paris: Éditions de l'Herne.

Gelas, N. (2009), 'De l'insoumission au sentiment tragique: variations sur la figure du clown dans *Les Enchanteurs* et *Les Clowns lyriques*', *Deeds and Days (Darbai ir Dienos)* 51: 151–60.

Gilbert, M. (1989), *Second World War*, London: Weidenfeld and Nicolson.

Gioanola, E. (1997), 'La crisi dell'identità: dal *Fu Mattia Pascal* a *Uno, nessuno e centomila*', in *Pirandello, la follia*, 65–94, Milano: Jaca.

Giovanelli, P. D. (1997), 'L'ossessione del corpo nella poetica pirandelliana', in M. Cantelmo (ed.), *L'isola che ride. Teoria, poetica e retoriche dell'umorismo pirandelliano*, 69–88, Roma: Bulzoni.

Glynn, M. (2007), *Vladimir Nabokov. Bergsonian and Russian Formalist Influences in His Novels*, New York: Palgrave Macmillan.

Gnocchi, A. (1995), *Don Camillo & Peppone: L'invenzione del vero*, Milano: Rizzoli.
Gnocchi, A. and M. Palmaro (2008), *Giovannino Guareschi. C'era una volta il padre di Don Camillo e Peppone*, Casale Monferrato: Piemme.
Gogotishvili, L. (1992), 'Varianty i invarianty M. M. Bakhtina', *Voprosy filosofii*. No. 1: 114–34.
Grayson, J. (1977), 'Major Reworkings: *Laughter in the Dark*', in *Nabokov Translated. A Comparison of Nabokov's Russian and English Prose*, 23–58, Oxford: Oxford University Press.
Guareschi, A. and C. (2009), *Giovannino nostro babbo*, Milano: Rizzoli.
Guareschi, A. and C. (2011), 'Istruzioni per l'uso del *Grande Diario*', in *Il grande diario. Giovannino cronista del Lager 1943-1945*, 3–7, Milano: BUR Rizzoli.
Guareschi, G. (1946), 'Addio, Giovannino', *Candido* 23: 1.
Guareschi, G. ([1949] 1958), *My Secret Diary*, trans. F. Frenaye, London: Gollancz.
Guareschi, G. ([1949] 2009), *Diario clandestino 1943-1945*, Milano: BUR Rizzoli.
Guareschi, G. ([1954] 2009), *Corrierino delle famiglie*, Milano: BUR Rizzoli.
Guareschi, G. ([1955] 2011), 'Colloquio nel bagno', in *Ritorno alla base*, introd. G. Lugaresi, Milano: BUR Rizzoli, 206–13.
Guareschi, G. (1965), 'Va' fuori o stranier!', *Oggi* 28: 72.
Guareschi, G. (1967), 'Era giovane, bellissimo... ', *Oggi* 30: 65.
Guareschi, G. ([1989] 2011), *Ritorno alla base*, introd. G. Lugaresi, Milano: BUR Rizzoli.
Guareschi, G. ([1993] 2009), *Chi sogna nuovi gerani?: autobiografia*, ed. C. and A. Guareschi, Milano: BUR Rizzoli.
Guareschi, G. ([1995] 2011), *Vita con Giò. Vita in famiglia e altri racconti*, Milano: BUR Rizzoli.
Guareschi, G. (2011), *Il grande diario. Giovannino cronista del Lager 1943-1945*, Milano: BUR Rizzoli.
Guareschi, G. (2015), *L'umorismo*, ed. A. Paganini, Poschiavo: L'ora d'oro.
Hickman, M. B. (2005), *The Geometry of Modernism. The Vorticist Idiom in Lewis, Pound, H.D., and Yeats*, Austin: University of Texas Press.
Hobbes, T. ([1650] 1839–1845), 'Human Nature', in Sir W. Molseworth (ed.), *The English Works of Thomas Hobbes of Malmesbury*, vol. 4, 1–76, London: Bohn.
Holland, N. (1982), *Laughing, a Psychology of Humor*, Ithaca: Cornell University Press.
Holquist, M. (1990), 'Introduction: The Architectonics of Answerability', in M. Holquist and B. Liapunov (eds), *Art and Answerability. Early Philosophical Essays* by M. M. Bakhtin, ix–xlix, trans. B. Liapunov, Supplement trans. K. Brostrom, Austin: University of Texas Press.
'Humoristic, adj. and n.', *OED Online*, Oxford University Press, www.oed.com/view/Entry/89410 (accessed 24 April 2019).
'Humoristic, adj. and n.', *OED Online*, Oxford University Press, www.oed.com/view/Entry/89413 (accessed 24 April 2019).

Huston, N. (1995), *Tombeau de Romain Gary*, Arles: Actes Sud.
Huston, N. (2010), 'La danse de Gengis Cohn ou comment Gary se traduit', in P. Assouline (ed.), *Lectures de Romain Gary*, 35–43, Paris: Gallimard.
Hyde, G. M. (1977), *Vladimir Nabokov: America's Russian Novelist*, London: Boyars.
Jameson, F. (1979), *Fables of Aggression. Wyndham Lewis, the Modernist as Fascist*, Berkeley: University of California Press.
Jardon, D. (1988), *Du comique dans le texte littéraire*, Bruxelles: De Boeck-Duculot.
Kauffmann, J. (2005), 'L'humour (juif), arme des désarmés', *Imaginaire et inconscient* 15: 93–104.
Kauffmann, J. (2009), 'Horrible, humour noir, rire blanc. Quelques réflexions sur la représentation littéraire de la Shoah', in A. Lauterwein (ed.) with the collaboration of C. Strauss-Hiva, *Rire, mémoire, Shoah*, 129–40, Paris: Éditions de l'éclat.
Kermode, F. (1967), *The Sense of an Ending: Studies in the Theory of Fiction*, New York: Oxford University Press.
Lafourcade, B. (1982), 'Afterword', in W. Lewis, *The Complete Wild Body*, 403–14, Santa Barbara: Black Sparrow.
Lafourcade, B. (1984), 'Afterword: A Cock-and-bull Story', in W. Lewis, *Snooty Baronet*, 255–70, Santa Barbara: Black Sparrow.
Laufer, L. (2005), 'L'éloge du masque, ou de l'art de ruser avec la mort', in J.-F. Hangouët and P. Audi (eds), *Les Cahiers de l'Herne. Romain Gary*, 38–53, Paris: Éditions de l'Herne.
Lecarme-Tabone, É. (2005), *Éliane Lecarme-Tabone commente* La vie devant soi *de Romain Gary*, Paris: Gallimard.
Lewis, W., ed. ([1914] 1981), *Blast* 1, foreword B. Morrow, Santa Barbara: Black Sparrow.
Lewis, W. (1927), *The Wild Body: A Soldier of Humour, and Other Stories*, London: Chatto and Windus.
Lewis, W. ([1928a] 1965), *The Childermass*, London: Calder.
Lewis, W. ([1928b] 2010), *Tarr*, ed. and introd. S. W. Klein, Oxford: Oxford University Press.
Lewis, W. ([1930] 1970), *Satire and Fiction*, preceded by *The History of a Rejected Review* by R. Campbell, Folcroft: Folcroft Library.
Lewis, W. ([1932] 1984), *Snooty Baronet*, ed. B. Lafourcade, Santa Barbara: Black Sparrow.
Lewis, W. ([1934] 1964), *Men Without Art*, New York: Russell & Russell.
Lipps, T. ([1903] 1964), 'From the Foundations of Aesthetics (1903), Part VI, Chapter 7: The Comical and Related Things', trans. L. Chadeayne, in P. Lauter (ed.), *Theories of Comedy*, 393–7, Garden City: Anchor.
Lugaresi, G. (2011), 'Scrivere per sopravvivere', introduction, in G. Guareschi, *Ritorno alla base*, 5–11, Milano: BUR Rizzoli.
Macchia, G. (1981), *Pirandello o la stanza della tortura*, Milano: Mondadori.
Marcheschi, D. (1992), 'Introduzione', in L. Pirandello, *L'umorismo*, v–xxxii, Milano: Mondadori.
Mathieu-Lessard, J. (2016), 'Humour Doubles: On the Role of the Two Selves in Giovannino Guareschi's Journalistic Fiction', *Post-Scriptum. Revue de recherche*

interdisciplinaire en texte et médias (20). http://www.post-scriptum.org/20-05-humour-doubles/

Morin, C. (2006), *L'humour avec soi. Analyse sémiotique du discours humoristique et de la supercherie chez Gary-Ajar*, Montréal: Nota Bene.

Morreall, J. (1983), *Taking Laughter Seriously*, Albany: State University of New York Press.

Morson, G. S. and C. Emerson (1990), *Mikhail Bakhtin: Creation of a Prosaics*, Stanford: Stanford University Press.

Nabokov, V. ([1938] 1960), *Laughter in the Dark*, New York: New Directions.

Nabokov, V. (1947), *Bend Sinister*, New York: Henry Holt.

Nabokov, V. (1959), *Invitation to a Beheading*, trans. D. Nabokov in collaboration with the author, New York: Putnam.

Nabokov, V. ([1967] 1989), *Speak, Memory. An Autobiography Revisited*, New York: Vintage.

Nash, W. (1985), *The Language of Humor*, New York: Longman.

Noguez, D. (1996), *L'arc-en-ciel des humours. Jarry, Dada, Vian, etc*, Paris: Hatier.

Noonan, W. (2011), 'Reflecting Back, or What Can the French Tell the English About Humour?', *Sydney Studies in English* 37: 92–115.

Östman, A.-C. (1994), *L'utopie et l'ironie. Étude sur* Gros-Câlin *et sa place dans l'œuvre de Romain Gary*, Stockholm: Almqvist & Wiksell.

Parkin, J. (1997), *Humour Theorists of the Twentieth Century*, Lewiston: Mellen.

Perry, A. R. (2001), 'Freedom of Imprisonment: Giovannino Guareschi and the Primacy of Conscience', *Italian Culture* 19 (2): 67–80.

Perry, A. R. (2005), '"No, niente appello!": How De Gasperi Sent Guareschi to Prison', *Italianist* 2 (25): 239–59.

Perry, A. R. (2007), *The Don Camillo Stories of Giovannino Guareschi. A Humorist Portrays the Sacred*, Toronto: University of Toronto Press.

Perry, A. R. (2009), '"C'era una volta la prigionia": Guareschi's Resistance in the *Favola di Natale*', *Italica* 86 (4): 623–50.

Perry, A. R. (2012), '"Io sono qui muto e solitario": Giovannino Guareschi's Prison Writings, 1954–1955', *Modern Italy* 17 (1): 85–102.

Perry, A. R. (2016) 'Giovannino's "Libertà": Guareschi's Personal Freedom in Opposition to Power', *Annali d'italianistica* 34. *Speaking Truth to Power from Medieval to Modern Italy*, 401–24.

Pirandello, L. ([1904] 1993), *Il fu Mattia Pascal*, Torino: Einaudi.

Pirandello, L. ([1905] 1990), 'Stefano Giogli, uno e due', in M. Costanzo (ed.), *Novelle per un anno*, vol. 3, tome 2, 1115–24, Milano: Mondadori (I Meridiani).

Pirandello, L. ([1920] 1974), *On Humor*, trans. A. Illiano and D. P. Testa, Chapel Hill: University of North Carolina Press.

Pirandello, L. ([1920] 1992), *L'umorismo*, ed. and introd. D. Marcheschi, Milano: Mondadori.

Pirandello, L. ([1922a] 2006), 'Il teatro moderno, Tilgher, Bracco, un nuovo romanzo, l'America', *Saggi e Interventi*, 1149–53, ed. F. Taviani, Milano: Mondadori (I Meridiani).

Pirandello, L. ([1922b] 1993), *Enrico IV*, Torino: Einaudi.

Pirandello, L. ([1926] 1973), *Uno, nessuno e centomila* in *Tutti i romanzi*, vol. 2, 737–902, ed. G. Macchia and M. Costanzo, Milano: Mondadori.

Pirandello, L. ([1926] 1992), *One, No One, and One Hundred Thousand*, trans. and introd. W. Weaver, New York: Marsilio.

Pritchard, W. H. (1968), *Wyndham Lewis*, New York: Twayne.

Rasson, L. (2008), *L'écrivain et le dictateur: Écrire l'expérience totalitaire*, Paris: Imago.

Rinn, M. (2009), 'L'humour pathétique de Romain Gary: sémio-pragmatique des figures de la véhémence', *Protée* 37 (2): 79–89.

Ritchie, G. (2009), 'Variants of Incongruity Resolution', *Journal of Literary Theory* 3 (2): 313–32.

Roumette, J. (2011), '"La hausse des cris": Romain Gary et l'irrespect carnavalesque', *Littératures* 65: 93–113.

Rowling, J. K. (1999), *Harry Potter and the Prisoner of Azkaban*, Vancouver: Raincoast.

Sartre, J.-P. ([1947] 2000), *Huis clos* suivi de *Les mouches*, Paris: Gallimard.

Schoolcraft, R. (2002), *Romain Gary. The Man Who Sold His Shadow*, Philadelphia: University of Pennsylvania Press.

Schopenhauer, A. ([1819] 1969), *The World as Will and Representation*, Volume I, trans. E. F. J. Payne, New York: Dover Publications.

Shentoub, S. A. (1989), 'Introduction', in J. Altounian et al. (eds), *L'humour dans l'œuvre de Freud*, 7–16, Paris: Edition Two Cities ETC.

Somigli, L. (1995), *Per una satira modernista. La narrativa di Wyndham Lewis*, Firenze: Cadmo.

Stendhal. (1864), *La chartreuse de Parme*, Paris: Michel Lévy Frères.

Strachey, J. (1960), 'Editor's Preface', in S. Freud, *Jokes and Their Relation to the Unconscious*, 3–8, New York: Norton.

Stuart, D. (1978), *Nabokov: The Dimensions of Parody*, Baton Rouge: Louisiana State University Press.

Toker, L. (1989), *Nabokov: The Mystery of Literary Structures*, Ithaca: Cornell University Press.

Toker, L. (1995), 'Nabokov and Bergson', in V. E. Alexandrov (ed.), *The Garland Companion to Vladimir Nabokov*, 367–73, New York: Garland.

Toker, L. (2005), 'Nabokov's Worldview', in J. W. Connolly (ed.), *The Cambridge Companion to Nabokov*, 232–47, Cambridge: Cambridge University Press.

Williams, C. T. (1967), 'Nabokov's Dialectical Structure', *Wisconsin Studies in Contemporary Literature* 8 (2): 250–67.

Wyllie, B. (2010), *Vladimir Nabokov*, London: Reaktion.

Zupančič, A. (2008), *The Odd One In. On Comedy*, Cambridge and London: MIT Press.

Index

Bakhtin, Mikhail 6–7, 13, 29, 120, 166, 180 n.9
   'Author and Hero in Aesthetic Activity' (in *Art and Answerability*) 119, 161
   'Epic and Novel' (in *The Dialogic Imagination*) 35, 37
   'Forms of Time and of the Chronotope in the Novel' (in *The Dialogic Imagination*) 11, 34–6, 84, 92–3, 95, 105–9, 111–12, 117, 168, 180 n.1
   'From Notes Made in 1970–71' (in *Speech Genres and Other Late Essays*) 6, 35, 38–40, 106, 174
   'From the Prehistory of Novelistic Discourse' (in *The Dialogic Imagination*) 34–5
   Problems of Dostoevsky's Poetics 39, 105–6, 118, 177–8 n.17
   Rabelais and His World 3, 6, 34–41, 82, 105, 108–9, 116, 143, 163, 177–8 n.17, 180 n.4
Baudelaire, Charles 78
Bergson, Henri 3–4, 6–7, 23–4, 30, 34, 37, 39–40, 92, 139–40, 166, 179 nn.11–12
   durée 179 n.13
   élan vital 16–17
   Le rire 13–20, 25, 32, 74, 175 nn.1–2, 176 nn.3–5, 183 n.15
body 11–12, 29, 31–2, 35, 38–41, 85–9, 112, 116, 121–66, 168–70, 172–3, 184 n.23
Brombert, Victor 8–9, 170, 175 n.5

carnival (*see also* Bakhtin) 13, 34–40, 84, 106–9, 113–16, 143, 163, 177–8 n.17, 181 n.13, n.15
chiasmus 10, 113, 141, 148, 169
comic
   See also Bergson, *Le rire*
   Ferroni, Giulio 6

   See also Freud, *Jokes and Their Relation to the Unconscious*
Jardon, Denise 13, 23, 51, 75, 81, 170
   See also Lewis, *The Wild Body*
Lipps, Theodor 177 n.12
Schopenhauer, Arthur 4, 137

doubles (*see also* pairs and split selves) 10, 23, 39, 69, 78–9, 87, 119, 132, 159, 169–70, 176 n.9, 182 n.17, 183 n.12
dybbuk 11, 121–3, 126, 130, 132, 161, 182 n.2
   Ansky, Shalom 182 n.2

Freud, Sigmund 6–7, 28–30, 34, 37, 40–1, 61, 83, 103, 114, 123–4, 130, 148, 162–3, 166, 177 n.12, 182 n.5, 183 n.8
   'Der Humor' 1, 3–4, 13, 19–23, 50, 55, 60, 131, 155, 159, 171, 176 n.8
   The Ego and the Id 155, 159–60
   Jokes and Their Relation to the Unconscious 4, 13, 19–22, 51, 171, 176 nn.7–9

Gary, Romain 2, 8, 10, 175 n.6, 178 n.7, 180 nn.9–10, 181 nn.12–13, 182 n.5, 182–3 n.6, 183 n.9
   'Être deux c'est pour moi la seule unité concevable' 116
   Les clowns lyriques 10–11, 83–5, 103, 106–120, 123, 168, 180 n.9, 180–1 n.11, 181 nn.12–15, 182–3 n.6, 184 n.27
   Les couleurs du jour 180 n.10, 180–1 n.11
   The Colours of the Day 117, 180–1 n.11, 181 n.16
   La danse de Gengis Cohn 9, 11, 23, 103, 121–35, 145, 161, 163, 165, 168, 170–1, 182 nn.1–4, 182–3, n.6, 183 nn.7–8, n.10

Les racines du ciel 9, 11, 43–4, 62–71, 75, 80–2, 99, 129, 134, 167, 179 n.8
La tête coupable 134, 182 n.1
Pour Sganarelle 114, 123, 130, 163, 180 n.10, 182 n.1, n.4, 185 n.39
Guareschi, Alberto and Carlotta
Giovannino nostro babbo 44, 55
'Istruzioni per l'uso del *Grande diario*' 47
Guareschi, Giovannino 2, 10, 38, 64, 96, 122, 165, 169, 184 n.26, n.28, 185 n.29, n.32, n.35, nn.37–8
'Addio, Giovannino' 184 n.22
Candido 149, 154, 184 n.22, n.24, 185 n.30, n.36
Chi sogna nuovi gerani? 149, 185 n.36
'Colloquio nel bagno' 149–55, 162, 184 nn.22–3
Corrierino delle famiglie 184 n.28
Diario clandestino 1943–1945 9, 11–12, 23, 43–62, 71, 81–2, 147–8, 153, 167, 170–1, 178 n.1, nn.4–6, 184 n.23
'Era giovane, bellissimo…' (in *Vita con Gio*') 149, 156–8, 160, 162, 185 n.31
Il grande diario 47, 52
Mondo piccolo (Don Camillo) 44–5
moustache 38, 50, 147, 149, 155–63, 169
Ritorno alla base 50, 60, 80, 149, 160, 178 n.1, 184 n.25, 185 n.33
'Umorismo razionato' 60–1
'Va' fuori o stranier!' 185 n.34

heterotopias (Foucault) 95
humour (theories of)
  Critchley, Simon 7, 41
  Escarpit, Robert 176 n.6
  See also Freud, 'Der Humor'
  See also Freud, *Jokes and Their Relation to the Unconscious*
  Hobbes, Thomas 4, 136, 183 n.13
  Morin, Christian 51, 81, 171
  Morreall, John 4, 6, 175 n.2
  Nash, Walter
    Jonathanisms 48, 51, 81, 178 n.3
    logical malpractices 101, 168
  Noguez, Dominique 176 n.9

Noonan, Will 175 n.1
Parkin, John 20
See also Pirandello, *L'umorismo*

Internati Militari Italiani (IMI) 45–6, 49–50, 57, 147–8, 158
irony 14–16, 51, 53, 117–18, 129, 149, 151–2

laughter (theories of)
  See also Bakhtin, *Rabelais and His World*
  See also Bergson, *Le rire*
  Bown, Alfie 175 nn.2–3
  Holland, Norman 6, 23, 175 n.4
  See also Lewis, *Blast* 1 / Vorticist manifesto
  See also Lewis, *The Wild Body*
Lewis, Wyndham 2–3, 5–7, 10, 13, 29–34, 37, 40–1, 180 n.5, n.7
  Blast 1 / Vorticist manifesto 5, 7, 29–31, 40, 64, 75, 82, 92, 129, 177 nn.13–14
  The Childermass 103–4
  metaphysical satire (*Men Without Art*) 3, 5, 7, 29, 33–4, 40–1, 93, 96, 102, 166, 169
  Satire and Fiction 33, 102
  Snooty Baronet 10–11, 83–5, 96–106, 111, 116, 118–19, 165, 168, 170, 180 n.6, n.8
  The Wild Body 5, 7, 29, 31–4, 40, 92, 101–2, 104, 140–2, 144, 161, 166, 177 nn.15–16

masks (see also Bakhtin, 'Forms of Time and of the Chronotope in the Novel') 11, 36, 50, 74, 83–5, 89, 91–2, 94–8, 104–7, 111, 113, 116, 118–20, 168, 172, 180 n.1, n.8
  clown 74, 106–118, 180 nn.9–10, 181 n.15
  fool 83–96, 141–3, 146
  rogue 105–6

Nabokov, Vladimir 2, 10, 179 n.11, 183 n.13
  Bend Sinister 71–2, 145, 184 n.19

Invitation to a Beheading 8–9, 11, 23, 38, 43–4, 71–80, 82, 105, 135, 139–40, 167, 169–71, 175 n.6, 179 n.10, nn.12–14, 183 n.12, 184 n.19
Laughter in the Dark 10, 12, 121–2, 134–47, 161–3, 168–9, 175 n.6, 183 n.11, n.14, 183–4 n.16, 184 n.17
Speak, Memory 77
nose 26, 38, 86–8, 158, 180 n.4

oscillation 2–3, 5, 12, 26, 41, 44, 60, 82, 118, 121, 123, 126, 146, 161, 166, 168, 171–3, 177 n.12, 181 n.12

pairs (*see also* doubles and split selves) 49, 103–4, 113–20, 123, 130, 134, 161–2, 168, 183 n.12
paradox 102, 120, 146, 154, 169, 180 n.5
Pirandello, Luigi 2–3, 6, 10, 182 n.17
  Enrico IV 180 n.8
  Il fu Mattia Pascal 88, 180 n.8
  'Il teatro moderno, Tilgher, Bracco, un nuovo romanzo, l'America' 94
  L'umorismo 3, 5, 7, 13, 19, 23–30, 34, 40–1, 55, 61, 85–6, 88, 93, 95, 102–3, 118, 146, 166, 172, 176 n.10, 177 nn.11–12

Uno, nessuno e centomila 10–11, 26, 29, 38, 83–96, 98, 103–6, 111, 118–19, 147, 153, 167–8, 170, 180 nn.1–3, 182 n.17
prison cell 2, 7–9, 11–12, 43, 70–83, 153–4, 162, 165, 167, 172–3

repetition 15–17, 48–52, 54, 69, 74–5, 79–81, 170–1, 176 n.3, 177 n.12, 178 n.1
Rowling, J. K. 1–2, 173–4

Sartre, Jean-Paul 8, 116, 170
satire (*see also* Lewis, Metaphysical satire) 3, 5, 7, 13–15, 29, 31, 33–4, 39–40, 101–2, 166, 169, 177 n.15
split selves (*see also* doubles and pairs) 19, 22–3, 77–9, 81–2, 114, 123–4, 130–2, 147–8, 154–5, 158–60, 162, 165–6, 169, 184 n.22
Stendhal 8
syllepsis 10, 129, 158, 162, 169

war camps 2, 8–9, 11–12, 43–71, 81, 83, 122, 147–9, 151, 156–9, 162, 165, 167–9, 171, 178 n.4, 185 n.37

Zupančič, Alenka 41, 81, 177 n.12, 179 n.9

CPSIA information can be obtained
at www.ICGtesting.com
Printed in the USA
LVHW050508011221
704868LV00012B/1326

9 781501 371998